DON'T
PANIC

BOOKS BY DOUGLAS ADAMS

Deeper Meaning of Liff, The (with John Lloyd)
Dirk Gently's Holistic Detective Agency
Hitchhiker's Guide to the Galaxy, The
Hitchhiker's Guide to the Galaxy, The: A Trilogy in Four Parts
Hitchhiker's Guide to the Galaxy, The: The Original Radio Scripts
Last Chance to See (with Mark Carwardine)
Life, the Universe and Everything
Long Dark Tea-Time of the Soul, The
Meaning of Liff, The (with John Lloyd)
Mostly Harmless
Restaurant at the End of the Universe, The
So Long, and Thanks for All the Fish
Utterly, Utterly Merry Comic Relief Christmas Book, The (Editor)

OTHER BOOKS BY NEIL GAIMAN

Fiction
American Gods
Coraline
Good Omens (with Terry Pratchett)
Neverwhere
Smoke and Mirrors
Stardust

Graphic Novels
Black Orchid (art by Dave McKean)
Books of Magic (art by various)
Day I Swapped My Dad for Two Gold Fish, The (art by Dave McKean)
Death: The High Cost of Living (art by various)
Death: The Time of Your Life (art by various)
Harlequin Valentine (art by John Bolton)
Last Temptation, The (art by Michael Zulli)
Miracleman: The Golden Age
Neil Gaiman and Charles Vess' Stardust
Neil Gaiman's Midnight Days (art by various)
Sandman: A Game of You (art by various)
Sandman: Brief Lives (art by various)
Sandman: Dream Country (art by various)
Sandman: Endless Nights (art by Moebius, Bill Sienkiewicz and others)
Sandman: Fables and Reflections (art by Dave McKean and others)
Sandman: Preludes & Nocturnes (art by various)
Sandman: Season of Mists (art by various)
Sandman: The Doll's House (art by various)
Sandman: The Dream Hunters (art by Yoshitaka Amano)
Sandman: The Kindly Ones (art by Mark Hempel and others)
Sandman: The Wake (art by various)
Sandman: World's End (art by various)
Signal to Noise (art by Dave McKean)
Tragical Comedy or Comical Tragedy of Mr Punch, The (art by Dave McKean)
Violent Cases (art by Dave McKean)

DON'T PANIC

DOUGLAS ADAMS
& THE HITCHHIKER'S
GUIDE TO THE GALAXY
NEIL GAIMAN

ADDITIONAL MATERIAL BY
DAVID K. DICKSON & MJ SIMPSON

TITAN BOOKS

DON'T PANIC
1 84023 742 2

Published by
Titan Books
A division of
Titan Publishing Group Ltd
144 Southwark St
London
SE1 0UP

This hardcover edition first published October 2003
10 9 8 7 6 5 4 3 2 1

© 2003 Neil Gaiman.

The right of Neil Gaiman to be identified as the Author of the Work has
been asserted by him in accordance with the Copyright, Designs & Patents
Act 1988.

Dedication

Because she's threatened me with consequences too dreadful to consider
if I *don't* dedicate a book to her...
And because she's taken to starting every transatlantic conversation with
"Have you dedicated a book to me yet?"...
I would like to dedicate this book to intelligent life forms everywhere.
And to my sister, Claire.

The Hitchhiker's Guide to the Galaxy and all extracts from the works of Douglas
Adams are copyright © Douglas Adams 1987-2002 and used by permission.

Front cover image © 1999, Jill Furmanovsky (www.rockarchive.com)

Visit our website: **www.titanbooks.com**

Did you enjoy this book? We love to hear from our readers.
Please e-mail us at: readerfeedback@titanemail.com
or write to Reader Feedback at the above address.

No part of this publication may be reproduced, stored in a retrieval system,
or transmitted, in any form or by any means without the prior written
permission of the publisher, nor be otherwise circulated in any form of
binding or cover other than that in which it is published and without a
similar condition being imposed on the subsequent purchaser.

A CIP record for this title is available from the Library of Congress.

Printed and bound in Great Britain by MPG Books Ltd, Bodmin, Cornwall

CONTENTS

CONTENTS

FOREWORD

Seventeen years ago a young writer was asked to write a *Hitchhiker's Guide to the Galaxy* companion. Douglas Adams had agreed some years before that Titan could publish such a book, but the original writer, Richard Hollis, hadn't written it for reasons I'm still not clear on to this day, and someone at Titan had asked Kim Newman if he wanted to write it. He didn't — but, he pointed out, who knew someone who had already interviewed Douglas several times.

So Nick Landau, of Titan Books, called me, and asked if I was interested. I wanted to write this book more than anything. I said yes.

Douglas Adams opened his address book to me. I talked to his colleagues, and went through his filing cabinets. I read dozens of scripts and photocopied all of Douglas's press clippings. I played the *Hitchhiker's* computer game to the end, and battled with primitive word processing programs trying to find one that would let me do footnotes. My favourite bits were interviewing Douglas, though, and the way he'd manage to be funny, and serious, and faintly baffled, all at the same time.

You will find many of the great Hitchhiker's anecdotes in this book (although several of them, such as the tale of the thousands of people blocking the streets for the first Forbidden Planet book signing, had not yet evolved in early 1987 when the greater part of the book was written).

Don't Panic! has been updated and expanded twice. David K. Dickson wrote chapters 24-26 in 1993, and in 2002 MJ Simpson wrote chapters 27-30, and overhauled the entire text.

When Douglas died I found myself being interviewed, in newspapers and on the radio, Douglas's favourite medium, being asked to explain who he was and what he did, and why his absence was a tragedy. Perhaps, it occurs to me now, at the end of the day, one of the most magical things about Douglas's writing, as with that of his literary hero P. G. Wodehouse, was that you knew the person writing was on your side, that he was not laughing at you, but that you were in on the joke.

Back in 1987 Douglas was bemused by the existence of this book, and doubly bemused by its success. What he would make of a world in which we have not only this but MJ Simpson's not-actually-authorised-but-by-no-means-unauthorised Douglas Adams biography, *Hitchhiker*, and Nick Webb's forthcoming actually-officially-authorised biography *Wish You Were Here*, I hesitate to think.

I wish he were still around. I'd send him an e-mail and ask him. And he'd write back something serious and funny and faintly baffled, all at the same time.

Neil Gaiman
July 8, 2003
Late

INTRODUCTION

The Hitchhiker's Guide to the Galaxy is the most remarkable, certainly the most successful book ever to come out of the great publishing companies of Ursa Minor. It is about the size of a paperback book, but looks more like a large pocket calculator, having upon its face over a hundred flat press-buttons and a screen about four inches square, upon which any one of over six million pages can be summoned almost instantly. It comes in a durable plastic cover, upon which the words

DON'T PANIC

are printed in large, friendly letters.

There are no known copies of *The Hitchhiker's Guide to the Galaxy* on this planet at this time.

This is not its story.

It is, however, the story of a book also called, at a very high level of improbability, *The Hitchhiker's Guide to the Galaxy*; of the radio series that started it all; the six-book trilogy it comprises; the computer games, towel, and television series that it, in its turn, has spawned.

To tell the story of the book — and the radio series, and the towel — it is best to tell the story of some of the minds behind it. Foremost among these is an ape-descended human from the planet Earth, although at the time our story starts he no more knows his destiny (which will include international travel, computers, an almost infinite number of lunches, and becoming mindbogglingly rich) than an olive knows how to mix a Pan Galactic Gargle Blaster.

His name is Douglas Adams, he is six foot five inches tall, and he is about to have an idea.

0

THE HITCHHIKER'S GUIDE
TO EUROPE

The idea in question bubbled into Douglas Adams's mind quite spontaneously, in a field in Innsbruck. He later denied any personal memory of it having happened. But it's the story he told, and, if there can be such a thing, it's the beginning. If you have to take a flag reading THE STORY STARTS HERE and stick it into the story, then there is no other place to put it.

It was 1971, and the eighteen year-old Douglas Adams was hitch-hiking his way across Europe with a copy of *The Hitchhiker's Guide to Europe* that he had stolen (he hadn't bothered 'borrowing' a copy of *Europe on $5 a Day*; he didn't have that kind of money).

He was drunk. He was poverty-stricken. He was too poor to afford a room at a youth hostel (the entire story is told at length in his introduction to *The Hitchhiker's Guide to the Galaxy: A Trilogy in Four Parts* in England, and *The Hitchhiker's Trilogy* in the US) and he wound up, at the end of a harrowing day, flat on his back in a field in Innsbruck, staring up at the stars. "Somebody," he thought, "somebody really ought to write a *Hitchhiker's Guide to the Galaxy.*"

He forgot about the idea shortly thereafter.

Five years later, while he was struggling to think of a legitimate reason for an alien to visit Earth, the phrase returned to him. The rest is history, and will be told in this book.

The field in Innsbruck has since been transformed into an unremarkable section of autobahn.

> "When you're a student or whatever, and you can't afford a car, or a plane fare, or even a train fare, all you can do is hope that someone will stop and pick you up.
>
> "At the moment we can't afford to go to other planets. We don't have the ships to take us there. There may be other people out there (I don't have any opinions about Life Out There, I just don't know) but it's nice to think that one could, even here and now, be whisked away just by hitchhiking."
>
> — Douglas Adams, 1984.

1

DNA

Deoxyribonucleic acid, commonly known as DNA, is the fundamental genetic building block for all living creatures. The structure
of DNA was discovered and unravelled, along with its significance,
in Cambridge, England, in 1952, and announced to the world in
March 1953.

This was not the first DNA to appear in Cambridge, however. A
year earlier, on 11th March 1952, Douglas Noel Adams was born in
a former Victorian workhouse in Cambridge. His mother was a
nurse, his father a postgraduate theology student who was training
for holy orders, but gave it up when his friends managed to persuade
him it was a terrible idea.

His parents moved from Cambridge when he was six months old,
and divorced when he was five. At that time, Douglas was considered
a little strange, possibly even retarded. He had only just learned to
talk and, "I was the only kid who anybody I knew has ever seen actually walk into a lamppost with his eyes wide open. Everybody
assumed that there must be something going on inside, because there
sure as hell didn't seem to be anything going on on the outside!"

Douglas was a solitary child; he had few close friends, and one
sister, Susan, three years younger than he was.

In September 1959 he started at Brentwood School in Essex,
where he stayed until 1970. He said of the school, "We tended to

produce a lot of media trendies. Me, Griff Rhys Jones, Noel Edmunds, Simon Bell (who wrote the novelisation for Griff and Mel Smith's famous non-award winning movie, *Morons from Outer Space*; he's not a megastar yet, but he gives great parties). A lot of the people who designed the Amstrad Computer were at Brentwood, as well. But we had a very major lack of archbishops, prime ministers and generals."

He was not particularly happy at school, most of his memories having to do with "basically trying to get off games". Although he was quite good at cricket and swimming he was terrible at football and "diabolically bad at rugby — the first time I ever played it, I broke my own nose on my knee. It's quite a trick, especially standing up.

"They could never work out at school whether I was terribly clever or terribly stupid. I always had to understand everything fully before I was prepared to say anything."

He was a tall and gawky child, self-conscious of his height: "My last year at prep school we had to wear short trousers, and I was so absurdly lanky, and looked so ridiculous, that my mother applied for special permission for me to wear long trousers. And they said no, pointing out I was just about to go into the main school. I went to the main school and was allowed to wear long trousers, at which point we discovered they didn't have any long enough for me. So for the first term I still had to go to school in short trousers."

His ambitions at that time had more to do with the sciences than the arts: "At the age when most kids wanted to be firemen, I wanted to be a nuclear physicist. I never made it because my arithmetic was too bad — I was good at maths conceptually, but lousy at arithmetic, so I didn't specialise in the sciences. If I had known what they were, I would have liked to be a software engineer... but they didn't have them then."

His hobbies revolved around making model aeroplanes ("I had a big display on top of a chest of drawers at home. There was a large old mirror that stood behind them, and one day the mirror fell forward and crushed the lot of them. I never made a model plane after that, I was upset, distraught for days. It was this mindless blow that fate had dealt me..."), playing the guitar, and reading.

"I didn't read as much as, looking back, I wish I had done. And not the right things, either. (When I have children I'll do as much to encourage them to read as possible. You know, like hit them if they don't.) I read Biggles, and Captain W. E. Johns's famous science fiction series — I particularly remember a book called *Quest for the Perfect Planet*, a major influence, that was. There was an author called Eric Leyland, who nobody else ever seems to have heard of. He had a hero called David Flame, who was the James Bond of the ten year-olds. But when I should have been packing in the old Dickens, I was reading Eric Leyland instead. But there you go — you can't tell kids, can you?"

Douglas was also an avid reader of *Eagle*, at that time Britain's top children's comic, and home of *Dan Dare*. *Dan Dare*, drawn by artist Frank Hampson, was a science fiction strip detailing the battle between jut-jawed space pilot Dare, his comic sidekick Digby, and the evil green Mekon. It was in *Eagle* that Douglas first saw print. He had two letters published there at the age of eleven, and was paid the (then) enormous sum of ten shillings each for them. The short story shows a certain precocious talent (see page 6).

Of *Alice in Wonderland*, often cited as an influence, he said, "I read — or rather, had read to me — *Alice in Wonderland* as a child and I hated it. It really frightened me. Some months ago, I tried to go back to it and read a few pages, and I thought, 'This is jolly good stuff, but still...' If it wasn't for that slightly nightmarish quality that I remember as a kid I'd've enjoyed it, but I couldn't shake that feeling. So although people like to suggest that Carroll was a big influence — using the number 42 and all that — he really was not."

The first time that Douglas ever thought seriously about writing was at the age of ten: "There was a master at school called Halford. Every Thursday after break we had an hour's class called composition. We had to write a story. And I was the only person who ever got ten out of ten for a story. I've never forgotten that. And the odd thing is, I was talking to someone who has a kid in the same class, and apparently they were all grumbling about how Mr Halford never gave out decent marks for stories. And he told them, 'I did once. The only person I ever gave ten out of ten to was Douglas Adams.' He remembers as well.

EAGLE merry-go-round

EAGLE AND BOYS' WORLD 27 *February* 1965

SHORT STORY

" 'London Transport Lost Property Office' – this is it," said Mr Smith, looking in at the window. As he went in, he tripped over the little step and almost crashed through the glass door.

"That could be dangerous – I must remember it when I go out," he muttered.

"Can I help you?" asked the lost-property officer.

"Yes, I lost something on the 86 bus yesterday."

"Well, what was it you lost?" asked the officer.

"I'm afraid I can't remember," said Mr Smith.

"Well, I can't help you, then," said the exasperated officer.

"Was anything found on the bus?" asked Mr Smith.

"I'm afraid not, but can you remember anything about this thing?" said the officer, desperately trying to be helpful.

"Yes, I can remember that it was a very bad – whatever-it-was."

"Anything else?"

"Ah, yes, now I come to think of it, it was something like a sieve," said Mr Smith, and he put his elbow on the highly-polished counter and rested his chin on his hands. Suddenly, his chin met the counter with a resounding crack. But before the officer could assist him up, Mr Smith jumped triumphantly into the air.

"Thank you very much," he said.

"What for?" said the officer.

"I've found it," said Mr Smith.

"Found what?"

"*My memory!*" said Mr Smith, and he turned round, tripped over the step and smashed through the glass door!

D. N. Adams (12), Brentwood, Essex.

PENI

Dear Editor,

I wonder if any a penny from ea noticed that eac the opposite wa the exception o him today, the the same way a

BR

A fine
The w
It po
And

Ha
He

"I was pleased by that. Whenever I'm stuck on a writer's block (which is most of the time) and I just sit there, and I can't think of anything, I think, 'Ah! But I once did get ten out of ten!' In a way it gives me more of a boost than having sold a million copies of this or a million of that. I think, 'I got ten out of ten once...'"

His writing career was not always that successful.

"I don't know when the first thoughts of writing came, but it was actually quite early on. Rather silly thoughts, really, as there was nothing to suggest that I could actually do it. All of my life I've been attracted by the idea of being a writer, but like all writers I don't so much like writing as having written. I came across some old school literary magazines a couple of years ago, and I went through them to go back and find the stuff I was writing then. But I couldn't find anything I'd written, which puzzled me until I remembered that each time I meant to try to write something, I'd miss the deadline by two weeks."

He appeared in school plays, and discovered a love of performing ("I was a slightly strange actor. There tended to be things I could do well and other things I couldn't begin to do... I couldn't do dwarves for example; I had a lot of trouble with dwarf parts."). Then, while watching *The Frost Report* one evening, his ambitions of a life well-spent as a nuclear physicist, eminent surgeon, or professor of English began to evaporate. Douglas's attention was caught by six foot five inch future Python John Cleese, performing in sketches that were mostly self-written. "I can do that!" thought Douglas, "I'm as tall as he is!"*

In order to become a writer-performer, he had to write. This caused problems: "I used to spend a lot of time in front of a type-writer wondering what to write, tearing up pieces of paper and never actually writing anything." This not-writing quality was to become a hallmark of Douglas's later work.

* Although at first glance this theory may seem flippant, a brief examination shows that the field of British comedy is littered with incredibly tall people. John Cleese, Peter Cook, Ray Galton, Alan Simpson and Adams himself are all six foot five inches, Frank Muir is six foot six inches, as is Dennis Norden. Douglas often mentioned that the late Graham Chapman, at only six foot three inches was thus four per cent less funny than the rest.

But the die had been cast. Adams abandoned all his daydreams, even those of being a rock star (he was, in fact, a creditable guitarist), and set out to be a writer-performer.

He left school in December 1970, and, on the strength of an essay on the revival of religious poetry (which brought together on one sheet of foolscap Christopher Smart, Gerard Manley Hopkins and John Lennon), he won an exhibition to study English at Cambridge.

And it was important to Douglas that it was Cambridge.

Not just because his father had been to Cambridge, or simply because he had been born there. He wanted to go to Cambridge because it was from a Cambridge University society that the writers and performers of such shows as *Beyond the Fringe, That Was the Week That Was, I'm Sorry I'll Read That Again* and, of course, many of the *Monty Python's Flying Circus* team had come.

Douglas Adams wanted to join Footlights.

2

CAMBRIDGE AND OTHER
RECURRENT PHENOMENA

Before going up to Cambridge, Douglas Adams had begun the series of jobs that would serve him on book jackets ever after. He had decided to hitchhike to Istanbul, and in order to make the money to travel he worked first as a chicken-shed cleaner, then as a porter in the X-ray department of Yeovil General Hospital (while at school he had worked as a porter in a mental hospital).

The hitchhike itself was not spectacularly successful: although he reached Istanbul, he contracted food poisoning there, and was forced to return to England by train. He slept in the corridors, felt extremely sorry for himself, and was hospitalised on his return to England. Perhaps it was a combination of his illness with the hospital work he had been doing, but on his arrival home he began to feel guilty for not going on to study medicine.

"I come from a somewhat medical family. My mother was a nurse, my stepfather was a vet, and my father's father (whom I never actually met), was a very eminent ear, nose and throat specialist in Glasgow. I kept working in hospitals as well. And I had the feeling that, if there is Anyone Up There, He kept tapping me on the shoulder and saying, 'Oy! Oy! Get your stethoscope out! This is what you should be doing!' But I never did."

Douglas rejected medicine, in part because he wanted to be a writer-performer (although at least four top British writer-performers have been doctors — Jonathan Miller, Graham Chapman, Graeme Garden and Rob Buckman), and in part because it would have meant going off for another two years to get a new set of A-levels. Douglas went on to study English literature at St John's College, Cambridge.

Academically, Douglas's career was covered in less than glory, although he was always proud of the work he did on Christopher Smart, the eighteenth-century poet: "For years Smart stayed at Cambridge as the most drunken and lecherous student they'd ever had. He used to do drag revues, drank in the same pub that I did. He went from Cambridge to Grub Street, where he was the most debauched journalist they had ever had, when suddenly he underwent an extreme religious conversion and did things like falling on his knees in the middle of the street and praying to God aloud. It was for that that he was thrust into a loony bin, in which he wrote his only work, the *Jubilate Agno*, which was as long as *Paradise Lost*, and was an attempt to write the first Hebraic verse in English."

Even as an undergraduate, Douglas was perpetually missing deadlines: in three years he only managed to complete three essays. This however may have had less to do with his fabled lateness than with the fact that his studies came in a poor third to his other interests — performing and pubs.

Although Douglas had gone to Cambridge with the intention of joining Footlights, he was never happy with them, nor they with him. His first term attempt to join Footlights was a failure — he found them "aloof and rather pleased with themselves", and, being made to feel rather a 'new boy', he wound up joining CULES (Cambridge University Light Entertainment Society) and doing jolly little shows in hospitals, prisons, and the like. These shows were not particularly popular (especially not in the prisons), and Douglas later regarded the whole thing with no little embarrassment.

In his second term, feeling slightly more confident, he auditioned with a friend called Keith Jeffrey at one of the Footlights 'smokers' — informal evenings at which anybody could get up and perform. "It was there that I discovered that there was one guy, totally unlike the rest of the Footlights Committee, who was actually friendly and helpful, all the things the others weren't, a completely nice guy named Simon Jones. He encouraged me, and from then on I got on increasingly well in Footlights.

"But Footlights had a very traditional role to fulfil: it had to produce a pantomime at Christmas, a late-night revue in the middle term, and a spectacular commercial show at the end of every year, as a result of which it couldn't afford to take any risks.

"I think it was Henry Porter, a history don who was treasurer of Footlights, who said that the shows that had gone on to become famous were not the Cambridge shows but subsequent reworkings. *Beyond the Fringe* wasn't a Footlights show, neither was *Cambridge Circus* (the show that launched John Cleese *et al*), it wasn't the Cambridge show but a reworking done after they'd all left Cambridge. Footlights shows themselves had to fight against the constraints of what Footlights had to produce every year."

Douglas rapidly earned a reputation for suggesting ideas that struck everyone else as hopelessly implausible. He felt straitjacketed by Footlights (and by the fact that nobody in Footlights seemed to feel his ideas were particularly funny) and, with two friends, he formed a 'guerilla' revue group called Adams-Smith-Adams (because two members of the group were called Adams, and the third, as you might already have guessed, was called Smith*).

As Douglas explained, "We invested all our money — £40, or whatever it was — in hiring a theatre for a week, and then we knew we had to do it. So we wrote it, performed it, and had a considerable hit with it. It was a great moment. I really loved that."

It was then that Douglas made an irrevocable decision to become a writer. This was to cause him no little anguish and aggravation in the years to come.

The show was called *Several Poor Players Strutting and Fretting*, and this extract from the programme notes has the flavour of early Douglas Adams:

* Will Adams joined a knitwear company upon leaving university; Martin Smith went into advertising, and was later immortalised as "bloody Martin Smith from Croydon" in a book written by Douglas.

> By the time you've read the opposite page (cast and credits) you'll probably be feeling restive and wondering when the show will start. Well, it should start at the exact moment that you read the first word of the next sentence. If it hasn't started yet, you're reading too fast. If it still hasn't started, you're reading much too fast, and we can recommend our own book 'How To Impair Your Reading Ability', written and published by Adams-Smith-Adams. With the aid of this slim volume, you will find that your reading powers shrink to practically nothing within a very short space of time. The more you read, the slower you get. Theoretically, you will never get to the end, which makes it the best value book you will ever have bought!

The following year Adams-Smith-Adams (aided in performance by the female presence of Margaret Thomas, who, the programme booklet declared, was "getting quite fed up with the improper advances that are continually being made to her by the other three, all of whom are deeply and tragically in love with her") took to the stage again in their second revue, *The Patter of Tiny Minds*. These shows were popular, packed out, and generally considered to be somewhat better than the orthodox Footlights' offerings.

Douglas's favourite sketches of this period were one about a railway signalman who caused havoc over the entire Southern Region by attempting to demonstrate the principles of existentialism using the points system, and another of which he said, "It's hard to describe what it was about — there was a lot of stuff about cat-shaving, which was very bizarre but seemed quite funny at the time."

It was shortly after this that Douglas Adams gave up performing permanently to concentrate on writing; this was due to his continuing upset with Footlights, and specifically with the 1974 Footlights Show. As he explained, "It is something that happened with Footlights that I still get upset about, because I think that Footlights should be a writer-performer show. But, in my day, Footlights became a producer's show. The producer says who's going to be in it, and who he wants to write it, they are appointed and the producer calls the tune. I think that's wrong, that it's too artificial. My year in Footlights was full of immensely talented people who never actually got the chance to work together properly.

"In my case, Footlights came to us — Adams-Smith-Adams — and said, 'Can we use all this material that the three of you have written?' and we said, 'Fine, okay,' whereupon they said, 'But we don't want you to be in it.'"

As things turned out, Martin Smith did appear in the show (alongside Griff Rhys Jones and future Ford Prefect, Geoffrey McGivern), but neither of the Adamses appeared, something that Douglas Adams was always slightly bitter about.

Douglas was still hitchhiking over Europe, and taking strange jobs to pay for incidentals. In another bid to get to Istanbul, he took a job building barns, during the course of which he crashed a tractor, which broke his pelvis, ripped up his arm, and damaged the road so badly it needed to be repaired. He wound up in hospital once more, but knew that it was far too late for him to become a doctor.

In Summer 1974, Douglas Adams left Cambridge: young, confident, and certain that the world would beat a path to his door, that he was destined to change the face of comedy across the globe.

Of course it would, and he did. But it did not seem that way at the time.

3

THE WILDERNESS YEARS

Following his graduation from Cambridge, Douglas Adams began doing the occasional office job, working as a filing clerk while trying to work out what to do with the rest of his life. He wrote a number of sketches for *Week Ending* — a radio show that satirised the events, chiefly political, of the past week. Due to his inability to write to order, and the fact that, although many of his sketches were funny, they were unlike anything ever broadcast on the show before, almost none of these sketches ever went out on the air.

The Footlights show of that year, *Chox*, not only got to the West End — the first Footlights show in a long time to do so — but it was also televised (Adams remembered fondly the enormous sum of £100 he was paid for the television rights to his sketches), and later spun off into a short-lived radio series called *Oh No It Isn't*. The show was, in Adams's words, "a dreadful flop", but a number of former Footlights personnel came to see it.

Among them was Graham Chapman. Chapman was a six foot three inch-tall doctor who, instead of practising medicine, found himself part of the Monty Python team (he was Arthur in *Monty Python and the Holy Grail*, and Brian in *Monty Python's Life of Brian*). At that time the future of Monty Python was uncertain, and the members of the team were diversifying and experimenting with projects of their own. Chapman liked Adams's work, and invited him over for a drink. Douglas came for the drink, got chatting, and began a writing partnership that was to last for the next eighteen months. It looked like it was Adams's big break — at twenty-two he was working with one of the top people in British comedy.

Unfortunately, very few of the projects that Douglas and Graham worked on were to see the light of day.

One that did — or nearly did — was *Out of the Trees*, a television sketch show that starred Chapman and Simon Jones. It was shown once, late at night on BBC 2, with no publicity, garnered no reviews, and went no further.

"My favourite bit from that show was a lovely sketch about Genghis Khan, who had become so powerful and important and successful as a conqueror he really didn't have any time for conquering anymore, because he was constantly off seeing his financial advisors and so on — it was partly a reflection of what one heard Graham muttering about the other members of Monty Python. I was very fond of that sketch.*

"The second episode of *Out of the Trees* was never even made, although there was some nice stuff in it. My favourite sketch was called 'A Haddock at Eton', about a haddock given a place at Eton to show the place was becoming more egalitarian. It got terribly bullied. Only it gets a rich guardian anyway, so the whole exercise is rather futile."

While *Out of the Trees* was not exactly a success, *The Ringo Starr Show* was even less noteworthy. It didn't even get to the pilot stage. The show was to be an SF comedy, starring Ringo as a chauffeur who carried his boss around on his back, until one day a flying saucer landed and mistakenly gave Ringo the powers of his ancestral race — the power to travel through space, to do flower arranging, and to destroy the universe by waving his hand.**

It would have been an hour-long American television special, but

---

* This sketch, rewritten into a short story, incorporated into the *Hitchhiker's* canon and illustrated by Michael Foreman, appeared in *The Utterly Utterly Merry Comic Relief Christmas Book*.

** The full script of *Our Show for Ringo Starr* was later published in the book *OJRIL: The Completely Incomplete Graham Chapman*.

the project fell through. Douglas remembered the show with affection, and later salvaged one of his ideas from it in *Hitchhiker's*: this was the Golgafrincham 'B' Ark sequence. Other Chapman-connected projects of this time include some work on the *Holy Grail* record, for which a sketch of Douglas's was highly rewritten by various hands: in its original form, it concerned the digging up of Marilyn Monroe's corpse to star in a movie...

Douglas also helped write ("nearly came to blows over") parts of Chapman's autobiography, *A Liar's Autobiography*. He co-wrote an episode of *Doctor on the Go*. It was doubtless his (not particularly major) contribution to the record, and his two walk-on parts in the last series of *Monty Python's Flying Circus* that caused the original American promotion of *Hitchhiker's*, five years later, to bill him as a member of the Python team. (For completists, or people who are interested, Douglas played a surgeon in a sketch that never gets started, and later, in a scene where a rag-and-bone man is hawking nuclear missiles from a horse and cart, Douglas was one of the squeaky-voiced little 'pepperpot' ladies, as the Pythons call them.)

It is worth noting at this point that Douglas had not really earned much money. His £17-a-week rent was being paid from his over-draft. He was not happy. The collaboration with Graham Chapman, far from being the break it had seemed, was a failure that left Douglas convinced that he was a twenty-four year-old washout. The collaboration's collapse was due to many factors, including Chapman's then troubles with alcoholism, Douglas's increasing lack of money, the uncertainties about the future of *Monty Python's Flying Circus*, and just plain bad luck.

At about the time that Douglas Adams and Chapman finally split up, Douglas was invited to Cambridge to direct the 1976 Footlights revue. In the past, the director's job had been to go to Cambridge every weekend for two or three months, take whatever show Footlights had roughly worked out so far, pull it into shape and stage it professionally.

Unfortunately for Douglas, in the two years since he had left Cambridge, the Footlights clubroom, which was the hub of the society, had closed down and been redeveloped into a shopping centre. Footlights had become homeless and dispossessed, and had almost ceased to exist.

"Whereas in my year, 1974, there were tremendous battles and competition to get in, I wound up in 1976 knocking on people's doors, saying, 'Have you beard of Footlights and would you like to be in the May Week Revue?' It was terrible. I got some people — Jimmy Mulville and Rory McGrath from *Who Dares Wins*, Charles Shaughnessy, who's now a daytime soap heart-throb in America on a show called *Days of Our Lives* — and the final show had some good bits, but they were few and far between, and the whole experience was pain and agony. I had to conjure something out of nothing. At the end of the show I was completely demoralised and exhausted."

At this point, Douglas went to the Edinburgh festival, with John Lloyd, David Renwick and others, with a fringe show called *The Unpleasantness of Something Close*, for which Andrew Marshall was to write some sketches. The show made no money and Douglas's income for the year was now approaching £200. His overdraft was nearing £2,000.

With his flatmate, John Lloyd, he worked on a film treatment for the Stigwood Organisation — an SF comedy based on *The Guinness Book of Records* — which never got off the ground, the attitude being, "Who was John Lloyd, and who was Douglas Adams?" Together they also wrote pilots for a television situation comedy to be called *Snow Seven and the White Dwarfs*, about two astronomers living in isolation together in a fictitious observatory situated on top of Mt. Everest. ("The idea for that was minimum casting, minimum set, minimum number of sets, and we'd just try to sell the series on cheapness. That failed to come to anything.")

While demoralised and very broke, Douglas answered a classified ad in the *Evening Standard* and found himself a bodyguard to an oil-rich Arabian family — a job which involved sitting outside hotel rooms for twelve hours a night, wearing a suit, and running away if anybody turned up waving a gun or grenade. (So far as it can be established, nobody ever did.) The family had an income of £20,000,000 a day, which cannot have done much for Douglas's morale, although it provided him with numerous anecdotes and another profession for the book jacket biographies.

"I remember one group of family members had gone down to the restaurant in the Dorchester. The waiter had brought the menu and they said, 'We'll have it.' It took a while for the penny to drop that they actually meant the whole lot, the a la carte, which is over a thousand pounds' worth of food. So the waiters brought it, the family tried a little bit of all of it, then went back up to their room. Then they sent out one of their servants to bring back a sackful of hamburgers, which is what their real obsession was."

All of Douglas's attempts to persuade television producers that a comedy science fiction series might not be a bad idea had come to nothing. His overdraft was enormous. He couldn't pay the rent. He had almost convinced himself that he was not and never would be a writer, and that he needed a 'proper job'. It was coming on towards Christmas 1976, and a highly depressed Douglas Adams went to his mother's house in Dorset, where he did not have to pay any rent, to live for the next six months, coming into London as necessary.

He was a twenty-four year-old flop.

4

GHERKIN-SWALLOWING, WALKING BACKWARDS AND ALL THAT

John Lloyd is probably the most influential producer in British comedy today. His successes include *Not the Nine O'Clock News*, *Black Adder*, and *Spitting Image*. He was also associate producer of the *Hitchhiker's* television series, and co-wrote Episodes Five and Six of the first radio series with Douglas Adams. He also co-wrote *The Meaning of Liff* with Douglas Adams, of which more later.

Lloyd was a member of Footlights in 1973. He had intended to become a barrister, but was infected by show business, and on graduating worked as a freelance writer, and as a producer in BBC Radio Light Entertainment.

He is a phenomenally busy man. I wound up interviewing him for this book at nine o'clock one Monday morning at the *Spitting Image* studios in London's Limehouse Docks, squeezed into a crowded schedule while people with urgent problems gestured at him from outside the glass partitions of his office.

"I knew Douglas, although not very well, at university. I was at Trinity, Cambridge, while he was at St John's, which is the next college along. Douglas did some of the unfunniest sketches ever seen on the Footlights stage — according to the people in Footlights. He'd do very long sketches... there was one about a tree, I remember, and another about a postbox. He'd stand up at these Footlights smokers and harangue the audience with these long, rather wearisome sketches, which didn't go down at all well in Footlights at that time, which was almost all singing and dancing.

"And so he went off with Martin Smith and Will Adams and they did two absolutely brilliant college revues, packed out, at the same time I was doing the Trinity revues. (Footlights at that time was a bunch of nancy boys — they had this awful club where they'd all go and pretend to be Noel Coward; but when that got knocked down to build a car park, Footlights became more peripatetic, and it began to attract a broader spectrum of people.)

"It was thought — especially by Douglas — that the Adams-Smith-Adams's revues were much better than Footlights' — and indeed they were. There was one amazingly funny bit in the interval where they told jokes very slowly to drive people out of the audience into the bar.

"I'd met Douglas a few times at parties, but it was only when I'd left university that I used to go and have lots of hamburgers with Douglas in a hamburger bar called Tootsies in Notting Hill, and we got to know each other extraordinarily well. We eventually wound up sharing a flat.

"I was working as a radio producer and Douglas was doing things like writing with Graham Chapman — an absolutely bizarre experience, as they used to get phenomenally drunk. Graham had a room in his house entirely devoted to gin: it was just gin bottles (he later went on the wagon) that lined the walls, and occasionally when I was working in BBC Radio I'd go up there at lunchtime. They'd have a few gins before lunch, then they'd go to the pub and do all the crosswords in every paper. Then they'd get roaring drunk, and usually Graham would take his willy out and put it on the bar... it was quite entertaining.

"After work, I'd come back from the office, and usually Douglas had had a very large number of baths and cups of tea and eaten all the food, and we'd sit around and write in the evenings. There were three of us sharing a house: my girlfriend, Douglas, and me. I was fully employed, but Douglas was struggling rather; he was very poor, and getting broker and broker, and his overdraft was going up and up, and he was getting more and more desperate. We had all these projects: Douglas and Graham had written a treatment for a film of the *Guinness Book of Records*, which fell through, so Douglas and I started doing it. We did rather well — the Stigwood Organisation liked it, and they invited us to come to Bermuda and discuss it, and we were incredibly excited. It was dreadfully disappointing. We never heard anything more from them, and we never even got paid for it.

"It would have been a science fiction thing, about a race of aliens who were the most aggressive aliens in the whole universe, who somehow got hold of a copy of the *Guinness Book of Records* and who immediately came down to challenge the world at wrestling and boxing and stamping on people's knuckles, that kind of thing. And the United Nations (John Cleese was going to be general secretary of the UN, I remember) agreed to compete, but they wanted to do all the silly events, like gherkin-swallowing, walking backwards and all that. So they had a *Guinness Book of Records* Olympics, and the aliens won all the sensible events, but lost at all the silly things.

"Then we decided to go and live in Roehampton. We were very happy, until we started advertising for a fourth person to share the house, and we had a succession of weird people. There was one very bizarre person — one day we got back from work to find he'd ripped up every carpet in the house (the house was rented from a little old lady) and he'd thrown them out of the window, as he said they were 'smelly'. The last straw came when we came home to find he'd chain-sawed the front hedge down, because, he said, it was untidy.

"At that time I was producing *Week Ending*, and I was always trying to get Douglas to produce stuff. At that time, I'd write lots of quickies for all sorts of comedy shows, while Douglas wouldn't. At the time, I thought he was wrong, I thought you had to be able to do everything which I could, and he couldn't, or wouldn't. I fitted in quite easily, and I got Douglas to write for *Week Ending*. He wrote a very funny sketch about John Stonehouse, the idea being that he was pretending to be dead all the time, but it just wasn't right for the show. It was very funny, but wrong.

"Then we went our separate ways. I was a radio producer. He was an unsuccessful writer. Anyway, we remained good friends. But

Douglas was at the edge of despair at that time, he was absolutely broke (if he wanted a drink I'd have to buy it for him). He had started applying for jobs in shipping in Hong Kong and so on, as he'd totally given up on being a writer.

"And then Simon Brett came along..."

5

WHEN YOU HITCH UPON A STAR

"1976 was my worst year. I'd decided I was hopeless at writing and I'd never earn any money at it. I felt hopeless and helpless and beached. I was overdrawn and in a bad way.

"In *Hitchhiker's* there's an element of writing myself back up out of that. I was surprised and delighted to find a lot of letters from people in the early days would say, 'I was terribly depressed and upset until I sat down and read your book. It's really shown me the way up again.' I wrote it to do this for myself, and it's seemed to have the same effect on a lot of other people. I can't explain it. Perhaps I've inadvertently written a self-help book."

There are a number of people without whom *Hitchhiker's*, at least in the form we know it, would never have appeared.

John Lloyd is one; Geoffrey Perkins another. But without doubt, the most important is Simon Brett, who was, in 1976, producer of a Radio 4 comedy programme, *The Burkiss Way*. Simon Brett deserves more space than can conveniently be given here. He's been a producer and director on radio and television. He has written for radio and television shows as diverse as *Frank Muir Goes Into...* and the cult show *After Henry*. As an author, he is best known for his excellent mysteries, including the series of murder mysteries starring Charles Paris (a lousy actor but a great detective) which, with their accurate and incisive scrutiny of life inside television, radio and theatre in Britain today, should be compulsory reading for anyone interested in the environments that *Hitchhiker's* comes out of; he has written a number of humour books, and some notable pastiches, including his sequel to Geoffrey Willan's and Ronald Searles's *Molesworth* books.

Brett had met Adams through John Lloyd, at that time a junior radio producer himself, and felt, as he explained to me, that, "Douglas was a talent without a niche. I'd encouraged him to write for *Week Ending* as he really didn't have any outlets for his humour, but it wasn't his thing, it can be a restricting market. Then I started *The Burkiss Way* for which he did a few sketches — one was the 'Kamikaze Briefing', another was a parody of Von Daniken, about the world being created by fluffy kittens in bow ties singing 'Rain-drops Keep Falling On My Head'."

Brett had the wit to see that Douglas needed a show of his own, rather than to try to cram his own strange talent into someone else's format, and on 4th February 1977 Douglas travelled up from Dorset to see Simon, who wanted to know if he had any ideas for a comedy show.

While Douglas had promoted the idea of a comedy science fiction series to all manner of unimpressed television producers, he had not even thought about it as a radio possibility, feeling that radio was too conservative a medium ever to be interested in science fiction. So, initially, the ideas he suggested to Simon were very conservative. And then...

And then history differs. As far as Douglas remembered, Simon Brett said, "Yes, those ideas are all very well, but what I always wanted to do was a science fiction comedy." According to Brett it was Douglas who suggested it, and he who agreed. It doesn't much matter, really. The subject was broached, both were enthusiastic, and Douglas went off to come up with an idea.

The initial idea was one that Douglas had had lying around for a while: "It was about this guy's house being demolished and then the Earth being demolished for the same reason. I decided to do a series of six shows, each of which would deal with the destruction of the Earth for a completely different reason.

"It was going to be called *The Ends of the Earth*. It's still not a bad idea.

"But it was while I was tinkering with the story idea for the first one that I thought, to give the story perspective there really ought to be somebody on Earth who is an alien who knows what's going on.

"Then I remembered this title I'd thought of while lying in a field in Innsbruck in 1971 and thought, 'OK, he's a roving researcher for *The Hitchhiker's Guide to the Galaxy*.' And the more I thought about it, the more that seemed to be a promising idea for a continuing story, as opposed to *The Ends of the Earth*, which would have been a series of different stories."

Adams did a three-page outline for the first episode of *The Hitchhiker's Guide to the Galaxy*, with an additional page of future plans for the show (as can be seen, almost nothing remains the same from the arrival in the Vogon hold onwards)*. The outline, with the name 'Aleric B' crossed out and the last-minute replacement, 'Arthur Dent', written in above it went to the BBC programme development group. Douglas was lucky in having two allies in the group: Simon Brett; and producer John Simmonds, the chief producer, who was, although fairly conservative, a big fan of Douglas's 'Kamikaze Briefing' sketch for *The Burkiss Way*.

                          KAMIKAZE
                          FX WILD FLURRY OF FLAMENCO MUSIC WHICH CONTINUES FOR SOME TIME.

VOICE: Japan 1945
                          FLAMENCO RESUMES.
                          Japan!
                          FLAMENCO MUSIC CONTINUES. WE VAGUELY SEE THE NARRATOR GOING INTO THE BAND AND, FOR INSTANCE, ATTACKING THE PIANO. JAPANESE MUSIC STARTS RELUCTANTLY AND STOPS VERY SOON.
VOICE: Thank you. Japan 1945. The war was moving into its

* See Appendix I.

final stage. The Japanese nation was in a desperate situation… I didn't say stop the music. (HE GOES BACK TO THE BAND AGAIN.) Now look, what is it? Is it the money, come on. (FLAMENCO STARTS AGAIN.) No, flamenco won't do! What do you mean the chords are easier? Look, we've got all these Japanese instruments for you, why don't you play something on this lot? (QUICK FLAMENCO RIFF ON JAPANESE INSTRUMENTS.) Alright, we're going to have a chat about this. You lot (characters now on stage) carry on.

SET CONSISTS OF A BENCH IN A BRIEFING ROOM ON WHICH SITS ONE KAMIKAZE PILOT WITH HIS GEAR AND HEADBAND ON. ON THE BENCH ARE LAID OUT THE HEADBANDS OF MANY OTHER PRESUMABLY DECEASED KAMIKAZE PILOTS. A COMMANDER STANDS TO ADDRESS THE 'MEETING'.

COMM: Now, you all know the purpose of this mission. It is a kamikaze mission. Your sacred task is to destroy the ships of the American fleet in the Pacific. This will involve the deaths of each and every one of you. Including you.

PILOT: Me sir?

COMM: Yes you. You are a kamikaze pilot?

PILOT: Yes sir.

COMM: What are you?

PILOT: A kamikaze pilot sir.

COMM: And what is your function as a kamikaze pilot?

PILOT: To lay down my life for the Emperor sir!

COMM: How many missions have you flown on?

PILOT: Nineteen sir.

COMM: Yes, I have the reports on your previous missions here. (FLIPS THROUGH EACH ONE.) Let's see. Couldn't find target, couldn't find target, got lost, couldn't find target, forgot to take headband, couldn't find target, couldn't find target, headband slipped over eyes, couldn't find target, came back with headache...

PILOT: Headband too tight sir.

COMM: Vertigo, couldn't find target, all the rest, couldn't find target. Now I don't think you've been looking very hard.

PILOT: Yes I have sir, I've looked all over the place!

COMM: You see, it's not actually that difficult bearing in mind that we do have a highly sophisticated reconnaissance unit whose job it is to tell you where to find the targets.

PILOT: Well, it's not always accurate sir, sometimes one can search for hours and not see a single aircraft carrier.

COMM: Well where exactly have you been looking for these aircraft carriers?

PILOT: Er, well sir...

COMM: (FLIPPING THROUGH NOTES.) ...I mean, I notice for instance that you seem to have more or less ignored the sea. I would have thought that the sea was quite a promising area.

PILOT: Yes sir...

COMM: And that the airspace directly above Tokyo was not. And another thing...

PILOT: Yes sir?

COMM: Skip the victory rolls.

PILOT: Sir, you're being unfair, I have flown over the sea lots of times. I actually attacked an aircraft carrier once.

COMM: Ah yes, I have the details of your 'attack' here. Mission nineteen. Let's see. Take off 0500 hours, proceeded to target area, nice start. Target spotted 0520 hours, good, climbed to a height of 6000ft, prepared for attack, went into a power dive, and successfully... *landed* on target.

PILOT: I had to go wee wees sir. Caught short. But I took off again immediately sir. Good job too — one of our lads crashed straight into it. Poor devil didn't stand a chance.

COMM:	What?
PILOT:	No sir — and that really got me upset, and I was going to let 'em really have it — I was going to whip it straight out, fly in low and lob it straight through the dining room porthole — that would have sorted them out.
COMM:	You were going to do what?
PILOT:	Cut it straight out and let 'em have it, whee splat right in the middle of their breakfast. They'd have known we meant business then alright sir.
COMM:	What were you going to cut straight out and throw into their breakfast?
PILOT:	My stomach sir. Oh yes, I'd like to see the expressions on their faces when the great squelchy mass plummeted right into…
COMM:	Wait… wait a moment, let me just get this clear in my mind. You were going to cut out…
PILOT:	My stomach, yes sir, kamikaze… (DOES HARA-KIRI GESTURE.)
COMM:	You were going to cut out your stomach and… throw it at the enemy?
PILOT:	Yes sir, straight at them.
COMM:	Any particular reason?
PILOT:	Die for the Emperor sir.
COMM:	And what purpose would that serve?
PILOT:	Make the enemy feel guilty sir.

— 'Kamikaze Briefing' radio script.

The BBC approved the making of the pilot on 1st March 1977, and by 4th April Douglas had finished the first script: it was essentially the *Hitchhiker's* script that we know now — with a couple of exceptions, the longest and most striking of which is the 'parallel universes' speech of Ford's (see pages 41-43), which gives the gradually eroded rationale for Ford rescuing Arthur in the first place. (Originally, it should be noted, he liked Arthur and wanted to enlist him as a fellow reporter for the *Guide*; by the time Douglas came to write the computer game, all Ford wanted to do was return Arthur's towel and get out before the planet was demolished.) There was also a much longer dialogue between Arthur and Prosser, the Council representative, which was wisely cut, as the style of humour owed more to Monty Python than to Adams himself.

PROSSER: But you found the notice, didn't you?

ARTHUR: Yes. It was on display in the bottom of a locked filing cabinet stuck in a disused lavatory with a sign on the door saying 'Beware of the Leopard'. Ever thought of going into advertising?

PROSSER: It's not as if it's a particularly nice house anyway.

ARTHUR: I happen rather to like it.

PROSSER: Mr Dent, you may choose to scoff at Local Government.

ARTHUR: Me? I wasn't scoffing.

PROSSER: I said you may choose to scoff at Local Government.

ARTHUR: Alright, maybe I was a bit.

PROSSER: May I continue?

ARTHUR: Yes alright.

PROSSER: You may choose to scoff at Local Government...

ARTHUR: Is this you continuing?

PROSSER: Yes! I said...

ARTHUR: Ah, I'm sorry, it's just that it sounded more like you saying the same thing again.

PROSSER: Mr Dent!

ARTHUR: Hello? Yes?

PROSSER: Have you any idea how much damage that bulldozer would suffer if I just let it roll straight over you?

ARTHUR: How much?

PROSSER: None at all.

— *Hitchhiker's* pilot radio script.

From April to August there were a number of delays. The pilot episode was made, but after that it was mainly a waiting game — the waiting in question being caused by the upper echelons of the BBC taking Summer holidays, which meant that the committees, bodies and groups who were to give the go-ahead to *Hitchhiker's* were unavailable. This had the effect of driving Douglas half-mad, and not paying him any money; it also had the effect of making him send the pilot script to the script editor of *Doctor Who*, to see if any money might be forthcoming from that direction.

However, on the last day of August 1977, word came down from the BBC hierarchy that the series of six episodes had been commissioned. Simon Brett would not be producing it: he was leaving the BBC to go to London Weekend Television as a producer. He recommended that Geoffrey Perkins, the most junior of the department's producers, be given the job. And luckily for everybody concerned, he was.

6

RADIO, RADIO

NARRATOR:	On this particular Thursday, something was moving quietly through the ionosphere miles above the surface of the planet. Only two people on the surface of the planet were aware of it. One was a deaf and dumb lunatic in the Amazon basin who now leapt off a fifty-foot cliff in horror, and the other was Ford Prefect.

— Pilot radio script.

One thing that everyone involved in the creation of *Hitchhiker's* is clear on is how definite Douglas Adams was on what kind of show it was he wanted: how it would sound, what it would be. (Another thing they are clear on is that he had no idea where it was all going.) But he was sure that it would be full of ideas, full of detail, experimental — a 'sound collage', unlike anything done on radio before. Epoch-making. A milestone in radio comedy.

But first he had to write it.

This was not to prove as easy as it may sound.

Douglas Adams's introduction to the radio scripts book gives an impression of this time, a period that he described as "six months of baths and peanut-butter sandwiches". Six months spent at his mother's house in Dorset filling waste-paper baskets with sheets of half-typed paper, of relentless self-editing, of depression. He would leave notes around for himself to find with messages such as:

> If you ever get the chance to do a proper, regular job...
> take it.
> This is not an occupation for a healthy, growing lad.

and underneath those notes, other notes, reminding him:

> This is not written after a bad day. This is written after an
> *average* day.

After producing the pilot, Simon Brett had gone to London Weekend Television, leaving Geoffrey Perkins in control. Perkins, a twenty-five year-old Oxford graduate, had been rescued from a life in the shipping industry by an invitation to come and work in radio, and was the most junior of the Light Entertainment producers. He knew Douglas vaguely, mainly as an "embarrassment to the BBC at the time", but was interested enough in the show to make a pitch for it, and, slightly to his surprise, he got it. Possibly because no one else had much idea of what the show was about, nor how to do it.

Geoffrey himself had no idea how to go about producing *Hitchhiker's*, but was relieved to discover, over a meal with Douglas before the second show, that neither of them knew what they were doing. This made things much easier.

Douglas, for his part, was nervous of changing producers so soon. But if on that second show (their first) they were wary of each other, they quickly discovered that, as far as putting the show together went, their minds worked very much on the same lines, complementing each other, and working well together. They also became good friends.

Was there anything that Douglas had particularly wanted to say during the first series of *Hitchhiker's*? "I just wanted to do stuff I thought was funny. But on the other hand, whatever I find funny is going to be conditioned by what I think about, what my concerns or preoccupations are. You may not set out to make a point, but points probably come across because they tend to be the things that preoccupy you, and therefore find a way into your writing.

"I wanted to — I say this in the introduction to the script book — I felt you could do a great deal more with sound than I had heard being done of late. The people who were exploring and exploiting where you could go with sound were people in the rock world — the Beatles, Pink Floyd, and so on.

"I had the idea of scenes of sound. That there would never be a moment at which the alien world would let up, that you would be in it for half an hour. I'm not saying we necessarily achieved that, but I think that what we achieved came about as a result of striving after that.

"We did spend an awfully long time getting the effects right, and the background atmosphere, and orchestrating all the little effects — the way Marvin spoke, and all that kind of stuff. It was taking so long we were continually having to steal studio time from other shows and pretending we were actually doing far less than we were: there was no way we could justify using that amount of time (time doesn't actually equal money to the BBC, but it comes close — there's a complicated but dependent relationship), so what we were doing was completely out of line with what normally happens.

"As much as anything, we were actually having to invent the process by which we worked, because nobody was doing multi-track recording, electronic effects, and so on. We went about it the wrong way at the beginning, simply because we didn't *know*, and then, as we began to understand it, we evolved a way to do it. It wasn't simply doing it the wrong way and finding the right way, it was more dependent on when we were able to get bits of equipment — we didn't have any 8-track recorders to begin with, and the final version didn't come about until we had an 8-track tape recorder. After a while, I took more of a back seat, because everyone knew how to do it, but I was always there, just sticking my oar in and making trouble."

Geoffrey Perkins tells a slightly different story, explaining that, "Douglas was thrown out of the director's cubicle from about halfway through the first series onwards, because he'd get quite excited about putting bits and pieces into scenes. You'd just finish a scene and he would say, 'I've been thinking... we should go back and do it again.'

'Why?'

'Because I think we should have something going *Bloobledooble-doobledoobleblobledoobleblob!* in the background...'

"We used to mix the programmes and cut them down, which wasn't a great way to do it because everything had music and effects behind it. I started off in the early programmes asking what we should cut, and he'd come back with a list of odd words here and there ('the's and 'and's and 'but's and things) and we couldn't do that. He'd say, 'But there's nothing else I want to cut!' In the end I stopped asking him. So I can come across as the vandal of the programme."

Douglas Adams had found a natural foil in Geoffrey Perkins, and the ideal *Hitchhiker's* producer. Perkins went on to be a writer-performer in Radio 4's seminal comedy *Radio Active* and BBC 2's *KYTV*, then became the BBC's Head of Comedy and now works for the production company Tiger Aspect. He was probably the only Radio 4 producer who would spend two days simply getting a sound effect right, and one of the few people who could bully, exhort and cajole scripts out of Douglas, and get them almost on time.

The show was something very different. In the past (and today, for that matter) as a rule a radio comedy show is rehearsed in an afternoon, recorded in front of an audience that evening, then edited the following day before being broadcast. Not only was *Hitchhiker's* not recorded in front of an audience (as Geoffrey Perkins has pointed out, all they would have seen was an empty stage, a number of actors hiding in cupboards, and some microphone leads), it was put together with almost lapidary detail, using (albeit in a somewhat Heath Robinson fashion) the miracles of the BBC Radiophonic Workshop, lots of tape, and scissors.

Douglas Adams said of Perkins's role, "As producer on a show of that kind, he was a very crucial and central part of it. When I was writing the script, he was the person I would go and argue with about what I was going to have in it and what I wasn't. I'd do the script and he'd say, 'This bit's good and that bit's tat.' He'd come up with casting suggestions. And he'd come up with his own ideas about what to do with bits that weren't working. Like throw them out. Or suggestions about how I could rewrite. I'd be guided by him, or by the outcome of the argument.

"One of Geoffrey's strengths is that he is very good at casting. In some cases, I had very specific ideas about casting, and in other cases I had none. Where I had ideas we'd follow them or argue, and I'd win or he'd win. When we were in production I'd be there, but at that point it was very much a producer's show.

"The producer gives instructions to the actors, and generally if you have anything you want to say, or suggestions or disagreements or points you want to make, then you'd say it to Geoffrey, and he'd decide whether or not to ignore it. Very rarely do you as a writer actually start giving instructions to the actors; it's protocol. To be honest, I'd sometimes step over it, but you can't have more than one person in charge. When I wrote the script I was in charge, but when it was made, Geoffrey was in charge, and the final decisions were his, right or wrong. But we rapidly arrived at a working relationship there. Sometimes we'd get very annoyed at each other, and sometimes we'd have a really terrific time — it's exactly the sort of working relationship you would expect."

Perkins says of his involvement with *Hitchhiker's*, "It's really impossible to say how much involvement I had in the story. We used to have meetings and talk grand designs — abortive plots which never quite worked out. It's a blur of lunches. I changed gerbils to mice because Douglas's ex-girlfriend kept gerbils..."

The first episode casting had been done by Douglas with Simon Brett, crucial casting since it involved the roles of Arthur Dent, Ford Prefect and The Book.

The making of the series is covered so well by Geoffrey Perkins's notes in the *Original Radio Scripts* book that it seems redundant to cover the ground again. (Go out and buy a copy of the book if you want to know what happened* — you'll get two introductions, lots of notes, and the complete texts of the first two radio series. Well,

---

* This may prove problematical as the *Radio Scripts* book is currently out of print.

almost complete. There are bits in this book that aren't in there. But you've already got this book.)

The BBC were unsure what they had on their hands: a comedy, without a studio audience, to be broadcast in stereo; the first radio science fiction serial since *Journey into Space* in the 1950s; half an hour of semantic and philosophical jokes about the meaning of life and ear-inserted fish? They did the only decent thing and put it out at 10.30 on Wednesday evenings, when they hoped nobody would be listening, with no pre-publicity, and expected it to uphold Radio 4's reputation for obscurity.

They were undoubtedly surprised when it didn't. After the first episode was broadcast, Douglas went into the BBC to look at the reviews. It was pointed out to him that radio almost never got reviews, and that an unpublicised science fiction comedy series was less likely to get reviews than the shipping forecast. That Sunday, two national newspapers carried favourable reviews of the first show, to the amazement of everybody except Douglas and the listeners.

The series rapidly began to pick up a following, accumulating an enormous audience chiefly by word of mouth — people who liked it told their friends. Science fiction fans liked it because it was science fiction*; humour fans liked it because it was funny; radio fans got off on the quality of the stereo production; Radiophonics Workshop fans doubtless had a great time**; and most people liked it because it was accessible, fast, and funny.

* In addition to its other awards, *The Hitchhiker's Guide to the Galaxy* was placed second in the 1979 Hugo Awards for best dramatic presentation, losing to *Superman*. The awards were made at the World Science Fiction Convention, held that year in Brighton, England. When the awards announcements were read, the crowd hissed the winner and cheered *Hitchhiker's*. Christopher Reeve, collecting the trophy, suggested that the awards had been fixed, whereupon a roar of agreement went up in the hall. It is a safe bet that if a few more Americans had heard of the show then it would have won.

** "They talk a lot about 'the wizardry of the Radiophonics Workshop' but ninety-five per cent of the first series was natural sound. And I had no idea about sound... at the end of the fourth episode I had the most wonderful explosion — the whole episode built up to it. It sounded magnificent in the studio. Then when it was broadcast the compression hit it and cut most of it out." — Geoffrey Perkins.

By the time the sixth episode had been broadcast, the show had become a cult.

While the first four episodes were written by Douglas on his own, the last two were not. This came about in the following manner: Douglas had sent off the pilot script for *Hitchhiker's* to the *Doctor Who* script editor earlier in the year, hoping to get a commission out of it to do some scripts. The commission came through; unfortunately, it came through at the same time that the six episodes of *Hitchhiker's* were commissioned, which meant that as soon as Douglas Adams had finished the first four episodes of *Hitchhiker's* he had to write the four episodes of a *Doctor Who* story, *The Pirate Planet*.

As a result, he was facing deadline problems with the final two episodes of *Hitchhiker's*; he knew how Episode Six ended, but he had "run out of words". In addition, he had just been made a radio producer. He turned to his ex-flatmate, John Lloyd, for help.

Lloyd remembers: "It's odd, but *Hitchhiker's* was always liked. That's the funny thing about it. It never had to struggle at all. Douglas struggled to write it, though; it took him about nine months to write the first four episodes. But everyone, from the first day, thought it was great — and the department was very conservative at the time. Anyway, after nine months Douglas was getting desperate, as he'd caught up with the deadline (and passed it, as is his wont) and they'd already started broadcasting. They were already up to programme two or three, and finally Douglas despaired.

"He rang me up and said, 'Why don't you do this with me?' I think what Douglas had wanted was to prove he was a writer in his own right. In the past he had done all this stuff and people had said, 'It's Chapman (or whoever).' But now he had proved it.

"He'd just started on the fifth episode when I came in.

"I'd been working for a couple of years on a silly science fiction book of my own, that had tons and tons of chapters, all unconnected, and I dumped it on his lap and said, 'Is there anything here you think might make a scene or two?'

"So we sat in the garage I was using for a study at that time, and wrote the fifth episode together more or less line by line. Things like the 'three phases of civilisation' and the Haggunenon Death

Flotilla, who evolved into different creatures, we sat down and worked it out word by word. It was actually incredibly quick, although very painstaking. Then I was busy on production for Episode Six, so although he used stuff I wrote for it, he really put the whole thing together.

"The pressure was fantastic. We were writing it hours before it was due to be recorded. (Later on, in the second series, things got really silly: he was writing *during* the recording.)

"Having written the thing, that was more or less it, and it had been great fun. As Douglas said, it was a tremendous relief for him not to have to do it on his own, and we both enjoyed it, and I didn't think that much about it. It was just a job, and we'd written together before.

"By the broadcast of the first three or four episodes the place had gone absolutely mad. I think six publishing companies rang up, and four record companies (which is extraordinary with radio — usually by the time you've done six series of thirteen episodes, people have just about heard of it). *Hitchhiker's* just went *whoosh!* And Douglas and I were getting on tremendously well, and were tremendously excited. When the first publisher called we went out and bought a bottle of champagne. It was so exciting. We were going to do the book together. And then Douglas had second thoughts.

"He decided he had to do it on his own — he felt the first four episodes were different in kind, and that the last two, although enjoyable enough, didn't have the same sense of loneliness and loss and desperation that characterises *Hitchhiker's* in a funny way. Like Marvin, who Douglas says is Andrew Marshall, but there is a big chunk of Douglas as well. The thing about *Hitchhiker's* is the wonderful bittersweet quality he gets in. The thing is terribly sad at certain points, it really means something. And I think that he felt that the other two episodes were light by comparison."

Douglas Adams's version of these events is essentially the same. "After the *Doctor Who* episodes I was absolutely wiped out. I knew roughly what I wanted to do in the last two episodes so I asked John if he'd help and collaborate, and we wrote together a bit of the Milliways sequence and the Haggunenon section. And then after that I took over and did the 'B' Ark stuff and the prehistoric Earth stuff."

The Haggunenon sequence from Episodes Five and Six is omitted from all later versions of the story (replaced by Disaster Area's stuntship), although it has been used in some of the theatrical adaptations of the show.

THE CASTING FOR THE RADIO SERIES

PETER JONES

"That was very curious. We didn't know who to cast. I remember saying that it should be a Peter Jonesey voice, and who could we get to do a Peter Jonesey voice? We thought of all sorts of people — Michael Palin, Michael Hordern, all kinds of people. Eventually Simon Brett's secretary got very annoyed hearing us talking on and on like this and not spotting the obvious. She said, 'What about Peter Jones?' I thought, 'Yes, that would be a way of achieving it, wouldn't it?' So we asked Peter, he was available, and he did it.

"Peter was extraordinary. He always affected not to understand what was going on at all. And he managed to transmute his own sense of 'I don't know what this is about' into 'I don't understand why this happened,' which was the keynote of his performance. He's great to work with, a very talented guy. He's never had the recognition he should have had. He's terribly good.

"He rarely met the other actors at all, because he'd be doing his bits completely separately. It was like getting session musicians in on a multi-track rock album, sitting alone in a studio doing the bass part."

STEPHEN MOORE

"He was Geoffrey Perkins's suggestion. I had no idea who to suggest for Marvin. A wonderful actor, absolutely brilliant. Not only did he do Marvin so well, but whenever I had a character that I didn't have enough clues about, or didn't know how it should be played, we'd say, 'Let's give it to Stephen and see what happens.'

"Stephen would find the character immediately and would make it really excellent. One of my favourite things that he did was the Man in the Shack — I knew what the character said, and why he said it, but I had not the faintest idea of how he would sound or what sort of a voice he would have."

MARK WING-DAVEY

"The thing that made me think of him for Zaphod was a part he had in *Glittering Prizes*. He played a guy who was a film and television producer who always took advantage of people and was very trendy. He did that so well I thought he would be good for Zaphod."

DAVID TATE

"He was one of the backbones of the series. He can do any voice: he could, if he wanted to, be a very successful actor. He's deliberately chosen to be just a voice. He's remarkable. In *Hitchhiker's* he played a large number of parts and always got them spot on. He played Eddie, he played the disc jockey 'broadcasting to intelligent life-forms everywhere', he played one of the Mice, one of the characters in the 'B' Ark. We had him there every week."

RICHARD VERNON

"He's so funny. He carved himself a niche playing all sorts of grandfatherly elderly types — Slartibartfast in *Hitchhiker's*. He's not actually as old as he appears. I originally wrote that part with John Le Mesurier in mind."

SUSAN SHERIDAN

"It's funny, Trillian was never that well-rounded a part. Susan never found anything major to do with the role, but that wasn't her fault, it was my fault. A succession of different people have played Trillian in different ways. It's a weak part and that's the best I can say. She was a delight to work with."

ROY HUDD

"He played the original Max Quordlepleen. He had to come into the studio and do his bit all by himself. To this day he still claims he doesn't know what it was all about..."

— Douglas Adams.

7

A SLIGHTLY UNRELIABLE PRODUCER

ARTHUR:	Ford, I don't know if this sounds like a silly question, but what am I doing here?
FORD:	Well, you know that. I rescued you from the Earth.
ARTHUR:	And what has happened to the Earth?
FORD:	It's been disintegrated.
ARTHUR:	Has it?
FORD:	Yes, it just boiled away into space.
ARTHUR:	Look. I'm a bit upset about that.
FORD:	Yes, I can understand. But there are plenty more Earths just like it.
ARTHUR:	Are you going to explain that? Or would it save time if I just went mad now?
FORD:	Keep looking at the book.
ARTHUR:	What?
FORD:	"Don't Panic".
ARTHUR:	I'm looking.
FORD:	Alright. The universe we exist in is just one of a multiplicity of parallel universes which co-exist in the same space but on different matter wavelengths, and in millions of them the Earth is still alive and throbbing much as you remember — or very similar at least — because every possible variation of the Earth also exists.

ARTHUR:	Variation? I don't understand. You mean like a world where Hitler won the war?
FORD:	Yes. Or a world in which Shakespeare wrote pornography, made a lot more money and got a knighthood. They all exist. Some of course with only the minutest variations. For instance, one parallel universe must contain a world which is utterly identical to yours except that one small tree somewhere in the Amazon basin has an extra leaf.
ARTHUR:	So one could quite happily live on that world without knowing the difference?
FORD:	Yes, more or less. Of course it wouldn't be quite like home with that extra leaf...
ARTHUR:	Well, it's hardly going to notice.
FORD:	No, probably not for a while. It would be a few years before you really became strongly aware that something was off balance somewhere. Then you'd start looking for it and you'd probably end up going mad because you'd never be able to find it.
ARTHUR:	So what do I do?
FORD:	You come along with me and have a good time. You'll need to have this fish in your ear.
ARTHUR:	I beg your pardon?

— Pilot radio script.

From mid-1977 to the end of 1980 it often becomes difficult to disentangle what Douglas Adams was doing when. But about the time that the first *Hitchhiker's* radio series was broadcast, which was about the same time that *The Pirate Planet* was recorded, Douglas was offered a job as a radio producer in Radio 4's Light Entertainment department. He took the job. As he explained, "I felt I had to do it, because I'd set out to be a freelance writer, had one disaster after another, ended up having to be supported by my parents and so on, and I thought, 'Well, here is someone offering me a solid job with a regular paycheck, which may not be exactly what I want to do, but

I'm not showing any success in doing what I want to do, and this is pretty close to what I want to do; I am in trouble and I will take this job.' Also John Lloyd and Simon Brett had paved the way for me getting the job offer, and I owed it to them.

"I started as a radio producer with *Hitchhiker's* going out and *Doctor Who* shortly to go out. Everybody who starts as a radio producer has to start doing *Week Ending*, so I produced *Week Ending* for a few weeks. As the most junior member of the department I was getting all the bum jobs, like a programme on the history of practical jokes which involved going out and interviewing Max Bygraves and Des O'Connor. I thought, 'What am I doing here?' But a lot of people had put themselves out to get me the job, and it was a staff job, not a contract job."

According to his contemporaries, Douglas tended to be a slightly unreliable producer ("He tended to think you could go on forever."), but even so it came as a slight shock to the department when, after six months, he left to become script editor of *Doctor Who*. This, as Simon Brett commented, put quite a few noses out of joint.

However, he returned to radio very soon after leaving it for one final production job: the Radio 4 Christmas Pantomime*. It turned out to be the project Douglas most enjoyed from that time. It was called *Black Cinderella II Goes East*, and was co-produced by John Lloyd. For no particular reason, it was written and cast entirely from ex-Footlights personnel.

"It was an excuse for such an odd bunch of people — apart from the obvious ones, we had John Cleese playing the Fairy Godperson; Peter Cook playing Prince Disgusting and Rob Buckman playing his brother, Prince Charming; The Goodies — Graeme Garden, Tim Brooke-Taylor and Bill Oddie — played the Ugly Sisters; Richard Baker, who used to play piano in Footlights, was the narrator; and John Pardoe MP, who was then Deputy Leader of the Liberal Party, played the fairy-tale Liberal Prime Minister (on the grounds that you only get Liberal Prime Ministers in fairy-tales); Jo Kendall played the

---

* Footnote for Americans, who may not understand how a pantomime can be performed on radio: this is one of those problems you're just going to have to learn to live with.

Wicked Stepmother... It was terrific, but for some reason the BBC and the *Radio Times* gave it no publicity at all, and it was buried without a trace."

After slightly less than six months, Douglas's first proper job had come to an end.

8

HAVE TARDIS, WILL TRAVEL

It has already been mentioned that, while *Hitchhiker's* was still in the pilot stage, Douglas found himself with time on his hands, during which he needed money and work.

"So once it looked like I had a finished script I thought 'Where else can I generate some work?' I sent the *Hitchhiker's* script to the then *Doctor Who* script editor, Bob Holmes, who thought it was interesting and said, 'Come in and see me.' This was just as Bob, who'd been script editor there for a long time, was on the verge of leaving and handing over to Tony Reed. So I met the two of them and Graham Williams, the producer, and talked about ideas. The one I came up with that they thought was promising was *The Pirate Planet*, so I went away and did a bit of work on it, and they thought it was promising but there was something wrong. So I did more reworking and took it back, and they still thought it was promising but needed more work, and this was going on for weeks, and eventually the inevitable happened..."

The plan had been to do some *Doctor Who* work as a fill-in until *Hitchhiker's* was ready to go into production, and the rest of the *Hitchhiker's* scripts needed to be written. As a plan, this was an abysmal failure.

At the end of August 1977, the six scripts for *Hitchhiker's* were commissioned. Within the week, four episodes of *Doctor Who* were also commissioned. This was the start of a period of non-stop work, confusion and panic that was to last for the next three years.

The Pirate Planet was a less than successful story, which managed to mix such elements as a telepathic gestalt of yellow-robed psychics, a bionic pirate captain, a planet that ate planets, and a centuries-gone evil queen imprisoned in time stasis, into a bit of a mess. The plot elements had obviously been worked out carefully, then edited down to the point of incomprehensibility by the time they reached the screen. There were *Hitchhiker's* in-jokes; there were some appalling performances; there was a murderous robotic parrot. It was teeming with ideas, and might have made a fairly decent six-parter.

Douglas Adams always had a soft spot for it, as he explained, "In a way I preferred writing the *Doctor Who* scripts to *Hitchhiker's* because I would be made to get the plot straight first. In *The Pirate Planet*, the plot was much more tightly worked out than was apparent in the final show because it had to be cut back so far in terms of time. But actually getting the mechanics to work at that time I really loved, and felt very frustrated that a lot of that didn't show in the final thing."

The *Doctor Who* people were impressed enough to offer Douglas a job as script editor. He had only just been given a job as a radio producer. He did not know what to do: "I'd only just taken this job in radio, and it seemed a pretty awful thing to do to leave after six months and go to television. I got very mixed up about that — I didn't know what to do. Various people gave me conflicting advice — some people said, 'This is obviously what you must do because it's much more along the line of what you claim as your strengths,' and other people said, 'You can't desert radio immediately, just like that.' David Hatch said the latter to me very strongly, because he was head of the department, and he had given me the job.

"But I did take the job, and the next person to desert the department was David Hatch, which made me feel a little better."

Remembering his experiences with *The Pirate Planet*, Douglas assumed that the writing of the scripts and coming up with the ideas was the responsibility of the writer, and that the script editor's job was chiefly that of making sure that the scripts arrived and were twenty-five minutes long.

"Then I discovered that other writers assumed that getting the storyline together was the script editor's job. So all that year I was continually working out storylines with writers, helping others with scripts, doing substantial rewrites on other scripts and putting yet other scripts into production. All simultaneously.

"It was a nightmare year — for the four months that I was in control it was terrific: having all these storylines in your head simultaneously. But as soon as you stop actually coping, then it becomes a nightmare. At that time, I was writing the book, script-editing the next series of *Doctor Who*, there were the stage productions of *Hitchhiker's* going on and the records were being made. I was writing the second series of *Hitchhiker's* and I was very close to blowing a fuse at the time. I was also doing some radio production with John Lloyd. The work overload was absolutely phenomenal."

The overload was also reflected in Douglas's dissatisfaction with *Doctor Who* at that time: "The crazy thing about *Doctor Who*, one of the things that led to my feelings of frustration, was doing twenty-six episodes a year with one producer and one script editor. It's a workload unlike any other drama series; if you are doing a police series, say, you know what a police car looks like, what the streets look like, what criminals do. With *Doctor Who*, with every story you have to reinvent totally, but be entirely consistent with what's gone before. Twenty-six shows, each of which has to be new in some extraordinary way, was a major problem. And there was no money to do it with: in real terms *Doctor Who*'s budget has been shrinking, but somehow or other you have to deliver the goods. Twenty-six a year is too many. I was going out of my tiny mind."

Douglas wrote three *Doctor Who* stories, although only two were actually screened*. The first was *The Pirate Planet*. The second was *City of Death*, co-written with Graham Williams, the producer. The

* Four, if you count *Doctor Who and the Krikkitmen*. See the chapter on *Life, the Universe and Everything* for further details.

third is the legendary 'lost' *Doctor Who* story, *Shada**.

City of Death was broadcast under the departmental pseudonym of 'David Agnew', and was written in the following circumstances: "When I was script editor, one of our regular stalwart writers (who we'd left alone as he was a reliable guy) turned out to have been having terrible family problems — his wife had left him and he was in a real turmoil. He'd done his best, but he didn't have a script that was going to work, and we were in deep trouble. This was Friday, and the producer came to me and said, 'We've got a director coming on Monday, we have to have a new four-episode show by Monday!' So he took me back to his place, locked me in his study and hosed me down with whisky and black coffee for a few days, and there was the script. Because of the peculiar circumstances and Writers' Guild laws, it meant that it had to go out under the departmental name of David Agnew. It was set in Paris and had all sorts of bizarre things in it, including a guest appearance by John Cleese in the last episode."

City of Death, in contrast to Douglas's first script, was an adult and intelligent script, in which little was redundant or unnecessary. The humour is never forced, and it is obviously being written by a *Doctor Who* veteran, not a newcomer. In addition to the cameo appearances of John Cleese and Eleanor Bron in the last episode, it contains no less than seven Mona Lisas (all of which are genuine, although six have 'This is a fake' written underneath the paint in felt pen), and life on Earth having been created by the explosion of an alien spaceship (something the Doctor must go back in time to prevent being prevented). It also contains a detective. That Douglas always had high regard for this story can be seen from the fact that certain plot elements were reused in Douglas's first non-*Hitchhiker's* novel, *Dirk Gently's Holistic Detective Agency*, as were some elements of *Shada*, a six-part story that was abandoned half-way through the production because of industrial problems (strikes).

"Once you get beyond a certain point it becomes more expensive to remount the thing than it is to do the whole production again from the word go. That's because when you are casting, you're doing

---

* BBC Enterprises finally released all available material on video in 1992, accompanied by the original script.

it from who's available — when you remount, you have to cast the people you've already got, and this becomes terribly difficult."

Shada was a return to Cambridge for Douglas and the Doctor, featuring a retired Time Lord whose TARDIS was his study, and a book that held the secrets to the Time Lord prison planet. The scripts for *Shada* (especially in early drafts) show an amusing and intelligent show — although Adams's script is far more comfortable with the temporal confusion of Professor Chronotis than with the villains, or, indeed, the plot. (The character of Chronotis, the retired Time Lord, is something else that Douglas would resurrect for *Dirk Gently's Holistic Detective Agency*.)

Adams aroused resentment from many of the shows hardcore fans, who criticise his stint as script editor for resulting in a show that was too silly, self-indulgent, and more like a comedy than *Doctor Who* should be. Tom Baker's Doctor, even more than Patrick Troughton's, was a cosmic clown, always ready with a whimsical remark in the face of danger.

Adams disagreed with this: "I think it's slightly unfair. In the things I wrote for *Doctor Who*, there were absurd things that happened in it, and funny things. But I feel that *Doctor Who* is essentially a drama show, and only secondarily amusing. My aim was to create apparently bizarre situations and then pursue the logic so much that it became real. So on the one hand, someone behaves in an interesting, and apparently outrageous way, and you think at first that it's funny. Then you realise that they mean it, and that, at least to my mind, begins to make it more gripping and terrifying.

"The trouble is that as soon as you produce scripts with some humour in them, there is a temptation on the part of the people making the show to say, 'This is a funny bit. Let's pull out the stops, have fun, and be silly.' One always knows as soon as someone says that that they are going to spoil it.

"So those episodes of *Doctor Who* weren't best served by that way of doing the shows. I can understand people saying, 'They weren't taking it seriously,' but in writing it I was taking it terribly seriously. It's just that the way you make something work is to do it for real... I hate the expression 'tongue-in-cheek'; that means 'It's not really funny, but we aren't going to do it properly.'"

Douglas worked on *Doctor Who* for fifteen months. During the course of this time, he wrote the first *Hitchhiker's* book, the second radio series, the theatrical adaptation, produced *Black Cinderella II Goes East*, and acted as script editor, writer and rewrite man for the Doctor. At the end of this time he had, much to his and no doubt everyone else's surprise, not gone mad, become prone to fits or to throwing himself off tall buildings. By this time, *Hitchhiker's* was enough of a success for Douglas to give up the only proper job he had held for more than a few months.

So he did.

9

H2G2

Shortly after the *Hitchhiker's* radio series first went on the air, Douglas Adams and John Lloyd were approached by New English Library and Pan Books, both prominent English paperback publishers, about doing a book of the series. After lunching with both of them, a deal was agreed with Pan, chiefly because they liked Nick Webb, the editor who approached them*.

The book was to start out on an unhappy note. Douglas had never written a book before, and, feeling nervous about it, had asked John Lloyd to collaborate on it.

John had agreed. As he tells it: "I'd been working in radio very hard for five years, and had gotten bored with it — I could see myself a crusty old radio producer at ninety — so I was very excited about the prospect of doing this book together. Then one night we had rather a strange conversation. Douglas said to me, 'Why don't you write your own novel?' I said, 'But we're writing this *Hitchhiker's* book together...' and he said, 'I think you should write your own.'

"The next day I got his letter saying, 'I've thought about it very hard and I want to do the thing on my own. It's a struggle, but I

* Nick Webb left Pan almost immediately, embarking on a game of musical publishers that would take him, in traditional publishing fashion, around most major British paperback publishers.

want to do it my own, lonely way.' It was the most fantastic shock — as if the bottom had dropped out of my whole life. We'd been trying to write together for so long that when this letter came I simply could not believe it. Even the fact that he'd written the letter at all seemed amazing, seeing that we went down the pub every night, and, as Douglas was at that time a radio producer in the office next door to me, we worked six inches away from each other.

"Looking back, I can't see why I reacted like that. It seems the most natural thing in the world for Douglas to have done it alone and I don't think *Hitchhiker's* would have been the success it was if we had written it together. I genuinely feel that.

"But at the time, I was shocked. I didn't speak to Douglas for two days, and I seriously considered getting a solicitor, and suing him for breach of contract. Then I met him in town a few days later. He said, 'How's it going?' I said, 'You'll be hearing from my legal representative.'

"Douglas was appalled! He thought I was over-reacting; I thought he was insensitive. These are the kinds of things that start wars...

"I saw an agent, and explained to him that we had agreed to the contract, and on the strength of that I'd drunk a lot of champagne, spent the money, and now wanted redress. My agent phoned Douglas's and made some fantastic demands: he said he wanted £2,000 now, and ten per cent of *Hitchhiker's* in perpetuity, so whenever the name *The Hitchhiker's Guide to the Galaxy* was used I'd get ten per cent. When he told me about this I was shocked — I hadn't wanted anything like that!

"At the time everyone, even Douglas's agent, thought that he was in the wrong. Even his mum. Then I ran into Douglas, and he said, 'What are you doing?' I said, 'You told me to get an agent!' He said, 'Yes, I told you to get an agent to write your own bloody book — not to sue me for mine!'

"Eventually we did a deal, whereby I took half of the advance, and that was the end of it.

"But we had booked a holiday in Greece that September to write the book together, and I had nowhere else to go. So, despite all that had happened, I went on holiday with Douglas. He stayed in his room and wrote *The Hitchhiker's Guide to the Galaxy*, and I went down to the bar and the beach and had a good time. Douglas showed me the first version of his first chapter, and I read it, and it was a Vonnegut novel. I told him that, and he tore it up and started again, and after that it started to come good. I have always thought the books were the best bits of *Hitchhiker's* by miles: you could see that they are so original, and so different that it was obvious that he had made the right decision.

(A number of other things occurred on this holiday, the most notable of which was the creation of what was to become *The Meaning of Liff*. But that will be told in its place.)

As Douglas explained, "It was very silly. On the one hand I thought, 'It might be a nice idea to collaborate,' and on sober reflection I thought, 'No, I can do it myself.' It was my own project, and I had every right to say, 'No, I'll do it myself.' John had helped me out, and been very well rewarded for the work. I rashly talked about collaborating, and changed my mind. I was within my rights, but I should have handled it better.

"You see, on the one hand, Johnny and I are incredibly good friends, and have been for ages. But on the other hand, we are incredibly good at rubbing each other up the wrong way. We have these ridiculous fights when I'm determined to have a go at him, and he is determined to have a go at me. So... I think it was an over-reaction on his part, but on the other hand the entire history of our relationship has been one or the other over-reacting to something the other has done."

So Douglas wound up receiving a £1,500 advance for his first book. (He would get over five hundred times that amount as an advance for his fifth novel.)

When the series had started, BBC Publications were offered the idea of doing the book, and quite sensibly turned it down. After the contracts were signed with Pan, BBC Publications asked to see the scripts, since it had occurred to them that they might possibly do a book of *Hitchhiker's*. On being told that Pan had already bought the book rights BBC Publications asked bitterly why the book had not been offered to them

ARTHUR:	You know, I can't quite get used to the feeling that just because I've spent all my life on the Earth I am therefore an ignorant country bumpkin.
TRILLIAN:	Don't worry Arthur, it's just a question of perspective.
ARTHUR:	But if I suddenly accosted a spider I found crawling under my bed, and tried to explain to this innocent spider in its spider world all about the Common Market, or New York, or the history of Indo China...
TRILLIAN:	What?
ARTHUR:	It would think I'd gone mad.
TRILLIAN:	Well?
ARTHUR:	It's not just perspective, you see. I'm trying to make a point about the basic assumptions of life.
TRILLIAN:	Oh.
ARTHUR:	You see?
TRILLIAN:	I prefer mice to spiders anyway.
ARTHUR:	Is there any tea on this spaceship?

— Cut from first radio series.

As with everything Douglas had done, the book was late.

Apocryphal stories have grown up about Douglas Adams's almost superhuman ability to miss deadlines. Upon close inspection, they all appear to be true.

The story about the first book is this: after he had been writing it for as long past the deadline as he could get away with, Pan Books telephoned Douglas and said, "How many pages have you done?"

He told them.

"How long have you got to go?"

He told them.

"Well," they said, making the best of a bad job, "finish the page you are on, and we'll send a motorbike round to pick it up in half an hour."

Many people have complained that the first book ends rather abruptly. That is the main reason why, although it is also true that Douglas knew he was going to have to keep the radio Episodes Five and Six (which he was still less than happy with) back for the end of the second book. If there *was* a second book.

Meanwhile, Pan were going through the normal pre-production actions of publishing: getting covers designed, accumulating quotes from celebrities to put on the covers, wondering how many copies they would sell.

The initial print run of sixty thousand copies betrayed a healthy optimism about sales, and showed that the publishers knew they were not dealing with just a new science fiction book (for which an initial print run is more like ten thousand), but with something slightly special. The earliest promoted cover design showed a Flash Gordon-type in a bulky spacesuit with his thumb stuck out, holding a sign that said, in crude letters 'ALPHA CENTAURI'. It was not used, although it was distributed on fliers at the 1979 World Science Fiction Convention.

Douglas had suggested a number of people who might be willing to give cover blurbs for *Hitchhiker's* to Pan. These included the Monty Python team, Tom Baker (then *Doctor Who*), and science fiction writers Christopher Priest and John Brunner.

None of these blurbs were ever used, although Terry Jones from Python turned in at least a page of possible quotes. These included:

> The funniest book I have ever read, today — Terry Jones

> Every word is a gem... it's only the order they're put in that worries me — Terry Jones

> Space age comedy for everyone... except for (insert the name of the man who writes worse poetry than the Vogons and whose name I can't remember) — Terry Jones

> Probably the funniest book in the universe — Terry Jones*
> *dictated by D. Adams

> One of the funniest books ever to have quoted what I said about it on the cover — Terry Jones

In the end the only quotes used were in some press releases:

> Really entertaining and fun — John Cleese

and

> It changed my whole life. It's literally out of this world
> — Tom Baker

The final cover design, by Hipgnosis and Ian Wright, better known for their record covers than their book covers, was ideal, and provided a uniformity of design with the first record, which was released at the same time as the book, during the second week of October 1979. The front cover showed the title in 'friendly' red letters, and on the back the words 'DON'T PANIC' appeared, in a similar, colour-videoscreen-style typeface.

It is worth commenting here on the anomalies of the title. The mould was cast by Adams, on his original three-page outline for the series, which was titled *THE HITCH-HIKER'S GUIDE TO THE GALAXY* (with hyphen) but referred to the book as *THE HITCHHIKER'S GUIDE* (without hyphen) throughout. The cover of the first book included the hyphen, but lost the apostrophe, while the spine, back and insides wrote *Hitch* and *Hiker's* as two words. The tradition continues to the present day. British copies of *So Long, and Thanks for All the Fish*, for example, hyphenated *Hitch-Hiker's* on the cover, but wrote it *Hitch Hiker's* inside; while the radio scripts book hyphenated all the way through, except at the back, where advertisements appear for the book under both titles, with hyphens and without.

In America, the problem is very sensibly avoided by referring to it as *Hitchhiker's* (with an apostrophe, without a hyphen, and making it into one word). Which is also, incidentally, the form used in this book (except when quoting a source which used one of the various spellings mentioned above). The matter will not be referred to again.

The book went straight to number one on the bestseller lists, and stayed there. This surprised a number of people, not least Douglas

Adams: "Nobody thought that radio had that much impact, but it does. I think a radio audience has a greater overlap with a solid reading audience than television does. All power to radio, it's a good medium."

Within the next three months, *The Hitchhiker's Guide to the Galaxy* sold over a quarter of a million copies. Douglas sent a note to booksellers when sales reached 185,000:

> I can only assume that you have all been giving away pound notes with every copy of *The Hitchhiker's Guide to the Galaxy*, or possibly even sending press gangs out into the streets, because I have just been officially notified that the sales have now passed the point of being merely absurd and have now moved into the realms of the ludicrous. Whatever you have been doing to get rid of them, thank you very much.

Although later Douglas was to express dissatisfaction with the instant success of the first book ("It was like going from foreplay to orgasm with nothing in the middle — where do you go after that?"), at the time he was jubilant.

The beauty of *Hitchhiker's* was that it came at just the right time. The success of *Star Wars* and *Close Encounters of the Third Kind* had created a willingness among the public to regard science fiction as an acceptable form of entertainment; science fiction readers had long been in need of something that was actually funny; and the radio audience who picked up the book discovered very quickly that there was far more in the first book than there had been in the radio series (in fact, it can come as something of a surprise, re-listening to the original radio series, to discover quite how many of the more familiar aspects of *Hitchhiker's* were not in it — towels, for example). The book garnered rave reviews. Douglas found himself compared to Kurt Vonnegut (a comparison that was to persist until the release of Vonnegut's *Galapagos* in 1985, at which point some reviewers started comparing Vonnegut, slightly unfavourably, to Douglas Adams), and the book found itself on many critics' 'year's best' lists for 1979.

If the radio series had been a cult success, then the book took

Hitchhiker's beyond that, to a place in the popular consciousness. It was not long before a lot of people found their perceptions of towels, white mice and the number 42 had undergone a major readjustment.

WHY WAS *HITCHHIKER'S* SO SUCCESSFUL?

John Lloyd:

"It's what William Goldman, in his book *Adventures in the Screen Trade* calls a non-recurrent phenomenon. Before *Hitchhiker's* came along there was no reason why it should, and once it's there it seems the perfect idiom for its time. I don't know why, but it catches the spirit of the moment. The title says it all for me — with hitchhiking and galaxies you have this curious mixture of post-hippie sensibilities and being interested in high tech, digital technology and all that stuff. But it's impossible to say why *Hitchhiker's* is so successful — it's just one of these great original products of a diseased mind. It makes no concessions to popularity, it just gets on and does it. Not once has Douglas toned the thing down so it would sell more copies. Douglas really was as surprised by its success as anyone — he had no idea whether it was any good or not. He used to sit around going, 'Is this good? Is this funny? What do you think of this script?' He really didn't know. But you can't explain it. And because you can't, you can't write another book like it. And that's what makes it a work of genius."

Jacqueline Graham (Press officer, Pan Books):

"Because it was such a wholly original idea, and you don't get too many of those. And because it was funny, but intelligently funny. And because it started as a sort of cult thing. Mostly because it's so original, and secondly because it makes you laugh."

Geoffrey Perkins:

"I know at the time we made the radio series I felt that it was the logical successor to *Monty Python*, really. There's no doubt that *Hitchhiker's* appeals to the same kind of audience and has the same sort of comedy. That was an initial reason for the success. The title plays an important part. Somebody once described it in an article as 'a programme somewhat clumsily entitled *The Hitchhiker's Guide to the Galaxy'*, which is a very erroneous judgement. I knew it hit a nerve from the start, when the letters started pouring in. The timing was obviously good. It was *Star Wars* time, there was a lot of interest in space. Also, when people think of space they tend to think of something very comic-strip and here was something very erudite and witty. That surprised people. But it appealed to everyone. The intellectuals compared it to Swift, and the fourteen year-olds enjoyed hearing depressed robots clanking around."

10

ALL THE GALAXY'S A STAGE

There have been three major productions of *Hitchhiker's* in the theatrical world. Two of these have been successful. The other was a disaster of epic proportions. It is somewhat unfortunate, in this case, that the disaster is the one that got noticed. The first production was put on at the ICA [Institute for Contemporary Arts] in London on 1st-9th May 1979, presented by Ken Campbell's Science Fiction Theatre Company of Liverpool. 'Staged' might be the wrong word for this production. The actors performed on little ledges and platforms, while the audience, seated on a scaffolded auditorium that floated around the ICA on air skates, filled with compressed air, was pushed around the hall at the height of 1/2,000th of an inch by hardworking stage hands.

The ninety-minute-long show was a great success.

Pan Galactic Gargle Blasters were on sale in the bar, and, for the eighty people who fitted into Mike Hust's airborne seating system, it was a great evening. Unfortunately, every hour brought 150 phone calls for tickets, all doomed to failure as the 640 tickets for the show's run had been sold out long before it opened. (Apparently an organisation with the same initials as the ICA, the International Communications Association, got so fed up with misrouted calls for tickets that they wound up closing their switchboard for a week, and stopped Communicating.)

The reviews were unanimous in their praise. A typical review from *The Guardian*, having praised the costumes and hovercraft, stated, "Chris Langham is an utterly ordinary Arthur... and is thus a beautiful counterpart to the cunning Ford (Richard Hope), the two-headed schizophrenic Beeblebrox (Mitch Davies and Stephen Williams, as a space-age version of a pantomime horse with two heads, two legs, and three hands) and the pyrotechnics of Campbell's production." At the time it was announced that they were hoping to revive the show "as soon as they could find a hall large enough to accommodate a 500 seater hovercraft".

This was, it should be borne in mind, before the publication of the book or the release of the first record, when nobody knew how much of a cult success *Hitchhiker's* was or was going to be.

The next performance began life some 300 miles due west in the Theatr Clwyd, a Welsh theatre company. Director Jonathan Petherbridge had taken the scripts of the first radio series and transformed them into a play, performed around Wales from 15th January until 23rd February 1980.

Announced as the "First Staged Production of Douglas Adams's Original Radio Scripts" the company would either perform two episodes an evening, or, on certain long evenings, the entire three hours of script in 'blockbuster' performances, during which "essential space rations" were handed out to the audience at half-hourly intervals. (Not only did the bar sell Pan Galactic Gargle Blasters, but the Coffee Lounge sold Algolian Zylbatburgers.) The Theatr Clwyd performance was so successful that they were offered the opportunity to take their production to London's prestigious Old Vic Theatre. Unfortunately, by this time Douglas had offered the stage rights to Ken Campbell, who had decided to stage another production at the Rainbow Theatre in London, a rock venue that seated three thousand people, in August.

Douglas Adams, displaying perfect hindsight, said, "I should have known better, but I had so many problems to contend with at that time I really wasn't thinking clearly. The thing at the Rainbow was a fiasco."

Douglas wrote additional material for the play (including the

Dish of the Day sequence in Milliways, which subsequently found its way into the literary and televisual version of the show).

An article appeared in *The Stage*, the theatrical newspaper, about the Rainbow production, in July 1980:

> A five-piece band backs the twenty-strong cast of *The Hitchhiker's Guide to the Galaxy*, a musical* based on the radio series that opens at the Rainbow for an 8 week run on July 16th 1980. Production has a £300,000 budget, and the front of the Rainbow will be redesigned as an intergalactic spaceport. Tickets £5, £4 and £3.
>
> The foyer of the theatre is being converted into the control deck of a spaceship, with banks of video screens, flying saucers hanging from the ceiling, and possibly a talking computer to advise passengers when the trip is going to begin. There will be usherettes dressed like aliens — 'Probably coloured green,' says co-producer Richard Dunkley — and a 'space bar' selling galactic-sized burgers and the now famous Pan Galactic Gargle Blaster.
>
> One of the diversions will be rock musician Rick Wakeman, soaring down from the roof on a flying saucer and dressed like the legendary Mekon, SF's most endearing little green man.
>
> This week workmen installed a vast revolving stage while others completed a backdrop for the day the Earth gets demolished.
>
> In California, the people who brought the Laserium to the London Planetarium were devising a spectacular new bag of tricks. Co-producer Philip Tinsley said, 'This will be the first show since *Rocky Horror* to appeal directly to young people.'

As the publicity for the show gained momentum a twenty-five-foot inflatable whale was thrown off Tower Bridge into the Thames, and

---

* No, it wasn't a musical, although there was a backing group.

made almost no splash in terms of news. ("The police were very, very cross", said *The Standard* in the ¾ of an inch they devoted to it.)

Then the show opened.

In retrospect this may have been a mistake. Such descriptions as "I cannot imagine a more tedious way to spend an evening" (*Daily Mail*), "clumsy without ever being cheerful" (*Time Out*), "embarrassing" (*Observer*), "never-ending and extremely boring" (*Standard*) melt into insignificance when placed beside the actual reviews, most of which dissected the show with fine and sharp scalpels and left nothing wholesome behind. A fairly average example of the put-downs was Michael Billington's in *The Guardian*, which stated that, "What happens on the Rainbow stage is certainly inchoate and barely comprehensible... Ken Campbell has directed this junk-opera and I can only say he gave us infinitely more fun in the days of his *Roadshow* when the highlight used to be a man stuffing a ferret down his trousers"*.

What went wrong? A number of things. The length, for one. The laser beams, sound effects and backing band for another. What was almost universally acknowledged as appalling acting for a third.

Douglas Adams explained it as, "The size of the Rainbow — a three thousand-seater theatre — and, because *Hitchhiker's* tends to be rather slow-moving and what is important is all the detail on the way... you put it in something that size and the first thing that goes out the window is all the detail. So you then fill it up with earth-quake effects and lasers and things. That further swamps the detail and so everything was constantly being pushed in the wrong direction and all the poor actors were stuck on the stage trying desperately to get noticed by the audience across this vast distance. If you'd put the numbers we were getting into a West End theatre they would have been terrific audiences — 700 a night, or whatever. But 700 people isn't much when the producers are paying for three thousand seats. So the whole thing was a financial disaster."

Ken Campbell, a man almost impossible to get hold of, claimed the reason for the success of the ICA and failure of the Rainbow was

* The man who stuffed the ferrets down his trousers was Sylvester McCoy, later the seventh televisual Doctor Who.

simpler than that. "In the ICA we put everybody on a hovercraft. We just never found a hovercraft big enough for the Rainbow," he told me in the shortest interview I did for this book*.

Four weeks into the run the show was in financial difficulties.

On 20th August *The Standard* reported co-producer Dunkley as saying, "I think we should struggle on. The cast and crew agree with me, and a certain number of them agreed to wait for their money. We had a very negative press, and it wasn't known at the beginning how many *Hitchhiker's* fans there were." The next day, however, *The Standard* reported that, "Last night the big musical** version of the cult radio show did not go on and after playing at times to twenty percent capacity [ie. 600 people] its season has been ended three weeks prematurely. Richard Dunkley reported that everybody concerned had lost a lot of money, but it was impossible to say how much."

It is easy to be wise after the event, but it would appear that the biggest mistake was that of trying to create a Cult Success. You don't gain a cult following for something big and bold and heavily hyped: a smaller, less flashy, less expensive production might well have succeeded where the galumphing Rainbow production failed.

As indeed, it has. Helping the fans and public to get over the Rainbow disaster was the Theatr Clwyd production. It surfaced again quietly a year later, and has been regularly and successfully staged by other theatre companies since. This adaptation, which, alone of all post '79 versions includes the Haggunenon sequence, and indeed actually has an inflatable Ravenous Bugblatter Beast of Traal, is uniformly popular with critics and public alike, and will, one hopes, still be revived and performed when the Rainbow fiasco has completely been forgotten.

FORD AND ZAPHOD: Zaglabor astragard!
                    Hootrimansion Bambriar!

* That was it.

** It wasn't a musical, honestly.

	Bangliatur Poosbladoooo!
ARTHUR:	What the hell are you doing?
FORD:	It's an ancient Betelgeuse death anthem. It means, after this, things can only get better.

THEY START TO SING AGAIN.

THE COMPUTER BANK EXPLODES.

END CREDITS.

— Alternative version.

At least twenty amateur stage productions are known to have been performed around the world over the years, variously adapted from the novel, the radio scripts or the Petherbridge script. *Hitchhiker's* has been presented on stage as far afield as Bermuda, Australia, Hawaii and Germany; it has been performed once as a one-man show and once as a musical*. There was also a stage production of Douglas's novel *Dirk Gently's Holistic Detective Agency* — retitled *Dirk* — in Oxford in 1995, which has enjoyed periodic revivals.

* This actually *was* a musical, although the audience wished it wasn't.

11

"CHILDISH, POINTLESS, CODSWALLOPING DRIVEL..."

On Monday, 21st January 1980, at 10.30 pm, the second series of *The Hitchhiker's Guide to the Galaxy* went on the air. It was heralded by a cover feature in the BBC television and radio listings magazine, *Radio Times* — it is almost unheard of for a radio programme to get such exposure, despite the name of the magazine — and the five episodes were broadcast at the same time every evening through the week.

This caused problems.

To begin with, as already detailed at length, in 1979 Douglas was under a great deal of pressure as far as other work commitments were concerned, and his normal tendency to put off writing until the last deadline had safely passed was displayed in full when it came to getting the scripts written. However, when he had agreed to produce the second radio series, Geoffrey Perkins had taken this into account.

Perkins went on holiday in September 1979, and before leaving spoke to David Hatch, controller of Radio 4, about the new series. Hatch wanted to know if they could have the second series of *Hitchhiker's* ready to be broadcast in January.

There had already been a seventh episode of *Hitchhiker's*, the 'Christmas Special', recorded on 20th November 1978, and broadcast on Christmas Eve. It had been recorded as a one-off, but had basically taken the plot strands from the end of Episode Six (ie.

everybody was either stranded back in time with no hope of ever returning, or had been eaten by a carbon-copy of the Ravenous Bugblatter Beast of Traal), and had started them off in a different direction, which involved Zaphod's mysterious quest to find the guy who was running the universe. ("This Christmas Programme was basically done by my moving into Douglas's flat. He scribbled upstairs and I was downstairs typing. That's how we got that together." — Geoffrey Perkins.)

Fit the Eighth, the first episode of the second series, reunited Zaphod, Ford and Arthur. Recording of the second series had begun in May 1979, so Hatch's request for the show to begin in January 1980 was not really that unreasonable. Geoffrey Perkins thought it was a good idea: "We were working on them at a fairly leisurely pace, and I said, 'Yes.' We needed a deadline, or we could have gone on till the crack of doom. I thought, 'We'll have made three episodes by then, and we'll do the rest of them over the next five weeks.'

"Then I went on holiday. I came back to find David had done a deal with the *Radio Times* — they would put us on the front cover if all the shows went out in a week. It was madness, really."

The second radio series was onerous for everybody. For Douglas Adams it was especially difficult: "I was terrified of doing the second series, because the first time it was just me in my own private little world writing this thing. Nobody expected it to be any good. The second series, the eyes of the world were upon me. It was like running down the street naked, because it had suddenly become everyone else's property as well."

Due to the deadlines there was another problem: much of the second series was a first draft. For the first series, Douglas had written and rewritten, self-editing mercilessly. On the second series, there simply wasn't the time. While Fit the Eighth had been started on 19th May 1979, Fit the Twelfth was still being mixed shortly before it was due to be broadcast, on 25th January 1980.

The recordings soon reached the point at which the cast had caught up with the author: "They were recording part of the show in one part of the studio, while I was in another part of the studio actually writing the next scene. And this escalated to the point where the last show was being mixed in Maida Vale about half an hour before it was due to be broadcast from Broadcasting House. At which point the tape got wound round the capstan, and they had to take the tape recorder apart to unwind it, then get it onto a motorbike to be taken to Broadcasting House. At one point, we nearly sent them the first half of the tape, then we were going to unwind the second half and get it down to Broadcasting House before they had finished playing the first half. Geoffrey Perkins, Paddy Kingsland and Lisa Braun all deserved medals for that!"

The reviews for the series were almost all excellent, despite the fact that many of the reviewers had only heard extracts from the six episodes (due to the fact that the bits they didn't hear hadn't yet been mixed but no-one was going to tell the reviewers that...).

The only voice raised against the series came from Mr Arthur Butterworth, who wrote to the *Radio Times*, saying, "In just about 50 years of radio and latterly TV listening and watching, this strikes me as the most fatuous, inane, childish, pointless, codswalloping drivel... It is not even remotely funny."

The *Radio Times* cover feature was a source of satisfaction to the cast and crew, but an irritant to Geoffrey Perkins, who felt the article was abysmal and overwritten, and requested that certain changes be made in it before it was printed "to prevent us all from looking like idiots".

A discussion on Radio 3's *Critics' Forum* programme found the panel of critics ranged between enthusiasm and bafflement. Perhaps the most perceptive comment was that of Robert Cushman, the chairman, who said "[*Hitchhiker's* has...] the sort of effect that a *Monty Python* programme actually has, of making everything that appears immediately after it on radio or television or whatever, seem absolutely ludicrous. It does have that marvellous cleansing thing about it."

The second radio series contained some excellent sequences, some of which, like the body debit cards and the robot disco, have not been repeated elsewhere. Other sections were unwieldy and overly strung out: the shoe material, for example, which correctly merited about half a page when it appeared in book form. Overall, though, it was less successful than the first series; something Douglas planned to sort out when he wrote the second book.

12

LEVEL 42

When the paperback of *The Hitchhiker's Guide to the Galaxy* appeared, the last page, instead of carrying the usual advertisements for other titles by the same publisher, carried an advert that read:

DON'T PANIC!

Megadodo publications, in association with Original Records, brought [sic] you the Double L.P. of the radio series. Fill out the form and send it off, with your cheque or postal order attached…

Despite the fact that it might well have meant the loss of Chapter 35 (on the back of which the advert was printed), a large number of people sent off for their mail-order copies of a record called *The Hitchhiker's Guide to the Galaxy*.

A number of record companies had expressed interest in making the vinyl version of the show, following the radio broadcasts. One company had already got an option on it, but, since they were not doing anything with it, Original Records stepped in and got the recording rights.

Geoffrey Perkins says of the first record, "It was very difficult. We knew it was going to be a double album, but we could not very well put half an hour on each side. So we sat down and worked out — reluctantly — which bits to cut. I was very happy with it. There were a number of things that were improvements, like the voice treatments. And when Trillian says, 'Please relax...' and we put this lovely little tune behind it. The infinite improbability sequence itself had only a fraction of the elements that went into the same scene on the radio series, but it's actually far more telling because they're clear. On radio we had thought that if we threw absolutely everything in, it would come out fascinating. Instead it came out a complete jumble — there were bits of everything in it; people had left records around in the studio from a previous show and we put a bit of that on, anything lying around. But when we mixed it all together it was a jumble and a lot of it was completely dropped. It was a definite wankoff." The cast of the radio show was almost the same as that of the record, although the late Valentine Dyall, radio's 'Man In Black', replaced Geoffrey McGivern as Deep Thought. (He was also to play Gargravarr, with a similar voice treatment, in the second series.)

Considering the record was only available by mail order, at least initially, it sold amazingly well. Over 120,000 units were sold in the first year, and it made a number of the music charts. The cover was an expanded version of the Hipgnosis book cover, including some entries from the *Guide* that have never appeared elsewhere. The record essentially covered the first four episodes of the radio series, edited down somewhat.

The second record, *The Restaurant at the End of the Universe*, was slightly less successful. Geoffrey Perkins again: "We all found the first record a very interesting experience. By the time we got to the second record, it was less so (partially because none of us had been paid for the first record).

"Now a lot of people like the second record, because it's more definitive and much more complete than the first.

"Unfortunately that is because it is far too long on each side. It's just a rough cut. We had decided to leave it a few days, and come back and edit it with a fresh mind — I went up to Edinburgh for the Festival, and when I came back, three days later, they had rushed through the record and cut it! I felt it was flabby, and I wanted to speed it up."

Adams agreed: "The second record is (a) very long on both sides, and (b) full of blah."

Perkins is still a fan of the first record: "The nice thing about doing the record was you stuck in bits that you knew people could only pick up on the second or third time through. Whereas the radio transmission had to be clear the first time."

In terms of plot, the second record is most similar to the last two episodes of the TV series: the Haggunenon material is missing, replaced by Disaster Area's stuntship.

The cover of the second record showed a yellow rubber duck, presumably in deference to the 'B' Ark Captain's immortal comment that "one's never alone with a rubber duck". As a publicity stunt related to the duck theme, on the release of the second record, the window of the HMV record shop in London's Oxford Street was filled by a display that involved a bathtub filled with twelve live week-old ducklings. The stunt, brainchild of Original Records' director Don Mousseau, finished rather earlier than expected when complaints were received from animal welfare groups.

When released in the US the records carried the text of a version of 'How to Leave the Planet' (see Appendix IV).

The two albums were not the only *Hitchhiker's*-connected records, though. There were also two singles released by 'Marvin the Paranoid Android', Stephen Moore. These were:

'Marvin' ("Ten million logic functions, maybe more. They make me pick up paper off the floor... You know what really makes me mad? They clean me with a Brillo pad. A car wash wouldn't be so bad... Solitary solenoid, terminally paranoid Marvin...") c/w 'Metal Man', about a spaceship out of control, trapped in a black hole, trying to persuade Marvin to rescue it. It got a limited amount of airplay, and made it into the lower reaches of the British charts.

'Reasons to Be Miserable' ("...give my brain a pain, very little turns me on, Marvin is my name..."), a titular parody of Ian Dury's 'Reasons to Be Cheerful', c/w 'Marvin I Love You', the story of Marvin's cleanout of old data tapes, discovering a love message ("Marvin

I love you, remember I'm programmed for you..."), a weird combination of narrative over electropop and 50s love song. This got a very limited airplay and didn't do very much at all.

Douglas Adams acted as consultant on the songs, and when asked about them would play a sweet lullaby on one of his many guitars (Marvin's song from *Life, the Universe and Everything*, with a tune by Douglas) maintaining that he always thought they should have released that as a single. If the *Life, the Universe and Everything* radio series ever gets made listeners may finally get to hear it.

(A fairly complete listing of all the songs used in *Hitchhiker's* can be found in the radio scripts book.)

13

OF MICE, AND MEN, AND TIRED TV PRODUCERS

"At first, I wasn't that interested in doing a visual version of *Hitchhiker's*. But while I was working on *Doctor Who* I began to realise that we have an enormous amount of special effects stuff which is simply not being used as it might be. If it turns out the way I'm beginning to visualise it, I think it could actually look very extraordinary."

— Douglas Adams, 1979.

"The *Hitchhiker's* television series was not a happy production. There was a personality clash between myself and the director. And between the cast and the director. And between the tea lady and the director..."

— Douglas Adams, 1983.

TELEVISION: EPISODE THREE.

MODEL SHOT:
THE HEART OF GOLD SPEEDING THROUGH A MURKY SKY. VERY FEW STARS, AND WHAT STARS THERE ARE ARE DARK AND VAGUE.
WE HEAR WHAT SOUNDS LIKE KISSING, AND THEN

A LITTLE RATTLING NOISE. JUST AS WE ARE BEGIN-
NING TO WONDER WHAT IS GOING ON, WE CUT
TO TRILLIAN'S CABIN. IT, AND THE OTHERS WE
SHALL SEE IN A MOMENT (REDRESSES) IS SMALL
AND CRAMPED. IT INCLUDES A BED WHICH
APPEARS TO FLOAT IN POSITION.

TRILLIAN IS GIVING HER ATTENTION TO A SMALL
MOUSE CAGE WITH A COUPLE OF WHITE MICE IN
IT. ONE OF THEM IS RUNNING IN A TREADWHEEL
(HENCE THE RATTLING NOISE) AND TRILLIAN IS
MAKING SOPPY SUCKING NOISES AT THEM (HENCE
THE KISSING NOISE). AFTER A MOMENT OR SO SHE
TURNS AWAY FROM THE CAGE. THE BED MOVES
TOWARDS HER INVITINGLY.

TRILLIAN: No thanks, I can't sleep.

SILENTLY A TV SCREEN ABOVE THE BED LIGHTS UP
WITH A PICTURE OF A FLOCK OF SHEEP MOVING
PAST CAMERA. SHE PUSHES A PANEL NEXT TO IT
AND THE PICTURE WINKS OUT AGAIN.

ONE OF THE UBIQUITOUS COMPUTER CONSOLES
NEXT TO HER BED LIGHTS UP.

EDDIE: Just trying to help. A little soothing music tuned to
your personal Delta rhythms?

MUSIC FLOODS THROUGH THE ROOM. SOME-
THING VERY NAUSEATING AND SACCHARINE.

TRILLIAN: No thank you.

THE MUSIC STOPS.

EDDIE: A story? Once upon a time there were three
computers — an analogue computer, a digital
computer and a sub-meson computer. They all lived
happily in a complex three-way interface…

TRILLIAN LEAVES THE ROOM IN IRRITATION.

EDDIE: Wait a minute… I haven't got to the really tiring bit yet.

CUT TO TRILLIAN WALKING DOWN THE DARKENED
CORRIDOR. SHE IS GOING TOWARDS THE BRIDGE.
SHE PASSES ANOTHER COMPUTER CONSOLE. IT

LIGHTS UP.

EDDIE: I can skip right on to the section where they try and find a binary model for the ineluctable modality of the visible. That's very, very soporific.

TRILLIAN IGNORES THIS AND ENTERS THE DOOR OF THE BRIDGE.

CUT TO THE INTERIOR OF THE BRIDGE. THIS TOO IS IN SEMI-DARKNESS. A COMPUTER CONSOLE LIGHTS UP.

EDDIE: Especially if I tell it in my slow... deep... voice... (HE MATCHES HIS VOICE TO THE DESCRIPTION, AND HIS CONSOLE LIGHTS DIM APPROPRIATELY.)

TRILLIAN: Computer!

EDDIE: (BRIGHTLY AGAIN.) Hi there!

ALL THE LIGHTS ON THE BRIDGE LIGHT UP SIMULTANEOUSLY WITH THIS. TRILLIAN WINCES.

TRILLIAN: Just tell me where we are, will you?

CUT TO MODEL SHOT, AS BEFORE, OF THE HEART OF GOLD IN MOTION THROUGH THE DIM SKY.

THIS TIME WE HEAR SNORING. NOT L.E.* SNORING, BUT DRAMA SNORING.

CUT TO ANOTHER SLEEPING CUBICLE.

THIS IS ARTHUR'S.

HE IS FAST ASLEEP. HANGING UP ON ONE WALL OF HIS ROOM ARE HIS CLOTHES, I.E. HIS TROUSERS AND DRESSING GOWN. THE PANEL AGAINST WHICH THEY ARE HANGING LIGHTS UP VERY DIMLY. LINES CRISS-CROSS IT. THEY ARE MEASURING HIS CLOTHES. AFTER A FEW MOMENTS, ANOTHER SUIT OF CLOTHES MATERIALISES NEXT TO THEM. THIS IS FAIRLY CONVENTIONAL SCIENCE FICTION GEAR, PROBABLY SILVERY.

CUT TO THE NEXT CUBICLE. FORD PREFECT IS HAVING DIFFICULTY SLEEPING BECAUSE OF

* Light Entertainment.

ARTHUR SNORING NEXT DOOR.

HE TURNS OVER. BECAUSE THE BED COVERING IS VERY THIN SPACE BLANKET HE IS FRUSTRATED IN HIS ATTEMPT TO WRAP IT ROUND HIS HEAD TO KEEP OUT THE NOISE. HE PICKS UP HIS TOWEL FROM BESIDE HIS BED AND PRESSES THAT AROUND HIS EARS.

CUT TO THE NEXT CUBICLE CABIN. THERE IS SNORING EMANATING FROM HERE TOO.

WE GO CLOSE UP ON ONE OF ZAPHOD'S HEADS. IT IS FAST ASLEEP AND SNORING. THE CAMERA PASSES OVER TO HIS OTHER HEAD WHICH OBVIOUSLY CANNOT SLEEP ON ACCOUNT OF THE SNORING OF THE FIRST HEAD.

QUIETLY, THE DOOR TO HIS CUBICLE SLIDES OPEN. TRILLIAN IS OUTLINED IN THE DOORWAY.

TRILLIAN:	Hey, Zaphod?
ZAPHOD:	Er, yeah?
TRILLIAN:	You know what you came to look for?
ZAPHOD:	Yeah?
TRILLIAN:	I think we just found it

ZAPHOD SITS UP.

ZAPHOD:	Hey, what?
TRILLIAN:	You called it "the most improbable planet that ever existed".

INTO OPENING CREDITS.

— Unused draft opening for TV series, Episode Three.

The television version of *Hitchhiker's* begins with a computer readout of time remaining until the end of the world, while the sun rises over a quiet English landscape.

The computer printout was faked; so was the English landscape. What the audience saw was imitation computer readout while a light bulb was lifted over a model of a landscape. The ingenuity and the casual faking of something that seems so natural exemplify the six television episodes of *Hitchhiker's*.

For many people the first, perhaps the only, exposure to *Hitchhiker's* came from the BBC television series. Certainly it was responsible, from its first airing in 1981 on BBC 2, for millions of extra sales of the books.

The idea was first mooted in late 1979, by John Lloyd, Associate Producer of the television series. He explains: "I was in TV at the time of the TV show, and I had done one series of *Not the Nine O'Clock News*, and I was looking around for something new to do — I didn't know at that time that *NTNOCN* was going to be the absurd success that it became, so I was wondering what to do next, and *Hitchhiker's* was the obvious thing — it had been a great success on radio, and would obviously be great fun to do visually.

"Douglas and I had always been fascinated by science fiction. Now this was before *Star Wars* and all that, we're still back in the time when people said that science fiction would never get anywhere commercially.

"Anyway, I wrote to my head of department saying, 'There's this great radio series, it would make great TV, it's just what I want to do.' He told me he didn't know anything about it, so I wrote him a memo saying what *Hitchhiker's* had done, and how it had been nominated for a Hugo award, and how it had been repeated more times than any other programme in history, that it had been a stage show and a bestselling book... this huge long list of credits. He said, 'All right, let's give it a go,' and he commissioned the first script, which Douglas wrote.

"It was an extraordinarily good script. Douglas had done what he did earlier with the books, which was to turn the radio series into something which you would never know had been based on a radio show. It used the medium to the fullest. My boss said that it was the best Light Entertainment script he had ever read — he was that excited!

"As I remember, Alan Bell started off as director and I was producer for the first episode, although it shaded into a co-production as I didn't have much experience with TV budgeting. But then the BBC went and scheduled the second series of *Not the Nine O'Clock News* on top of the recording of *Hitchhiker's*. *NTNOCN* was a real seven days a week job, and I couldn't do both.

"I was really angry about it. I felt at the time like the BBC felt that (as *NTNOCN* was beginning to get successful) they didn't want the junior producer in the department (me) to have two successes at once. So they used *Hitchhiker's* to give someone else some work. I was really furious as I became perforce 'Associate Producer'. Which meant nothing. I didn't have any clout at the BBC, being just a junior producer on attachment — theoretically they could have sent me back to radio. I said I'd try to keep an eye on the occasional recording and rehearsal, but frankly I didn't have the time, and basically I had nothing to do with the TV show.

"Alan Bell made a big point of this in the TV show, as when my credit comes up in the titles it explodes and shoots off into space...*

"Really, the only thing I did on the TV series was writing the original memo, and being in on a few early discussions to get things moving, and the BBC corporate machinations booted me out."

Lloyd has mixed feelings about the director and producer of the series, Alan J. W. Bell, and on how the television shows eventually turned out.

"I didn't like working with Alan. He's one of this breed of TV producers who... I'm not saying he isn't hardworking, because he is, but he wouldn't ever run over time, or overspend. He just wanted to get the job done. He's less interested in the script or the performance than he is in the logistics of how the programme gets made.

"In some of the rehearsals I attended actors were saying the words in the wrong order, and mispronouncing them, and Alan wouldn't correct them. He was much more interested in the technical side — and technically he knew an awful lot. He was very bold and brave on the technical side. Some of the actual shots in *Hitchhiker's* are wonderful.

"But it didn't work for me as a comic performance, because it wasn't being directed. They hadn't got old Perkins there; he's a real nitty-gritty man, the sort who would spend hours getting one sound effect right, worrying about the script and the attitude and all that,

* It is true that John Lloyd's Associate Producer credit does explode during the end titles. However, according to Alan Bell, this is pure coincidence.

things which Alan would see as trivial and irritating.

"I remember going to the editing of the pilot, and there were some terrible edits, and I told Alan he had to go back and do it again, because it just didn't work. His attitude was, 'We haven't got any time — we've got to go on.'

"Personally, I think *Hitchhiker's* on TV was not all it could have been. If it had been done properly it would have won all the awards. And the only evidence there is that it was a really original show are the computer graphics. Reading the scripts you'd think, 'Suddenly television has gone into the 1990s. This is unbelievable!' But then, most of the performances and filming were nowhere near as good as, say, *Doctor Who*.

"Alan is not a great original mind. Douglas is.

"To give Alan Bell credit, it was a difficult job to do logistically, and you can't Belgium with TV the way you can with radio — the way Geoffrey would keep going till the last minute and keep actors hanging around while stuff was written. You can't do that with TV — there's a limit. There does have to be a grip on things which Douglas, well... I've co-produced things with him on radio, and he does tend to be a bit daffy. He tends to think you can go on forever. I suppose he's been a bit spoiled.

"Alan did get the thing onto the air, which probably Douglas would never have done — and I can't say that I would have done, either!"

It was the first time that Douglas had worked with someone on *Hitchhiker's* who he felt was less than sympathetic to his ideas and work. He wanted John Lloyd as producer, and he wanted Geoffrey Perkins around: the radio people he knew understood *Hitchhiker's*.

This was not to be. Alan Bell was a television person, and had, as he admits, little time for people from radio who attempted to tell him his job.

Geoffrey Perkins explains, "Television people tend to think that radio people don't know anything, which has an element of truth in it, but they tend to know more about scripts than people in TV ever do. And the TV people tended to think that Douglas didn't know what he was talking about.

"Now, on radio, when Douglas burbled, one could say, 'Okay,

might try that,' or, 'No, shut up.' But the TV attitude was that he didn't know what he was talking about. I read the first TV script and I thought it was one of the best scripts I'd ever seen. He'd thought up all that graphics stuff. It was absolutely brilliant."

Ask people what they remember best of the *Hitchhiker's* TV series, and the answer is usually "the computer graphics". The graphics — sequences apparently from the screen of the actual *Hitchhiker's Guide* — were incredibly detailed, apparently computer-created animated graphics, full of sight gags and in-jokes, and presumably designed for people with freeze-frame and slow-motion videos, since there was no way one could pick up on the complexities of the graphics sequences in a single watching at normal speed.

Would one have noticed, for example, the cartoons of Douglas Adams himself, posing as a Sirius Cybernetics Corporation Advertising Executive, writing hard in the dolphin sequence, and in drag as Paula Nancy Millstone Jennings*? Could one have picked up on all the names and phone numbers of some of the best places in the universe to purchase, or dry out from, a Pan Galactic Gargle Blaster?

One of the phone numbers in the graphics of Episode Six was that of a leading computer magazine who phoned Pearce Studios, responsible for the graphics, to ask which computer it was done on, and whether a flat-screen television was built into the book prop used on the show. The comment beside the phone number was not flattering.

The computer graphics were all done by hand.

In January 1980, animator and science fiction fan Kevin Davies was working for Pearce Studios in Hanwell, West London, when he

---

* Douglas also made a couple of real-life appearances in the TV series. In Episode One he can be seen at the back of the pub, awaiting the end of the world with equanimity, in Episode Two he is the gentleman who withdraws large quantities of money from a bank, then takes off all his clothes and wades into the sea. Rumours of an out-takes tape (in which more of Douglas than is seemly is seen in this scene) abound. Douglas played this part because the actor who was meant to be doing it was moving house that day, and, an hour away from filming, Douglas stepped into the breach. As it were. During the filming of the series, and while he wasn't running naked into the sea, Douglas generally sat in a deckchair and did cross-words. Sometimes, according to a number of the actors and technicians, he fell off the chair, although none of them were quite sure why.

heard the blipping and bleeping of *Star Wars* droid R2D2 from the BBC cutting rooms down the corridor. He wandered down to the cutting rooms and met Alan J. W. Bell, at that point engaged in cutting a sequence of *Jim'll Fix It* in which a child got to visit the *Empire Strikes Back* set.

Bell discovered in Davies not only a *Hitchhiker's* fan with communicable enthusiasm, but also through Davies, he discovered Pearce Studios, led by Rod Lord, who were commissioned to do the graphics for the TV show (their quote for Episode One was half that of the BBC's own animation department, while the trial section produced by the BBC's own animators was so appalling it was unusable).

Pearce Studios, under animator Rod Lord, did not possess a graphics computer. What they did have was animators, who worked in a very computerish style.

WARNING! TECHNICAL BIT.

HOW IT WAS DONE

The sound track of Peter Jones's voice was broken down for timing, and notes of frame numbers per line of dialogue were taken. Pencil drawings were made, then punched acetate cels were laid on top, and the pictures were traced with pens. The lettering was a combination of dry transfer and set on an IBM typewriter. The artwork (black drawings and lettering on a clear cel) would then be photographically reversed out, to clear letters and drawings on black backgrounds.

These were back lit under an ordinary 16mm film rostrum camera, the colour being added with filter gels. Each line of lettering and each colour required a separate exposure and a separate piece of artwork (the Babel fish sequence, for example, needed about a dozen passes under the camera). The main difference between this animation and the more usual version was that instead of animating a single frame per drawing, several frames at a time were taken to give any moving objects the slightly jerky, staggered feel that people expect from computer graphics.

END OF TECHNICAL BIT.

(The television series was entered into the innovation category at the Golden Rose of Montreux TV Festival. It won absolutely nothing (the Golden Rose went to the US-made *Baryshnikov on Broadway*, in case anyone is interested) and apparently left foreign audiences confused and reeling. At home it did rather better. In the BAFTA Awards for 1981, *Hitchhiker's* received two of the ten awards. Rod Lord gained a BAFTA award for the graphics*, and Michael McCarthy received one for being Sound Supervisor of *Hitchhiker's*.)

I asked Paddy Kingsland, responsible for most of the music and sound effects in the TV series (and the pilot for the radio series, as well as the second radio series) what was so special about the *Hitchhiker's* sound effects, and what the differences were between radio sound and TV sound. "I suppose the difference between doing TV and radio was that for radio they'd say, 'We need The End of the World as a sound effect — go away and do it.'

"On TV The End of the World is composed of hundreds of shots with a close-up of the Vogon ship, then a close-up of screaming crowds, a shot of a laser in space, and so on. You don't just have one sound effect, you have a bit of this and a bit of that ending with a bang which actually then cuts off because you're back inside the spaceship again very quickly. The shape is all finished and all you can do is do stuff to fit the pictures that have been done.

"I thought the TV show was good in parts. I thought the computer graphic stuff was very good, very well thought out. And some of the performances were marvellous.

"But inevitably there were things that didn't hang together too well. It's a problem you get when you mix together film and TV studios and doing it all to a deadline — there's no time to sit back and look at the thing and say, 'Is that all right?' And if it isn't, to do it again.

"I don't think it had the magic of the radio series, because you could see everybody. Like Zaphod's extra head — that was one of the more spectacular failures of the TV show. A tatty prop can be

---

* Rod Lord received his second graphics BAFTA for the 'computer graphics' in the *Max Headroom* TV movie, four years later. Now I bet you thought those were computer generated...

amusing, but if you don't have the money to do it right it's sometimes better not to do it at all.

"I was pleased with the sound effects of the TV series, however. It was the detail that did it. Alan Bell had everybody miked up with radio mikes to start with so that they only got the voices of the people and none of the exterior effects. So we did things like overdubbing all the footsteps in the spaceships — which is never done for British TV.

"To give the effect of them walking through spaceships we got a couple of beer kegs from the BBC club and actually walked around on the beer kegs while watching the screen, so when they're walking along you get these metallic footsteps instead of the rather unconvincing wooden ones you would have got. It took ages to do, but it paid off.

"I did all the effects for the computer graphics — the film would arrive with nothing except for Peter Jones's voice. I had to go through it doing all the sound effects and the music tracks as well. All the little beeps and explosions and things, which took ages to do — quite time-consuming. The TV series was interesting to work on, although frankly I preferred the radio series."

The necessity of getting the *Hitchhiker's* scripts to the screen somewhere within the budget was responsible for a certain amount of technical innovation. Alan Bell is proudest of his development of a new special effects process of doing 'glass shots'.

A glass shot, in cinematic tradition, consists of erecting a tower with a painting done on glass, high in the studio, then filming through it, thus giving the illusion that the glass painting is part of the picture. (The long shot of the Vogon hold in the first episode, for example, was done like this.) It's a complicated, fiddly, and expensive process.

Bell's solution was simple: scenes requiring matte shots were filmed or taped, then a photographic blow-up of one frame would be made. From the photos, paintings would be made. The paintings would be photographed as slides, and the previously filmed segment would be matched up and inlaid into the painted shot. This was quicker and easier than painting on glass, and is perhaps best displayed in the 'pier at Southend' sequence, when only a small section of the pier was built in the studio. The rest is a perfectly aligned matte painting.

The plot of the television series is nearest to the plot of the two records. From Magrathea the travellers are blown straight to Milliways, and, leaving there in a stolen stuntship, we follow Arthur and Ford to prehistoric Earth, where the series finishes.

The places where the TV *Hitchhiker's* succeeded best and failed worst were places where Douglas had written something into the radio series that could not be done on television. The narration sequences are an excellent example: one does not need lengthy narrations on television; however, being stuck with them, Douglas needed to work out how to make them work, and came up with the graphics concept.

As Douglas explained: "What made it work was the fact that it is impossible to transfer radio to television. We had to find creative solutions to problems in a way you wouldn't have had to if you were writing something similar for television immediately.

"The medium dictates the style of the show, and transferring from one to another means you're going against the grain the whole time. It's the point where you go against the grain that you come up with the best bits. The bits that were the easiest to transfer were the least interesting bits of the TV show.

"The idea of readouts from the book itself done in computer graphics form was that kind of thing. So you get little drawings, diagrams, all the words the narrator is saying, plus further expansion — footnotes and little details — all coming out at you from the screen. You can't possibly take it all in.

"I like the idea of a programme where, when you get to the end of it, you feel you didn't get it all. There are so many programmes that are half an hour long and at the end of it you're half an hour further into your life with nothing to show for it. If you didn't get it all, that's much more stimulating.

"I wasn't as pleased with the TV series as I was with the radio series, because I missed the intimacy of the radio work. Television pictures stifle the picturing facilities of the mind. I wanted to step over that problem by packing the screen with so much information that more thought, not less, was provoked by the readers. Sometimes what you see is less exciting than what you envisage."

CUT TO MODEL SHOT OF THE SHIP.

THE MISSILES ARE ON THE POINT OF HITTING IT WHEN THE SKY EXPLODES WITH BEWILDERING COLOURS AND A MONTAGE OF TOTALLY INCONGRUOUS IMAGES. THESE SHOULD INCLUDE DISTORTED PICTURES OF THE PASSEN-GERS, STARS, MONKEYS, STAPLING MACHINES, TREES, CHEESE SOUFFLÉS... IN OTHER WORDS, A BRIEF VISION OF MADNESS. INCLUDED SHOULD ALSO BE A SPERM WHALE AND A BOWL OF PETUNIAS. WE GO BACK INSIDE THE BRIDGE.

EVERYTHING IS HIGGLEDY-PIGGLEDY. THERE ARE A VERY LARGE NUMBER OF MELONS LYING ABOUT.

THERE IS ALSO (THOUGH NO ONE CALLS ATTENTION TO IT) A GOAT WITH A SCALE MODEL OF THE EIFFEL TOWER STRAPPED TO ITS HEAD STANDING ABOUT. THIS GOAT IS NEVER EVER REFERRED TO, BUT IT WILL CONTINUE TO BE WITH THEM FOR MOST OF THE REST OF THE SERIES.

ZAPHOD: (DAZED.) What the photon happened?

— Unused draft for TV series script, Episode Three.

It was all too easy for Douglas to give Zaphod Beeblebrox an extra arm and an extra head during the radio series. No one ever saw him; it was a one-off throwaway line. But if one has the televisual task of trans-forming this into something that works on the screen one thanks one's lucky stars that Douglas did not give Beeblebrox five heads, or fifty...

Unable to find a bicephalic actor (or at least, one who could learn his lines), the BBC resorted to Mark Wing-Davey, Zaphod on radio, and built him an animatronic head and an extra arm (mostly stuffed, but occasionally, when all hands needed to be seen to be working, the hand of someone behind him, sticking an extra arm out, as can be seen quite clearly in the Milliways sequence of Episode Five).

ASTONISHINGLY ENOUGH, ONE WALL OF THE BRIDGE APPEARS TO GIVE DIRECTLY OUT ONTO QUITE A LARGE SUNNY PATIO, WITH GRASS, A DECKCHAIR, A TABLE WITH A LARGE BRIGHTLY COLOURED SUNSHADE, EXOTIC FLOWERS AND SO ON. SEATED IN THE DECKCHAIR WITH A DRINK IS AN EXTRAORDINARY LOOKING MAN. HE HAS TWO HEADS. OBVIOUSLY ONE OF THESE IS GOING TO BE A FAKE UNLESS WE CAN FIND AN ACTOR PREPARED TO UNDERGO SOME VERY EXOTIC SURGERY. THE REAL HEAD AND THE FAKE HEAD SHOULD LOOK AS FAR AS POSSIBLE ABSOLUTELY IDENTICAL: ANY SHORTCOMINGS IN THE REALISM OF THE FAKE HEAD SHOULD BE MATCHED BY THE MAKE-UP ON THE REAL ONE. THE FAKE SHOULD HAVE AN ARTIC-ULATED MOUTH AND ARTICULATED EYES.
— Unused draft for TV series script, Episode Two.

There was a problem with Zaphod's head. It looked false, and stuffed, and stuck there. This is not because it was a less than sterling piece of special effects work (although it wasn't that good), but also because things went wrong, and even when they didn't, the batteries tended to run down in rehearsals, so by the time a scene was filmed, the head just lolled around expressionlessly. As Douglas Adams said, "It was a very delicate mechanism, and it would work wonderfully for thirty seconds and then break down or get stuck and to get it working properly you'd have to spend an hour taking it apart and putting it back together again, and we never had that hour so we fudged as best we could."

As Mark Wing-Davey remembers, "The difficulty with the television series for me was Alan Bell (who we all know and love). I don't think he wanted the original members of the radio show at all, because he wanted the freedom to pick and choose a bit, but we were supposed to have first option so we came in and read for it. They didn't want any input from me on the way the character would look (I'd visualised him as a blonde beach bum). I quite liked the final design, but I refused to wear the eyepatch — I said, 'Give the other head the eyepatch, because I'm not having one! It's hard enough acting with another head, but with one eye as well...*'

"The other head was heavvvvvvy. Very heavy. I was wearing armour plating made of fibre glass, and because I wanted to be able to alternate the two right arms I had a special cut-out.

"There was a little switch hidden in the circuitry of my costume which switched the head on and off. We were under such pressure in the studio that occasionally I forgot to switch it on, so I'm acting away and it's just there. It cost £3,000 by the way — more than me!"

Costume design for the series was primarily the responsibility of Dee Robson, a veteran BBC designer with a penchant for science fiction. It was she who designed Ford Prefect's precisely clashing clothes — based on what could be found in the BBC's wardrobes, and it was she who gave Zaphod Beeblebrox yet another additional organ: examining the costume worn by Mark Wing-Davey reveals two trouser flies (one zipped, one buttoned) and, Dee's original costume notes explain, Zaphod has a "double crotch, padded to give effect of two organs".

As Mark Wing-Davey explained, "I said to wardrobe, you've seen Mick Jagger in those tight trousers — make me a pair. So I had these nine inch tubes down the front of the trousers for filming. When we got into the studio Dee came up to me to say she was 'worried about those... things. I thought they might be a bit obvious, so I've cut them down to six inches.'"

---

* This was decided after the initial animation had been done, so the Zaphod graphics in Episode One sport two eyepatches. Come to that, in the graphics of Episode One Arthur Dent doesn't have a dressing gown...

One of the most famous costumes, however, was Arthur Dent's: a dressing gown, over a pair of pyjamas. The dressing gown first appeared in the books following the television series: there is no mention of what Arthur is wearing in the first two books. That Arthur remained in the dressing gown throughout the TV series was Alan Bell's idea: Douglas had written a sequence on board the *Heart of Gold* in which the ship designed Arthur a silvery jump-suit. The whole sequence was scrapped, and Alan ensured that Arthur stayed in his dressing gown. As Bell explained, "What was special about Arthur was that he was in a dressing gown. Silver jump-suits are what they wore in *Star Wars*."

Alan J. W. Bell is a BBC Light Entertainment director and producer; having worked on such shows as *Maigret* and *Panorama* as a film editor, he won a BAFTA award for Terry Jones's and Michael Palin's *Ripping Yarns*, a BAFTA nomination for the long-running geriatric comedy *Last of the Summer Wine*, and a Royal Television Society award for *Hitchhikers*.

I met him initially in his office at the BBC, which still contains a number of items of *Hitchhiker's* memorabilia. It's a show he is proud of, and has many fond memories of. On his desk was a small plastic fruit machine which he urged me to try. I pulled the handle, but nothing happened; it should have squirted me with water. Alan pointed out to his secretary that it was her job to keep it filled, and we began the interview: this was BBC Light Entertainment.

"The first time I heard of *Hitchhiker's* was in a bar somewhere — I was asked if I'd heard it on the radio. I hadn't, so I listened to it, and I thought it was marvellous, inspired stuff, but there was no way it could be done on TV. It was all in the mind, all in the imagination.

"So about three months later I was asked to do it, and I said that I thought it couldn't be done, but they said 'We're going to do it,' so that was it. I had to do it.

"Now, I work for Light Entertainment, not Drama (who do *Doctor Who* and have experience of things like this), and we had no idea what the budgeting would be. All I could do was put down what I thought it would cost, and I was out by thousands of pounds. For the first episode, for example, we had to throw away £10,000 of model shots of spaceships, because they wobbled, and they looked like models. That first episode was about £40,000 over budget, which is vast in TV terms. But it had to be done right. Otherwise it would have been awful."

The first episode of *Hitchhiker's* was made very much as a pilot, and Alan Bell presented it to the heads of department at the BBC. Some of them didn't like it. They didn't understand it, nor for that matter did they realise it was meant to be funny. And the cost of the first episode — over £120,000 — was about four times as much as an equivalent episode of *Doctor Who*.

In order to demonstrate the humour of the show, Alan Bell arranged for a laugh track. This was done by assembling about a hundred science fiction fans in the National Film Theatre, playing them the first episode, and taping their reaction. As a warm-up to this a ten minute video was played, featuring Peter Jones reading hastily felt-penned cue cards in a bewildered fashion, assuring the audience that Zaphod Beeblebrox would be in the next episode, and, with the ubiquitous Kevin Davies, demonstrating the use of the headphones.

This is Peter Jones's only on-screen appearance in the *Hitchhiker's* television series, and is included in full on the DVD.

The audience loved the show, laughed on cue and generally had a good time, and while the BBC hierarchy had agreed that the next five episodes should be made (although they were made for more like £40,000 a show — one reason why the sets begin to get a little rudimentary towards the end), it did not insist on a laugh track. This was undoubtedly a Good Thing.

As Bell remembers, "The first episode was only a pilot, but by the time we had got half-way through, they had already commissioned the series, but we still didn't know the resources that would be required because all we had to go on were the radio scripts.

"When we'd finished it, the Powers That Be thought that the viewers wouldn't know that it was comedy unless we added a laughter track. So we hired the National Film Theatre and showed it on a big screen and gave all the audience headphones so they could hear the soundtrack nice and clearly, and they laughed all the way through. It did help that that audience was composed of fans..."

While much of the casting was the same on television and radio, there were a few variations.

"I wanted to keep everyone from the radio series, but sometimes people's voices don't match their physical appearance.

"For example, I wanted someone for Ford Prefect who looked slightly different, and when I saw Geoffrey McGivern I thought he looked too ordinary. Ford should be human but slightly unnerving, so we looked around for someone else. My secretary* suggested David Dixon. He was great, but I thought we'd change the colour of his eyes and make them a vivid blue, so we got special tinted contact lenses which looked marvellous in real life, but when it came to television the cameras just weren't sensitive enough to pick up on it — except in the pub scene at the beginning.

"Sandra Dickinson got the part of Trillian after we had interviewed about 200 young ladies for the role. None of them had performed it with the right feelings. The girl had to have a sense of humour. And then Sandra Dickinson came in and read it and made the lines more funny than any other actress who'd done an audition."

Sandra Dickinson was a surprising choice for Trillian; the character was described in the book as a dark-haired, dark-complexioned English woman; Sandra played it (as indeed she is in real life) as a small blonde American with a squeaky husky voice. As Douglas Adams said of her, "She could have done a perfect 'English Rose' voice, and looking back I think perhaps we should have got her to do it. But it was such a relief to find someone who could actually read Trillian's lines with some humour, and give the character some life, that we just had her do it as herself, and not change a thing."

Another surprise casting came with Episode Five: Sandra's husband, Peter Davison, the fifth and blandest Doctor Who. He played the Dish of the Day, a bovine creature which implores diners to eat it. As Alan Bell explains, "Sandra came to me and said that

---

* It should be noted that most of the really important pieces of casting in *Hitchhiker's* seem to have been done by secretaries. Whether this phenomenon is unique to *Hitchhikers*, or whether it is extant throughout the entertainment industry has not been adequately investigated, at least, not by me.

Peter wanted to play a guest part in *Hitchhiker's* and she suggested the Dish of the Day. I said, 'You cannot put Peter Davison in a cow skin!' but she said, 'No, really, he wants to do it!' I said OK, and we booked him. We didn't pay him star status; he just did it for the fun of it. And he played it very well."

Early on in the press releases for *Hitchhiker's*, great play was made of the fact that they would not be filming in the quarries and gravel pits in which *Doctor Who* has always travelled to distant planets. And they wouldn't have any of the plastic rocks that made *Star Trek's* alien worlds so strangely unconvincing.

Instead, they would go abroad. Iceland, perhaps. Or Morocco. The Magrathean sequences, one was assured, would be filmed somewhere exotic.

Alan Bell: "Douglas wanted us to film the Magrathean sequences in Iceland. So I looked up the holiday brochures, and it was very cold and there weren't any hotels of any note, but I had been to Morocco years before and I remembered there was a part of Morocco that was very space-like. We went to look, but we had so much trouble getting through customs — without cameras — and we met a Japanese film crew who said, 'Don't come because they deliberately delay you so you'll spend more money!' — they'd had all their equipment impounded for three weeks.

"So we ended up in this rather nice clay pit in Cornwall, where we also did the beach scenes: Marvin playing beach ball and Douglas going into the sea."

Most of the cast and crew have memories of the Cornish clay pit. Some of them have to do with the fact that there were no toilets down there. Others have to do with David Learner, the actor inside Marvin, who, due to the length of time it took to get in and out of the Marvin costume, was abandoned in the clay pit during the occasional rain showers during filming, protected from rust by an umbrella.

Prehistoric Britain was filmed in the Lake District, during a cold snap, which meant that Aubrey Morris (playing the Captain of the 'B' Ark, in his bath), and the extras clad in animal skins who played the pre-Golgafrincham humans, were all frozen to the bone, and spent all their time when not on camera bundled up in blankets and drinking tea.

The other interesting location was that of Arthur's house — discovered by Alan Bell while driving, lost, around Leatherhead. (The gate, which is all one sees knocked down by a bulldozer, was built especially.)

It was while the pub scenes at the beginning were being filmed that the union troubles began for *Hitchhiker's* — the precise nature of which no one seems clear on anymore, but which apparently involved a trip to the pub by some members of the cast and crew which might have been recreational, but which the union representatives assumed was professional, and as such they felt they should have been invited, or something.*

The computer room at the end of Episode Four (the Shooty and Bang Bang sequence) was actually filmed on Henley Golf Course. "We wanted somewhere near at hand which we could build and blow up," Alan Bell remembered. "It was just sufficiently out of London that we could warn the locals that if they heard a bang at two in the morning, don't pay any attention to it — it's only us! You can't see it on the show, but it's actually raining into the set — it was open at the top."

Union problems continued when the filming returned to the studios: "The Milliways set was actually the biggest set they've ever put into the BBC's biggest studio. The unions said they wouldn't put the set in, and we had to cut bits out, which was a pity.

"But the way we filmed it you never saw it all at once anyway, just parts at a time. My reason for that was that... well, if you've ever watched a variety show, they'll spend all their money on a set, the singer sings, the camera pulls back, and you see the set. And song after song you see the set, and you get bored with it.

"So I said, when we do *Hitchhiker's* we'll leave things to people's imaginations, so even though we had this huge set there isn't one

---

* The story changes according to who you talk to and I never really understood any of the versions. I also had the impression that nobody telling me quite understood their version either. This is one of the few examples of woolly reporting in an otherwise excellent book, and should not be counted against it.

shot where you see it all. Only parts of it, because then you think it's even bigger than it is. You never see the edges of it.

"Things got very rushed toward the end. The series was structured to be made on a daily basis, so that, once all the graphics work and location work for each episode was done, the studio filming could be done in one day in the studio. It should really have been five days at the studio, so there was an enormous panic to get everything done in time. And the Electricians' Union were in dispute, so at 10.00 pm every night the lights went out, the plugs were pulled, and that was it. There's a scene where you see Arthur Dent running to hide behind a girder — we actually used a shot of Simon Jones, the actor, running across the studio to get to his mark."

The show was a success. The fans loved it, it garnered excellent reviews, most people were pleasantly surprised and befuddled by the computer graphics, and it won the BBC a few awards in a year otherwise dominated by ITV's *Brideshead Revisited*.

Everybody waited expectantly for the second series. And waited. And waited. There are conflicting stories of why the second series never came to be made...

John Lloyd: "They asked Douglas to do a second series. As far as I know, he went to the BBC and said, 'I'd be delighted, but I never want to work with Alan Bell again.' And the BBC most untypically supported Alan — they said he was the only person to do it. That was the end of it. (I say untypically because if, say, a comedy star didn't get on with a producer he'd go to the head of department and they'd give him a new one. They'd do it for a star, but not for a writer.)"

Geoffrey Perkins: "Douglas wanted me to produce it. I heard that Alan Bell refused to direct if I were producer, and instead said how would I like to be script editor? This seemed to me the most thankless task imaginable — for the first TV series they didn't know how lucky they were — they already had the script from the radio series and records, they were in clover. They hadn't been through the whole thing of getting scripts out of Douglas. Now I knew that getting those scripts for the second series without any say in the way they were done would be an appalling, heartbreaking thing, possibly the most thankless task I could ever think up.

"I said no.

"My own impression is that the second series really got to brinkmanship. Douglas gave the BBC an ultimatum. They said no, fully expecting him to back down. And of course he didn't, and neither did they."

Alan Bell: "There was going to be a second series. It was all commissioned, we had fifty per cent more money, the actors were told the dates, and during that time Douglas went past his script deadline, and time was running out, we needed to have the information because otherwise, six weeks before production, what can you do? We needed sets built — there's no way you can build them in that time. The deadlines to deliver the scripts came and went, we gave him another three weeks and meetings were going on — and that was it, it had to be cancelled.

"It was going to begin with a test match in Australia, but we checked it out and the timing wasn't right, so we were looking at Headingly or somewhere. That was all I knew about the second TV series — it wasn't going to be the second radio series at all.

"Douglas is very strange. He believed that radio was the ultimate series and that TV let him down. I don't know. Maybe it did. I had to change a lot of things in production to make it stronger, like Slartibartfast's aircar: anyone who had seen *Star Wars* would think we'd stolen it from there, so I changed it to a bubble, and he was upset about that.

"We started making lists of his wild ideas. He wanted to make Marvin a chap in a leotard painted gold — if you see it on TV you'd know it was an actor. The fun of the script is that Marvin is a tin box that's depressed. If you see a man in a leotard you know it's an actor straightaway, and what's so unusual about an actor being depressed? And anyway there was that gold robot in *Star Wars*. That impasse went straight to the Head of Department.

"He wanted the Mice to be played by men in mouse skins. It wouldn't have worked. It would have looked like pantomime. He wanted it to be faithful to the radio, but you couldn't be faithful to the radio as it's visual, people have to walk from one side of the set to the other.

"So Douglas and I were fighting, not that that matters, because that's what life's all about. If you're on a production and everybody's enjoying themselves it's generally a load of rubbish, because people feel passionately about things. It was my job to throw out the bad ideas and keep the good.

"The change in role for the black Disaster Area stuntship was done by Douglas himself. John Lloyd was the co-writer of some episodes of the radio series, when Douglas was script editor of *Doctor Who* and also writing *Hitchhiker's*, and he was quite happy to farm out to John to write the bits he couldn't write, and the Black Ship bit was one of them. When it became a big success, Douglas very much regretted having shared the credit with John on those episodes so when it came to the TV series he wouldn't at any cost do anything that John Lloyd had written because he wanted it to be all Douglas Adams. I think if I was Douglas Adams I'd do exactly the same thing.

"We got on quite well, but I thought he was a hindrance. We used to tell him that the dubbing dates were in three weeks' time when we'd done it the day before, because if he came along he interfered all the time, and, I have to say, not necessarily for the better."

PRODUCTION SUGGESTION: Mice.
I've suggested using the eidophor images in case we can manage to do some very convincing puppetry to give us the appearance of talking mice, like the Muppets, or indeed Yoda in the otherwise terribly boring *Empire Strikes Back*. If we do that, then of course the mice must look as real as we can possibly make them, and not simply joke mice. That means that on the actual set, in the glass transports, we either use little life-size models, or indeed real mice, which would be preferable.

Obviously, if we can make them appear to be speaking convincingly, then it obviates the need for the very extreme voice treatments we had to use on radio, which were detrimental to the actual sense of the lines.

— Douglas Adams's production notes for TV series, Episode Five.

Douglas Adams: "A lot of what Alan says is simply not the case. Whether his memory is at fault or not, I don't know. All I would say is that as he cheerfully admits he will say what suits him rather than what happens to be the case. And therefore there's no point in arguing.

"I wouldn't start seriously moving on the second TV series until we'd sorted out various crucial aspects of how we were going to go about it. I felt very let down by the fact that though John Lloyd was meant to be producer he was rapidly moved aside, much to the detriment of the show. I'd always made it clear that I wanted Geoffrey Perkins, at the very least as a consultant.

"Neither of these things transpired in the first series. It was perfectly clear to myself and the cast that Alan had very little sympathy with the script. So I didn't want to go into the second series without that situation being remedied in some way, and the BBC was not prepared to come up with a remedy. That was the argument going on in the background, that was why I was not producing the scripts. I wasn't going to do the scripts until I knew we were going to do the series."

In 1984, when John Lloyd and Geoffrey Perkins were both involved, as producer and script editor respectively, in Central Television's *Spitting Image*, there were noises made that the *Spitting Image* company would have been interested in making a version of *Life, the Universe and Everything*. It would have been interesting — one feels that they would probably have been able to get Zaphod's head right — but the television rights were tied up with the film rights and nothing ever came of it.

14

THE RESTAURANT AT THE
END OF THE UNIVERSE

MARVIN: It's the people you meet that really get you down in
             this job. They're so boring. The best conversation I
             had was over thirty-four million years ago.
TRILLIAN: Oh dear.
MARVIN: And that was with a coffee machine.
ZAPHOD: Yeah, well, we're really cut up about that, Marvin.
             Now, where's our old ship?
MARVIN: It's in the restaurant.
ZAPHOD: What?
MARVIN: They had it made into teaspoons. I enjoyed that bit.
             Not very much though.
ZAPHOD: You mean they're stirring their coffee with my ship?
             The *Heart of Gold*? Hey, that was one of the creamiest
             space strutters ever stacked together.
                  — Cut from radio series script, Episode Five.

"Each time I come to a different version, I always think I could do it better; I'm very aware of what I feel I got wrong, what was thin or bad in the first version of it. Part of it is that I wrote it serially, so I was never sure where it was going. And no matter how frantically I'd plot it out, it would never adhere to the plot I had mapped out for it.

"You map out a plot, and you write the first scene, and inevitably the first scene isn't funny and you have to do something else, and you finally get the scene to be funny but it's no longer about what it was meant to be about, so you have to jack in the plot you had in mind and do a new one...

"After a while, it became pointless plotting too far in advance, because it never worked, since the vast body of the material arrived serially. I'd often reach a point where I'd go, 'If I knew I was going to wind up *here* I would have done something else *there*.' So writing the books is usually an attempt to make sense of what I've already done, which usually involves rather major surgery.

"Especially with the second book, I was trying with hindsight to make a bit of sense out of it all. I knew how it would end, with the prehistoric Earth stuff, and I found myself plotting the book backwards from there..."

The Restaurant at the End of the Universe is Douglas Adams's favourite of the *Hitchhiker's* books, although the circumstances under which it was written were somewhat less than ideal and they were to be far from unique.

"I had put it off and put it off and got extension after extension (all sorts of other things were going on at the time, like the stage show and the TV series), but eventually the managing director of Pan said, 'We've given you all these extensions and we have got to have it: sudden death or else, we have to have it in four weeks. Now, how far have you got with it?' I didn't like to tell him I hadn't started it; it seemed unfair on the poor chap's heart."

Jacqueline Graham, who was working for Pan, explains the predicament: "After the first book, our attitude was a mixture of resignation and exasperation with Douglas's lateness. By the second book, we expected him to be late, it was built into our planning, but at the same time we thought, 'Well, he can't do it again, surely! This time he'll start on time, or he'll have a schedule and stick to it...'

"But he didn't. The whole thing was tremendously late, and Douglas was getting into a bit of a state about it because it was getting later and later. He was sharing a flat at the time with a friend called Jon Canter, and Douglas found it impossible to work as the phone kept ringing and Jon was always there. In the end I said to him, 'Why don't you just move out?' as he had written the first book at his mother's. He thought that was a very good idea, so I rented him a flat, and moved him in that afternoon."

Douglas found the experience more than slightly weird: "I was locked away so nobody could possibly reach me or find me. I led a completely monastic existence for that month, and at the end of four weeks it was done.

"It was extraordinary. One of those times you really go mad... I can remember the moment I thought, 'I can do it! I'll actually get it finished in time!' And the Paul Simon album had just come out, *One Trick Pony*, and it was the only album I had. I'd listen to it on my Walkman every second I wasn't actually sitting at the typewriter — it contributed to the sense of insanity and hypnotism that allowed me to write a book in that time."

When the manuscript for *The Restaurant at the End of the Universe* was turned in, Douglas stated that that would be the final *Hitchhiker's* book. "It's the last of all that, I hope", he announced to one daily paper, "I want to try another field, now, like performing".

The book, again a paperback original from Pan, was a critical success. While most critic's had been a little wary of the first book initially, mostly not reviewing it at all, its sales had made it a major book. Oddly enough, the only part that British critics found too highly Monty Python, and too down-to-earth, was the colonisation of Earth by the Golgafrincham detritus; the 'oddly' because this is the section most American critics picked up on most easily and singled out for praise.

MARVIN TURNS FROM THE TELEPORT AND TRUDGES AWAY.

MARVIN: I suppose some people might have expected better treatment after having waited for five hundred and seventy-six thousand million years in a car park. But not me. I may just be a menial robot but I'm far too intelligent to expect anyone to think of me for a moment. Far too intelligent. In fact, I'm so intelligent I've probably got time to go through the five million things I hate most about organic life forms. One. They're so stupid…

— Cut from TV series script.

15

INVASION USA

"And now", began the press release, "for something completely different..."

As has been seen, Douglas Adams's contribution to Monty Python was neither major nor earth-shattering, consisting as it did of having had an old sketch rewritten by diverse hands for the soundtrack album of *Monty Python and the Holy Grail*, and two walk-on parts (once in drag and once in a surgical mask) in the final series.

This was not, however, the impression one got from the American PR for *The Hitchhiker's Guide to the Galaxy*, which represented Douglas as a "former scriptwriter for *Monty Python*". In addition to which, the initial press release for the hardback copy of *Hitchhiker's* (published by Harmony/Crown in October 1980) contained the following praise for the book:

Really entertaining and fun — John Cleese

Much funnier than anything John Cleese has ever written
— Terry Jones

I know for a fact that John Cleese hasn't read it
— Graham Chapman

Who is John Cleese? — Eric Idle

Really entertaining and fun — Michael Palin

An American fan might have been forgiven for supposing that Douglas Adams, not Terry Gilliam, was the sixth member of the *Python* team.

MONTY PYTHON AND *HITCHHIKER'S*

"It's funny. When I was at university I was a great *Python* fan. I still am, but that was obviously when Python was at its most active. So I have very much an outsiders view of *Python*; an audience's view. As far as *Hitchhiker's* goes I'm the only person who doesn't have any outsider's view whatsoever. I often wonder how I'd react to it if I wasn't me, but I still was me, so to speak, and how much I'd like it, and how much I'd be a fan or whatever. The way I would perceive it in among everything else. Obviously I can't answer that question. I have no idea, because I'm the one person who can't look at it from outside.

"You can see all the elements in *Hitchhiker's* in which it is a bit this or a bit that. I mean, it's an easy line for people wanting to categorise it in the press to say it is a cross between *Monty Python* and *Doctor Who*, and in a sense it is, there are all kinds of elements that go into making it what it is. But at the end of the mixing you have something which is different from anything else in its own peculiar way.

"But then, everything is like that. *Python* was a mixture of all kinds of things thrown together to give you something different from anything else. Even the Beatles (let's get really elevated here) were a mixture of all kinds of elements drawn from other things, mixed together and they created something which was extraordinarily different.

"Although *Hitchhiker's* does not have any real political significance, there is a theme there of the ubiquity of bureaucracy and paranoia rampant throughout the universe. And that is a direct debt to *Python*, along with the comparative style of 'individual events, little worlds'. The difference comes with the narrative structure, so the world of *Hitchhiker's* is based outside the 'Real World' while still co-existing with it. It's like looking at events through the wrong end of a telescope."

— Douglas Adams.

In 1980 a few American radio stations had already broadcast *Hitchhiker's* and National Public Radio was just waiting for its new stereo system to begin operating before it started to broadcast the radio series nationally. Even so, the show was not going to have the same effect on the States that it had had in England through radio, and a new tack was needed.

The book had done moderately well in hardcover on its release but did not reach the cult status it had in England and that, it was imagined, it had the potential of reaching in America. The radio series was finally broadcast by National Public Radio member stations in March 1981. (National response was so good that the twelve episodes were rebroadcast six months later.)

(Douglas Adams had paid his first visit to America in January 1981, on completion of the BBC television series. He lived in New York, had a wonderful time (despite contracting an ear infection) and visited Mexico before returning to England where he was to begin working on *Life, the Universe and Everything*.)

In many ways, the paperback release of *The Hitchhiker's Guide to the Galaxy* had a lot in common with the promotion of the cult film *The Rocky Horror Picture Show*. In order to get people along to *Rocky Horror* the film company realised that the public had to 'discover' it for themselves, there had to be a word-of-mouth campaign among the right sort of people.

It is peculiar that, even more than favourable reviews or national advertising (neither of which, admittedly, ever hurt sales), the factor that seems to sell most books is word-of-mouth promotion: people reading books and recommending them to friends. It was to be hoped that *Hitchhiker's* could have the same kind of impact that some of the 'campus classics' of the 60s and 70s had had — books that had built up high sales, and then remained perennial best-sellers. Could it be the next *Catcher in the Rye*? The next *Lord of the Rings*, or *Dune*?

Hitchhiker's needed advance word-of-mouth among science fiction fans and — more importantly — among the college crowd and the kind of people who would appreciate its humour. The solution? An advertisement in the 20th August *Rolling Stone*, giving away 3,000 copies of *The Hitchhiker's Guide to the Galaxy* ("FREE!") to the first people to write to the "Hyperspace Hitchhiking Club — Earth Div. c/o Pocket Books" by 27th August. This was combined with many "advance reading copies" and "give-away promotions" which were distributed by Pocket in the months before publication to ensure that people would begin to read *Hitchhiker's* and that they would, Pocket hoped, tell their friends how much they had enjoyed it.

Pocket did not skimp on the promotion, however. "England", they explained in their press release, "the country that gave America the Beatles and *Monty Python's Flying Circus* has just exported another zany craze — *The Hitchhiker's Guide to the Galaxy* by Doug Adams, a wild spoof available in October from Pocket Books".

The book was released in October, and did reasonably well.

Douglas was again in America at this time, in Los Angeles, while ABC tried to put together the ("thank heaven, abortive") American version of the television series.

"It was like every horror story you have ever heard," said Douglas. "They weren't really interested in how good it was going to be, they just wanted to do lots of special effects, and they also wanted not to have to pay for them."

The show was to be one of the many British comedy shows that had been turned into American comedy shows.* (There is a long and noble tradition of this, that includes dragging such shows as *Steptoe and Son*, *Fawlty Towers*, and *The Fall and Rise of Reginald Perrin* across the Atlantic, recasting them, rewriting them, and frequently

---

* It is interesting to note that quiz shows tend to cross the Atlantic in the opposite direction. Such shows as *The Price is Right* and *Hollywood ('Celebrity') Squares* have all reached the UK from the US.†

† It is equally interesting to note that, since the first edition of this book, several US sitcoms have been disastrously remade on this side of the Atlantic, while British quiz shows such as *Who Wants to be a Millionaire?* and *The Weakest Link* have been successfully exported to the USA. This suggests that it is the quiz aspect, rather than the made-in-Britain aspect, which is vital for success. We now return you to your book.

removing whatever it was that happened to make the show funny in the first place.)

Quite what ABC planned to do with *Hitchhiker's* is unknown. The script was to be by other people than Douglas, and was being written and put together by various committees.

"There were terrible stories coming back after meetings with executives, they'd make remarks like 'Would an alien be green?' Eventually everything got abandoned because the first episode's budget came to $2,200,000. It would have been the most expensive twenty-two minute show ever made. The script was terrible."

Douglas's sole contribution was to "come in and hang around the production office for a week". As he later pointed out, "It gives you an idea of the crazy proportion of this thing, when you think that they paid me four times as much for that one week as I was paid to write the whole series for radio!"

It was with the release of *The Restaurant at the End of the Universe*, shortly afterwards, that Douglas first made it onto the US bestseller lists, and, with the American broadcast of the BBC television series, *Hitchhiker's* popularity was assured.

Many people were surprised that something as essentially British as *Hitchhiker's* took off in America. Not Douglas Adams.

"One is told at every level of the entertainment industry that the American audience does not like or understand English humour. We are told that at every level except that of the audience, who, as far as I can see, love it. It's everybody else, the people whose job it is to tell you what the audiences like; but the people I meet here, and in the US, who are fans, are very much the same type of people.

"The most commonly heard plea from American audiences is 'Don't let them Americanise it! We get all sorts of pabulum over here…!'

"In terms of sales these days, it is more popular in America than England (it sells twice as many books to four times as many people, so it's either twice as popular, or half as popular). I think too much is made of the difference between US and UK humour. I don't think there's a difference in the way those audiences are treated. Audiences in the US (through no fault of their own) are treated as complete idiots by the people who make programmes. And when you've been treated as an idiot for so long you tend to respond that way. But when given something with a bit more substance they tend to breathe a deep sigh of relief and say 'Thank God for that!'

"There are things that the British think are as English as roast beef that the Americans think are as American as apple pie. The trick is to write about people. If you write about situations that people recognise then people will respond to it. The humour that doesn't travel is stuff like the Johnny Carson monologue, for which you needed to know precisely who said what about who that week and how it affected the performance of the LA Rams. If you don't have the information then it isn't funny.

"But anything that relies on how a person works is universally accessible. (How it works in translation is another matter, as in that respect comedy is a fragile plant, and very often I suspect it might not stand up in translation. I don't know. *Hitchhiker's* has been translated into all kinds of languages, and I've no idea which ones work and which ones don't.)"

As it is, *Life, the Universe and Everything* and Douglas's subsequent novels have sold amazingly well in the US. The computer game, which was a reasonable hit in the UK, was the number one game in the US for a year, selling over a quarter of a million copies. Throughout the 1990s much of Douglas's mail, and the greater part of his income, came from America.

16

LIFE, THE UNIVERSE AND EVERYTHING

ZAPHOD: There's nothing wrong with my sense of reality. I
            have it thoroughly serviced every fortnight.
            — Cut from radio series script, Episode Three.

The first two *Hitchhiker's* books were based on material developed for the radio series. When Douglas Adams agreed to write the third book he had sworn he would never write, he took the plot from a storyline he had had "knocking around for ages".

He had once suggested it as a *Doctor Who* story, but Graham Williams thought it was just "too silly". Later, when there was talk of a *Doctor Who* film to star Tom Baker, he had written the story as a film outline, *Doctor Who and the Krikkitmen* (see Appendix V). The film never materialised, but later, when talk began of the second *Hitchhiker's* television series, Douglas began to look at the *Krikkitmen* script as a *Hitchhiker's* vehicle.

As things turned out, for reasons explained at length elsewhere, there was not going to be a second television series. However, the process of turning *Doctor Who and the Krikkitmen* into *Life, the Universe and Everything*, had begun.

As far as plots go, the storylines are essentially the same.

Douglas divided the *Doctor Who* role between Slartibartfast,

Trillian and (for the final sequence) Arthur Dent, although what would have been the last half of the *Doctor Who* format became the final thirty pages of *Life, the Universe and Everything*.

(In the *Doctor Who* version, after having failed to prevent the Krikkitmen from taking the components of the Wicket Gate, the Doctor arrives with Sarah Jane on Krikkit and spends most of the rest of the story, in classic *Doctor Who* style, running around, getting captured, escaping, learning vital bits of plot, running around, getting captured, escaping, rescuing Sarah Jane, and so on.)

Life, the Universe and Everything was different in kind from the other *Hitchhiker's* books, in that it was not written serially. Douglas knew what was going to happen next, but this gave him a new problem, that of fitting the *Hitchhiker's* characters into the *Doctor Who* plot. *Hitchhiker's* characters are essentially feckless, and instead of, say, saving the universe they would tend instead towards going to a party (Ford), staying cool (Zaphod), looking bewildered (Arthur) or moaning (Marvin); this really left only Trillian, whose personality had never been fully explored (indeed, barely glanced at), as a substitute worldsaver.

More so, perhaps, than any other part of Douglas's oeuvre, the creation of *Life, the Universe and Everything* was fraught with difficulties: "As with everything, I put it off longer than I should have, and then I had a huge domestic crisis which knocked me for six; I couldn't think of anything funny to save my life; I wanted to jump off cliffs and things like that. It was an emotional episode which I'm not going to go into in any detail..."

(Although Adams later declined to discuss it, his then girlfriend had left him — as he said in an interview given about that time, "She went off with this bloke on, to me, the spurious grounds that he was her husband.")

As a result of this, Adams wrote a "very bleak" first draft of *Life, the Universe and Everything*: "I had the first draft of it three-quarters finished and then I had to go and do a major book promotion tour in the US for a month. I was suddenly confronted by the fact that this book was not anything like right at that point. And I had to phone up my publisher and say 'Look, it's not finished yet, I'm going to have to rewrite it, but I have to go now' — it was terrible!

"So I went away and did this tour, feeling terrible about the situation I'd left behind. Then I came back and sat down and wrote; and threw out practically every word of the first draft of *Life, the Universe and Everything*. Take, for example, in the first draft, the first twenty pages, which were Arthur waking up in his cave, two and a half million years ago. (I think it was just that was where I wanted to be at the time.) I rewrote it and rewrote it and rewrote, and at the end of twenty rewrites those thirty pages were the first two lines of the book, and that was it.

"What is amazing is that the third book ever got written at all, that it got into existence and was as good as it was. But it is patchy, simply because it was written in circumstances I wouldn't want to build a bookcase under, let alone write a book.

"But it's true of each book I've written that I've hated it, and then written the next book, and was so busy hating the next book I discovered I rather liked the previous book. There are problems in the third book which have to do with the way I handled the plot: since it was actually a plotted story, occasionally you can hear the grinding gears where I had to do something which had to establish a plot point, and at the same time had to be funny, and I'd have to overstretch to make it funny. That's the real problem: you can sort of hear the tyres screech around a few corners.

"The struggle between substance and structure reached a pitch with the third book, as it was the one where I had a very detailed plan of the logical structure, and virtually none of that actually got into the book. I always go off at tangents, but whereas before I'd follow the tangents and go on from there, this time I was determined to go back to the plot each time. The tangents remained purely as tangents.

"So there was a real fight going on between the way I felt I ought to be doing things and the way things naturally end up getting done. That's why it has a slightly bitchy feeling — I keep yanking it back to where it's going even though it hasn't shown any inclination to go there: an awful lot of the explanations in my outline never got anywhere near the book, and every time you get yanked back to the plot you don't get told what the plot is.

"I think I must be a very weird person.

"On the other hand, some of my favourite bits of actual writing are in that book: the Agrajag section, and the flying bit. I didn't revise any of the flying bit — it was all done first draft (although I cheated slightly, as, being aware I had written the entire sequence straight off, I felt slightly superstitious about it, and left things I could have revised).

"I wasn't pleased with the resolution of the Agrajag episode, it was a bit perfunctory, and I should have got that right. Overall I think *Life, the Universe and Everything* has some of the best and some of the worst *Hitchhiker's* writing in it."

Geoffrey Perkins suggested to me that *Life, the Universe and Everything* had a succession of endings (in Chapters 33 and 34) because Douglas had felt that the book wasn't long enough.

"No, that's not true. Actually, it's one of the longest of the books. It was almost the opposite — when I got the proofs back from Pan I read through and had the niggling feeling there was something wrong. If it had been a small thing wrong I would have spotted it immediately, but it was one of those things that was so big and wrong that it takes you a while to see exactly what it is.

"What it was was this: there were two chapters missing.

"Those two had disappeared and actually turned up later in America, by which time the number of pages in the final bound copy had actually been determined. And that is why, in the English edition, the text of the book carries on to the very last page. There aren't any ads or anything in the back of the book. But it's actually quite a long book.

"No, that stuff wasn't put in because the book wasn't long enough, but because there was a bit I wanted to put in that I hadn't managed to get in anywhere else, which was the story of The Reason. That's one of my favourite bits, that no one else seems to have responded to very well.

"When you write you often feel a constant salvage from impending catastrophe. I mean, there's a constant disastrous bit followed by disastrous bit, and just occasionally you come up with a bit of which you think, 'Oh, I'll pat myself on the back for that.' That bit was one of those. I actually thought it was quite neat.

"But the problem of the third book is that I have a plot which actually signifies something, and there are momentous events afoot, but I'd created such a feckless bunch of characters that before writing each scene I'd think, 'Well, OK, who's involved here?' and I'd mentally go around each of the characters in my mind explaining to them what was going on, and they would all say, 'Yeah? Well so what? I don't want to get involved.' Either they didn't want to get involved or they didn't understand.

"In the end, Slartibartfast had to become the character who had to get them all to get a move on, and that really wasn't in his nature either. You see, all the characters are essentially character parts. I had a lot of supporting roles and no main character."

ON WRITING HUMOUR

"Writing comes easy. All you have to do is stare at a blank piece of paper until your forehead bleeds.

"I find it ludicrously difficult. I try and avoid it if at all possible. The business of buying new pencils assumes gigantic proportions. I have four word processors and spend a lot of time wondering which one to work on. All writers, or most, say they find writing difficult, but most writers I know are surprised at how difficult I find it.

"I usually get very depressed when writing. It always seems to me that writing coincides with terrible crises breaking up my life. I used to think these crises had a terrible effect on my being able to write; these days I have a very strong suspicion that it's the sitting down to write that precipitates the crises. So quite a lot of troubles tend to get worked out in the books. It's usually below the surface. It doesn't appear to tackle problems at a personal level, but it does, implicitly, even if not explicitly.

"I'm not a wit. A wit says something funny on the spot. A comedy writer says something *very* funny two minutes later. Or in my case, two weeks later.

"I don't think I could do a serious book anyway. I'm sure that jokes would start to creep in. I actually do think that comedy is a serious business: when you are working on something you have to take it absolutely seriously; you have to be passionately committed to it. But you can't maintain that if you are going to stay sane. So when I talk about it to other people I tend to be flippant about it. I'm always so glad to have got through it, I say 'It's just jokes.' It's a relief.

"What I do now on many occasions is have, say, an inconsequential idea for a throwaway line that seems quite neat, then I go to huge lengths to create the context in which to throw that line away and make it appear that it was just a throwaway line, when in fact you've constructed this huge edifice off which to chuck this line. It's a really exhausting way of writing but when it works...

"Often the things that seem frivolous and whimsical are the hardest to get right. Take the opening section of *Life, the Universe and Everything*, which is something I'm quite pleased with. They are stuck on prehistoric Earth, and then suddenly they find themselves on Lord's Cricket Ground, which comes about because they chased a sofa across a field. It all sounds inconsequential or illogical or whatever, but completely belies the fact that I tried over and over again, and rewrote that bit over and over, going absolutely crazy with it until I eventually found the right elements to create the air of whimsical inconsequence, if you like. So I could come right up at the end of that long section with, 'They suddenly found themselves in the middle of the pitch at Lord's Cricket Ground, St John's Wood, London, with Australia leading and England needing so many runs to win' (I forget the exact quote). Now, in order to chuck away a line like that at the end of the chapter, you needed all that stuff about Ford coming back and explaining what he has been doing in Africa, which was obviously very unpleasant, and then him trying to explain about the flotsam and jetsam, and eddies in the space-time continuum (which was really a very silly joke, but you are allowed the odd silly joke) and the sofa, and so on.

"It required all that just to be able to suddenly say 'Bang! Here they were somewhere else,' because if you do just say that without getting all the rhythm right, then it doesn't work. It wouldn't have been enough for them to just be magically transported without it suddenly being a tremendous surprise coming at that moment.

"It's those kind of effects that take an awful lot of engineering, when you don't necessarily know what the answer is going to be, you are just thrashing around in the dark trying to find something somewhere that's going to help you get to that point. And when you are operating within a convention which says (or seems to say) 'anything goes', you have to be extremely careful how you use that. I think if I have a strength as a writer it is in recognising that and trying to deal with it, and if I have a weakness it's that I don't always deal with it as well as I would like to be able to.

"Anyway, the reason I liked that bit where they appeared at Lord's so much was that I knew what a huge problem I had solved and the fact that it wouldn't appear to the reader to be a transition from one bit to another. And the reader would feel, 'Well, that was easy, wasn't it? You say *Here they are in one place*, then *Here they are in another*?' But for that to be easy you have to do an awful lot of engineering."

— Douglas Adams, 1984.

When *Life, the Universe and Everything* was released the critical response was far less favourable than that for the first two books — and most of the critics said similar things:

> The third time around I found Arthur Dent and his ridiculous dressing gown — why hasn't he found a change of clothes somewhere along the line? — increasingly tedious*; never a very substantial hero, he is in danger of being shrivelled in the heat of his author's imagination. Perhaps Adams should now look beyond SF; I feel that his cynicism and detachment are too strong for a genre which depends so much on naivety and trust..." — Kelvin Johnston, *The Observer*

> ...the humour depends on a limited repertoire of gimmicks, and this third volume, though by no means

* As noted, *Life, the Universe and Everything* is the first place it is seen in print that Arthur is still wearing a dressing gown, something Douglas only discovered in the television series when the sequence that reclothed him on the *Heart of Gold* was cut.

lacking in enthusiastic drive, does little to suggest that the idea could or should be taken much further from here..." — Richard Brown, *Times Literary Supplement*

"Fans will relish the mixture as before... but signs of padding and self-parody suggest that Adams would be wise to avoid a fourth" — Martin Hillman, *Tribune*

Even the interviewers, most of them obviously fans, were complaining to Douglas that *Life, the Universe and Everything* was less funny than the earlier books. And Douglas, hating the book, couldn't have agreed with them more. In his defence, he pointed out how depressed he had been during the writing, how he felt he was no longer writing in his own voice, how writing a third *Hitchhiker's* book had been a major mistake, and one he would not repeat.

"After I wrote the second *Hitchhiker's* book, I swore on the souls of my ancestors that I would not write a third. Having written the third, I can swear on the souls of the souls of my ancestors there will not be another", was a typical quote, and, "I utterly intend not to write another sequel", was another.

What he wanted to do next, he told all the interviewers, would have nothing to do with the *Hitchhiker's* characters.

He'd write a stage play, perhaps. Or a film on something else. Definitely, indubitably, unarguably, nothing else with *Hitchhiker's* connections in any shape, colour or form. But it was not long before the souls of the souls of Douglas's ancestors were revolving in the graves of their graves.

17

MAKING MOVIES

"I went to Hollywood, and I kept thinking, 'This is just like going to Hollywood.' The experience of it conformed far more closely to the one that everyone said I'd have than the one I expected to have. I told people, 'This is going to work! It's going to be great!' But I fell foul of all the clichés of Hollywood..."

— Douglas Adams, on his return from LA,
November 1983.

In 1979 Douglas was approached with an offer he found almost irresistible: a *Hitchhiker's* film. All he had to do was sign a piece of paper, and he would have $50,000 in his hand. The only trouble was that what the director seemed to have in mind was "*Star Wars* with jokes".

"We seemed to be talking about different things, and one thing after another seemed not quite right, and I suddenly realised that the only reason I was going ahead with it was the money. And that, as the sole reason, was not good enough (although I had to get rather drunk in order to believe that). I was quite pleased with myself for not doing it, in the end. But I knew that we were doing it for TV anyway at that time.

"I'm sometimes accused of only being in it for the money. I

always knew there was a lot of money to be made out of the film, but when that was the whole thing prompting me to do it, when the only benefit was the money, I didn't want to do it. People should remember that."

FORD: What is it you're after?

ZAPHOD: Well, it's partly the curiosity, partly a sense of adventure, but mostly I think it's the fame and the money.

FORD: Money?

ZAPHOD: Yes, money in mind-mangling amounts.

FORD: Zaphod, last time I knew you, you were one of the richest men in the Galaxy. What do you want money for?

ZAPHOD: Oh, I lost it all.

FORD: All of it? What did you do, gamble it away?

ZAPHOD: No, I left it in a taxi.

FORD: Stylish.

— Cut from first radio series script.

A couple of years later, Terry Jones (of Monty Python, and a scriptwriter and director in his own right) decided that he would like to make a *Hitchhiker's* film. The concept was to do a story that was based solidly in the first radio series, but pretty soon Douglas began to have second thoughts. He had done it four times (radio, theatre, book, record) and had recently done it for a fifth time (television), so decided that, in order to avoid the problems of repetition that would occur if he wrote the same script again ("I didn't want to drag it through another medium — I was in danger of becoming my own word processor"), they would create a new story that would be "totally consistent with what had gone before, for the sake of those people who were familiar with *Hitchhiker's*, and totally self-contained for the sake of those who weren't. And that began to be a terrible conundrum, and in the end Terry and I said, 'It would be nice to do a film together... but let's start from scratch, and not make it *Hitchhiker's*.' Also, Terry and I have been great friends for a long time, but have had no professional links*. And there's a slight risk you take, when you go and do a professional job with a friend, that it might spoil things. So we didn't do it."

In 1982 Douglas went to California with John Lloyd to write *The Meaning of Liff*, and it was then that he was approached by two people with whom he got on extremely well, Michael Gross** and Joe Medjuck, about a *Hitchhiker's* film.

At the time Douglas was excited by the possibilities of what could be done with computers, having seen some amazing special effects and technical work (imagine *real* computer graphics, done with computers!), and decided that he *would* write the film. He moved to Los Angeles, taking his girlfriend Jane Belson with him, bought a Rainbow word processor, and began to write.

Mike and Joe were producers working for Ivan Reitman, then known only for *Animal House*, now better known for 1984's smash-hit *Ghostbusters*, and unfortunately there was not the same rapport between Adams and Reitman as there had been between Adams and the other two.

FRANKIE:	Now, Earth creature. As you know, we've been at this Ultimate Question business for seventeen and a half million years.
BENJY:	Oh, longer, surely.
FRANKIE:	No, it just seems longer.
	— White Mice dialogue, cut from first radio series.

Douglas later described 1983 as a 'lost year'. He and Jane hated Los Angeles, missed London and their friends. He found it hard to work,

* Terry Jones subsequently worked with Douglas twice: on a short story for *The Utterly Utterly Merry Comic Relief Christmas Book*, and on *Starship Titanic*.

** Gross was originally an artist and designer for *National Lampoon*, and was the man responsible for the famous cover showing a dog with a pistol to its head, captioned "Buy this magazine or we shoot the dog!"

spending much of his time learning how to work a computer, playing computer games, learning to scuba dive, and writing unsatisfactory screenplays.

Transforming *Hitchhiker's* into a film hit two snags. The first was that of organising the material: "There are inherent problems with the material. It's a hundred minute film, of which the first twenty-five minutes are concerned with the destruction of Earth; then you start a whole new story which has to be told in seventy-five minutes, and not overshadow what went before. It's very, very tricky, and I've had endless problems getting the structure right. With radio and television you have three hours to play with.

"The material just doesn't want to be organised. *Hitchhiker's* by its very nature has always been twisty and turny, and going off in every direction. A film demands a certain shape and discipline that the material just isn't inclined to fit into."

The other problem was that Ivan Reitman and Douglas Adams did not see eye to eye on the various drafts of the screenplay. Again Douglas started using the phrase of *"Star Wars* with jokes". Unfortunately this time he had already signed the contracts, was signed up as a co-producer, and had accepted amazingly large amounts of money to work on the film.

The versions of the script done in Los Angeles were attempts by Douglas Adams to meet Reitman half-way, of which he said, "They fell between two stools — they didn't please me, and they didn't please them."

FRANKIE: We've got to have something that sounds good.

ARTHUR: Sounds good? An Ultimate Question that sounds good?

FRANKIE: Well, I mean, *yes* idealism, *yes* the dignity of pure research, *yes* the pursuit of truth in all its forms, but there comes a point I'm afraid where you begin to suspect that if there's any *real* truth, it's that the entire multi-dimensional infinity of the Universe is almost certainly being run by a bunch of maniacs.

> And if it comes to a choice between spending
> another ten million years finding *that* out, and on the
> other hand just taking the money and running, then
> I for one could do with the exercise.
> — More White Mice dialogue, cut from TV series this time.

Los Angeles was getting Douglas more and more depressed. He began to feel he was losing touch with the very things that had made him write what he did anyway. Eventually he decided to leave.

"I didn't realise how much I hated LA until I left. Then the floodgates opened, and everything came out. It wasn't a good period for me, nor a productive period. I had a slight case of 'Farnham' — that's the feeling you get at four in the afternoon, when you haven't got enough done. So there came a point when we all decided to disagree, and I'd come back to the UK where I felt more in touch, and try to get it right to my own satisfaction."

> TWO: What are you talking about, professional ethics?
> VROOMFONDEL: Look, don't you mess with me about ethics. Let me tell you that I have got three first class degrees in Moral Sciences, Ethics, and Further Ethics, a PhD in A Lot Further Ethics, and have written three bestselling books on *Why Sex Is Ethical, Why More Sex Is Ethical* and *Five Hundred and Seventy Three More Totally Ethical Positions*, so I know what I'm talking about when I say that ethically that machine is a write-off. Get rid of it.
> — Cut from first radio series script.

Douglas returned to England, where he began to work once more on the screenplay of the film, in addition to beginning work on *So Long, and Thanks for All the Fish* and the *Hitchhiker's* computer game.

At that time he told me, "What I'm trying to do with the film is use a completely different selection process to that which went into the TV series. We are trying to show the stuff you didn't see in the TV series. So if you go back to the book, and find all the things not in the TV series... that's the film!

"Also, a lot of the film comes to have a completely different rationale. I've just put the scene with Marvin and the Battletank into the film, from the second book."

For some years after, things appeared to progress very slowly, if at all, with the film seemingly stuck forever in Development Hell. Then suddenly, in January 1998, it was announced that the film was back on track and would be made by Disney.

Disney?

Well, actually Hollywood Pictures, a division of the mighty Disney empire. (Anyone who believes that Disney only make cartoons about talking animals should bear in mind that *Pulp Fiction* was made by a division of the company.) The success of *Men in Black* had made comedy science fiction flavour of the month, and Douglas had signed a deal with Hollywood Pictures which his agent Ed Victor summed up as, "substantial and special". Jay Roach, who had made such a success of *Austin Powers: International Man of Mystery* and its sequel, was signed to direct, and Douglas professed himself very happy with both deal and director.

However, three years later the film was no closer to production, even though Douglas had actually moved to California to write the script. Occasionally, frustrating snippets of information about what was happening surfaced in interviews with Adams or Roach. Then, finally, Douglas announced that he had finished a draft of the script which really worked and everybody seemed to be happy with it.

That was in the Spring of 2001...

18

LIFF, AND OTHER PLACES

ZAPHOD: Soulianis and Rahm! Two ancient furnaces of light
               that have warmed this dead and barren planet
               through the countless millennia, guarding its price-
               less secrets. Just looking at it makes me feel I could
               really, you know really... write travelogues.

               — Cut from first radio series script.

Douglas Adams and John Lloyd collaborated on a number of projects. Some have already been mentioned. One, *Doctor Snuggles*, was
an animated television series for which two episodes were scripted
by Adams and Lloyd. *Doctor Snuggles* was "a cross between *Professor
Branestawm* and *Dr Dolittle*" and produced by a Dutch television
company for the international market.

One of their episodes apparently won them an award, although
neither of them ever saw either the award or the series.

Doctor Snuggles was essentially a children's series, and while the
Adams/Lloyd scripted episode I have seen ('Doctor Snuggles and the
Nervous River') was superior to the run of scripts for the series, fans
of Douglas Adams's or John Lloyd's work are missing nothing if they
haven't seen it. The plot, however, was science fiction: Doctor
Snuggles meets a nervous river too scared to go down to the sea

because huge chunks of the sea are disappearing. After a number of adventures, the Doctor goes off into space to discover that the water is being taken by aliens who thought we didn't want our water because we kept throwing rubbish into it. They give the water back, Doctor Snuggles ties it to the back of his spaceship and returns to Earth.

Another project of theirs was rather better known in Britain, but for some reason not a success in the US: a curious book entitled *The Meaning of Liff*.

It began during the holiday in Corfu, which John and Douglas had booked to write *The Hitchhiker's Guide to the Galaxy*, but during which, for reasons already chronicled, only Douglas wrote the book. They were sitting in a tavern, playing charades and drinking retsina with a few friends. They had been drinking retsina all afternoon, and after a while decided they needed a game to play that did not require as much standing up.

Douglas remembered an English exercise he had been set at school, fifteen years earlier, and suggested it as a game.

The rules were fairly simple: someone would say the name of a town, and someone else would say what the word meant.

As John Lloyd explained, "It was a fantastically enjoyable holiday. For a month we got drunk, and we'd stay up all night playing these incredibly long games of charades.

"Then we began playing this placenames game. Near the end of the holiday, I started writing them down, not having very much else to do. By the end of the holiday, we had about twenty of these things, some of the best ones in *The Meaning of Liff*, like 'Ely' — the first, tiniest inkling that something has gone terribly wrong.

"Many of them were to do with Greece, sitting in wickerwork chairs and so on. And we kept doing them after the holiday was over."

Douglas clarified the concept on a press release for *The Meaning of Liff*:

> We rapidly discovered there were an awful lot of experi-
> ences, ideas and situations that everybody knew and
> recognised, but which never got properly identified
> simply because there wasn't a word for them. They were

all of the, "Do you ever have the situation where...?" or, "You know what feeling you get when...?" "You know, I always thought it was just me..." All it takes is a word, and the thing is identified.

The vaguely uncomfortable feeling you get from sitting in a seat which is warm from somebody else's bottom is just as real a feeling as the one you get when a rogue giant elephant charges out of the bush at you, but hitherto only the latter has actually had a word for it. Now they both have words. The first one is 'shoebury-ness', and the second, of course, is 'fear'.

We started to collect more and more of these words and concepts, and began to realise what an arbitrarily selective work the Oxford English Dictionary is. It simply doesn't recognise huge wodges of human experience.

Like, for instance, standing in the kitchen wondering what you went in there for. Everybody does it, but because there isn't — or wasn't — a word for it, everybody thinks it's something that only they do and that they are there-fore more stupid than other people. It is reassuring to realise that everybody else is as stupid as you are and that all we are doing when we are standing in the kitchen wondering what we came in here for is 'Woking'.

Following John Lloyd's disappointment with the *Hitchhiker's* book, he was similarly disappointed over a comedy series he was meant to have been co-writing, *To the Manor Born*, starring Penelope Keith. Instead he found himself producing a BBC 2 satire show, *Not the Nine O'Clock News*, starring Pamela Stephenson, Rowan Atkinson, Mel Smith and Griff Rhys Jones. After a while *Not the Nine O'Clock News* became a major success (which, according to Douglas, meant that John in his turn spent a while being as obnoxious as Douglas had been in the early days of the success of *Hitchhiker's*), and spawned a number of records and books.

One of the books was the *NOT 1982* calendar. Lloyd found himself stuck for material to fill in space at the bottoms of some pages, and at the tops of some pages, and in quite a few of the middles, so he dug out seventy of the best definitions (he had accumulated about 150) and inserted them into the book as extracts from *The Oxtail English Dictionary.*

Faber and Faber, John's publisher, were very enthusiastic about the definitions.

"They said, 'This is the best idea in the whole calendar — why don't you do it as a book?' This time it was the reverse situation: I hadn't expected Douglas to be very interested in doing it as a book, so I expected to do it on my own. Then Douglas said, 'Let's do it together,' and I said, 'Yes!' I can't stand doing things on my own, which is one reason why I'm a producer and not a writer."

The Meaning of Liff was written in September 1982, in a rented beach hut in Malibu. The two of them sat on the beach, watched the ocean, drank beer, thumbed through a gazetteer, and thought up definitions. Douglas also started learning to scuba dive at this time. (He finished learning to scuba dive in Australia two years later, and collected a number of wise sayings on the subject of sharks.) It was published in November 1983 by Pan (in a co-publishing deal with Faber and Faber) in a remarkable format (153mm by 82mm); a very small, very slim, very black book, with a bright orange sticker on the cover that proclaimed, *"This Book Will Change Your Life!"*

The 'selling point summary' that went out to reps included: "Small format for discreet consultation on retrieval from inside pocket", "Authors expert in field" and "Possible early quote from John Cleese's psychoanalyst" as selling points.

On its release it went to number four in the *Sunday Times* best-seller lists. However, overall it didn't do as well as a *Hitchhiker's* book or, for that matter, a *Not the Nine O'Clock News* book.

As Douglas said at the time, "Normally I don't enjoy writing at all, but it was a real pleasure doing this book. But what's really nice is that my family and so on, who say, 'Yes dear, it's nice about *Hitchhiker's*' — John's say the same about *Not the Nine O'Clock News* — love *this* book. My kid brother and sister like it.

"It's selling briskly, but not as well as it could do. I think that's because people have no idea what it is — it's totally enigmatic and anonymous, unless you happen to recognise our names. In both cases the product is more famous than the names — but on the other hand it has terrific word-of-mouth.

"But I enjoy it. I can reread it, whereas normally I cringe when I read my stuff."

The Meaning of Liff also kicked off a minor controversy in the newspapers. Although it was well, and extensively, reviewed (primarily because it was so easily quotable — despite the presence of the word 'Ripon', described in *The Meaning of Liff* as: [of literary critics] 'To include all the best jokes from the book in the review to make it look as if the critic had thought of them'), there were also accusations of plagiarism.

Having just undergone a traumatic time trying to get a certain advertising agency to pay up for having stolen the idea for an ad campaign using the phrase *The Oxtail English Dictionary* (see 'Cannock Chase' in *The Meaning of Liff*), Adams and Lloyd were rather put out when it was widely pointed out that the idea had originated in an essay written by Paul Jennings, called *Ware, Wye and Watford* published in the late 1950s.

Douglas suggested that the teacher who gave him the exercise had probably got the idea from the Jennings book, and sent Jennings a note of apology.

(Miles Kington in *The Times* rushed to Adams's and Lloyd's defence, pointing out the essential difference between the two: that while Jennings had been primarily interested in the sound and flavour of the placename (he suggested that 'Rickmansworth' — as in "a small café in..." — was really the nominal rent paid to the Lord of the Manor for hay; it sounds right, but isn't particularly funny), Lloyd-Adams had been far more concerned in amassing meanings for which there were no words previously in existence, the actual word or placename they picked being less than important.)

An additional coincidence (although certain devoted fans have woven intricate conspiracy theories around it) was its release at almost exactly the same time as *Monty Python's The Meaning of Life*. The film's title sequence shows the title, carved, in classically modest Terry Gilliam fashion, into a huge slab of rock; initially reading *THE MEANING OF LIFF*, a lightning bolt adds the bottom bar of the final E. It was a meaningless coincidence, discovered by Douglas and Terry Jones slightly before the release of either of their products, but too late for anything to be changed. It was a coincidence but if you wish to concoct conspiracy theories (and what does happen in the forty-second minute of the film?) then go right ahead.

Although *The Meaning of Liff* was published in the US in a different format and with some extra words, it is the least known of Douglas's books there.

"I did some college readings in America. You would think that a high concentration of people who knew what I had written would be in those audiences, yet hardly anybody there had heard of *The Meaning of Liff*. I read sections, and they went over well. People kept asking me where they could find the book. No one could find it. I think it suffered from nobody knowing what to do with it."

'Liff', incidentally, is a town in Scotland. Its meaning? A book, the contents of which are totally belied by its cover. For instance, any book the dust jacket of which bears the words, "This book will change your life!"

Postscript: Adams and Lloyd, assisted by Stephen Fry, returned to *Liff* in their work for *The Utterly Utterly Merry Comic Relief Christmas Book*, co-edited by Douglas Adams, and in 1990 an expanded version, *The Deeper Meaning of Liff*, was published — even in America. In addition, *The Meaning of Liff* has been successfully translated into Dutch and Finnish editions, despite the fact that this is clearly impossible.

19

SLATFAT FISH

	CUT TO A BLURRY CLOSE-UP OF ZAPHOD LYING ASLEEP ON THE GROUND.
FORD:	Zaphod! Wake up!
ZAPHOD:	Mmmmmmmwwerrrr?
TRILLIAN:	Hey come on, wake up.
	SLOWLY THE PICTURE FOCUSES.
ZAPHOD:	Just let me stick to what I'm good at, yeah?
	HE GOES BACK TO SLEEP.
FORD:	You want me to kick you?
ZAPHOD:	Would it give you a lot of pleasure?
FORD:	No.
ZAPHOD:	Nor me. So what's the point? Stop bugging me.
TRILLIAN:	He got a double dose of the gas. Two windpipes.
ZAPHOD:	Hey, lose the talk, will you? It's hard enough trying to sleep anyway. What's the matter with the ground? It's all cold and hard.
FORD:	It's gold.
	PULL BACK RAPIDLY AS ZAPHOD LEAPS TO HIS FEET. WE SEE THAT THEY APPEAR TO BE STANDING ON A VAST SHINING PLAIN OF SOLID GOLD.
ZAPHOD:	Hey, who put all that there?
FORD:	It's nothing.

ZAPHOD:	Nothing? Gold by the square mile nothing?
TRILLIAN:	This world is an illusion.
ZAPHOD:	You pick now to become Buddhists?
FORD:	It's just a catalogue.
ZAPHOD:	A who?
FORD:	A catalogue. It's not real. Just a projection.
ZAPHOD:	How can you say that?

HE DROPS TO HIS KNEES AND STARTS FEELING THE "GROUND".

TRILLIAN:	We both came round a while ago. We shouted and yelled till somebody came...
FORD:	And then carried on shouting and yelling till they put us in their planet catalogue. They said they'd deal with us later. This is all Sens-O-Tape.

HE POINTS UP INTO THE SKY.

WE SEE THERE ARE SOME WORDS. THEY SAY:

"MAGRATHEAN PLANET CATALOGUE BK THREE.

DESIGN 35/C/6b. 'ULTRASULTAN'S ECSTASY'.

LANDFORMATION: GOLD.

OPTIONAL EXTRAS: SILVER MOON. ZAN-TEQUILA OCEANS.

ALL ORDERS PAYABLE IN ADVANCE."

ZAPHOD:	Ah, fetid photons, you wake me from my own perfectly good dream to show me somebody else's?
TRILLIAN:	We didn't wake you earlier. The last planet was knee deep in fish.
ZAPHOD:	Fish?
FORD:	Fish.
ZAPHOD:	Well, tell them to turn it off. Get us out of here!

HE YELLS UP AT THE SKY.

ZAPHOD:	Get us out of here!

IN THE SKY THE WRITING CHANGES. IT NOW SAYS:

"MAGRATHEAN PLANET CATALOGUE BK THREE.

DESIGN 35/C/7. 'LEATHERLAND'.

LANDFORMATION: FINEST ARCTURAN MEGA-OX HIDE.

OPTIONAL EXTRAS: STEEL MOUNTAIN STUDS."
WE SEE THAT THEY ARE NOW STANDING ON A
PLAIN OF SHINING BLACK LEATHER WHICH UNDU-
LATES AWAY INTO THE DISTANCE. GIANT STRAPS
AND BUCKLES ARE ALSO VISIBLE.

ZAPHOD: Get us out of here!
THE SKY WRITING CHANGES AGAIN. (I'M GIVING
THE DETAILS IN FULL, THOUGH IT IS NOT NECES-
SARY TO DWELL ON THEM LONG ENOUGH TO
READ THEM ALL.)
"MAGRATHEAN PLANET CATALOGUE BK THREE.
DESIGN 35/C/8. 'WORLD OF PLAYBEING'.
LANDFORMATION: EPIDERMITEX.
OPTIONAL EXTRAS: ASK FOR SPECIAL CATALOGUE."
WE SEE THAT THE NEW LANDSCAPE THAT HAS
MATERIALISED AROUND THEM IS SOFT AND PINK
AND CURIOUSLY UNDULATING. THERE ARE HILLS
AROUND THEM WHICH ARE GENTLY ROUNDED
WITH RED PEAKS.

ZAPHOD: Get us… hey, I think I could learn to like it here. What
do you think Ford?

FORD: I think it's a mistake to mix geography with pleasure.

ZAPHOD: What's that meant to mean?

FORD: Nothing. It's just a form of mouth exercise. Ask
Trillian.

ZAPHOD: Ask her what?

FORD: Anything you like. (HE WANDERS OFF ENIGMATI-
CALLY.)

ZAPHOD (TO
TRILLIAN): Is he trying to drive me mad?

TRILLIAN: Yes.

ZAPHOD: Why?

TRILLIAN: To stop all this driving us insane.
MEANWHILE A SLOGAN HAS RISEN ABOVE THE
HORIZON. IT SAYS IN LARGE LETTERS:
"WHATEVER YOUR TASTES, MAGRATHEA CAN

CATER FOR THEM. WE ARE NOT PROUD."

— Unused scene from early draft of TV series script, Episode Four.

Having written one *Hitchhiker's* book he had been unsatisfied with — *Life, the Universe and Everything* — and having sworn "never again" on the *Hitchhiker's* saga, why did Douglas Adams sign a contract to write the fourth book in the trilogy?

Firstly, he was under a great deal of pressure to write it, both from his agent and his publishers. On his return from the US, he explained, "I felt so disoriented being in Los Angeles, and so keen to be home and just sort of grab hold of things I knew again, it became very easy to give in to the temptation of sort of re-establishing what I knew I could do, by doing another *Hitchhiker's* book."

Secondly, he did have God's Final Message to His Creation; and since he was never going to tell people what the Ultimate Question was, he felt that that was something he should reveal.

Thirdly, the advance he was offered topped £600,000.

He signed the contract.

I asked him about the book in November 1983: "I can tell you more about the working title than what it's actually going to be about. The working title is *So Long, and Thanks for All the Fish*. It's about something left hanging at the end of the third book, which is Arthur's quest to find God's final message to His creation.

"My agent thinks *So Long, and Thanks for All the Fish* isn't the right title for the book, since the first three all have 'Galaxy' or 'Universe' in the title, so he wants me to call it *God's Find Message to His Creation*. I don't know, but I don't think that has the ironical ring to it, in the way that that most modest of titles *Life, the Universe and Everything* does. Or doesn't. However that sentence started. Also I do want it to be a quotation from the first book, as the titles of the other two books were."

While Ed Victor, Douglas's agent, was not too keen on *So Long, and Thanks for All the Fish* as a title, everyone else was — especially Douglas's American publisher (and five-sixths of the advance money had come from America). At this point Douglas had a title and a contract. And an idea, but not much of one.

DEEP THOUGHT: It occurs to me that running a programme like this is bound to create considerable interest in the whole area of popular philosophy, yes?

MAJIKTHISE: Keep talking…

DEEP THOUGHT: Everyone's going to have their own theories about what answer I'm eventually going to come up with, and who better to capitalise on that media market than you yourselves?

BY THIS TIME WE ARE QUITE CLOSE IN ON ONE OF DEEP THOUGHT'S TV SCREENS. A NEW SCENE COMES UP ON IT: A TV PROGRAMME CALLED "DEEP THOUGHT SPECIAL". AT THE BOTTOM OF THE SCREEN FLASHES THE WORD "SIMULATION" WHICH ALTERNATES WITH THE WORDS "MERELY A SUGGESTION". THOUGH NO SOUND COMES WITH THE PROGRAMME WE SEE THAT IT FEATURES BOTH VROOMFONDEL AND MAJIK-THISE AS IMPORTANT-LOOKING PUNDITS ON A DISCUSSION PROGRAMME. THEY APPEAR TO BE ARGUING ON EITHER SIDE OF A SWINGOMETER WHICH IS LABELLED "ANSWER PREDICTOR". AS THEY ARGUE THE SWINGOMETER NEEDLE MOVES BACKWARDS AND FORWARDS BETWEEN TWO EXTREMES MARKED "LIFE AFFIRMATION" AND "HOPE-LESSNESS AND FUTILITY". THESE DETAILS ARE NOT PARTICULARLY IMPORTANT IN THEM-SELVES IF WE CAN'T MAKE THEM OUT. THE IMPORTANT THING TO ESTABLISH IS THAT IT LOOKS IMPORTANT. THE REAL VROOM-FONDEL AND MAJIKTHISE ARE CLEARLY FASCINATED BY THIS PICTURE.

DEEP THOUGHT: So long as you can keep violently disagreeing with each other and slagging each other off in the popular press, and so long as you have clever agents, you can keep yourselves on the gravy train for life.

— From early draft of TV series script, Episode Four.

Life, the Universe and Everything had given Douglas the problem of trying to force jokes onto a carefully worked-out plot. This time he would just follow the story wherever it led him. For the first time, the book was to be released in the UK in a hardback edition first (rather than a later library and book-club hardback). The presses were booked. The deadlines were agreed. The final-final deadlines were agreed. The extensions-beyond-which-one-could-not-extend were agreed.

Douglas was late.

Although he had made a number of notes on the book, had toyed with various ideas, including pulling in some of the weirder stuff from the second radio series, and getting a computer spreadsheet programme to organise his ideas for him, he had not written it in his Islington home (incidentally, *Life, the Universe and Everything* is the only *Hitchhiker's* book Douglas wrote at home, as opposed to some-where else. It has been suggested that this was because he had only just moved in there, and it seemed like somewhere else).

He had gone down to the West Country, where earlier books had been written, but did not write it there.

Which was why the sales kit that went out to Pan Books' sales representatives in late Summer 1984 began as follows:

> The great test of a promotion person is to devise a promo-tion for a book about which one knows absolutely zilch.
>
> The same goes for a representative selling such a book. At the time of writing Douglas Adams is holed up somewhere, I believe, in the West Country, incommuni-cado, as they say.

Prayers are held every morning in the editorial department along the lines of, "Please God grant to Douglas Adams the gift of inspiration along with his daily bread so that he can deliver the manuscript in time for us to make publication date." We just hope we have a fund of goodwill up there! But of course you know that all the *Hitch Hiker* promotions have been devised without sight of a book. That's what makes working on them such fun...

In the sales pack were such assorted goodies as badges, and posters showing birds under glass bowls. Also there was Douglas's promo piece for the book, a plot description that began:

EVERYTHING YOU WANTED TO KNOW ABOUT THE
FIRST THREE BOOKS BUT NEVER THOUGHT TO ASK.

It deals with that most terrible and harrowing experience in life — trying to remember an address which somebody told you but you didn't write down.

At the end of *Life, the Universe and Everything* Arthur Dent was told where to find God's Final Message to His Creation, only he can't remember where it was. He tries everything he can to jog his memory, meditation, mind reading, hitting himself about the head with blunt objects — he even tries to combine them all by playing mixed doubles tennis — but none of it works.

Still it plagues him — God's Final Message to His Creation. He can't help feel[ing] it must be important.

In desperation he decides to throw himself off a cliff in the hope that his life will then flash before his eyes on the way down. As to what will happen when he reaches the bottom — he decides he'll meet that challenge when he gets to it. He lost all faith in the straight forward operation of cause and effect the day he got up intending to catch up on some reading and brush the dog and ended up on prehistoric Earth with a man from Betelgeuse and

135

a spaceship-load of alien telephone sanitisers.

He picks a nice day, a nice cliff, and does it... he falls... he remembers...

He remembers an awful lot of other things besides, which throws him into such a state of shock that he misses the ground completely and ends up in the top of a tree with scratches, bruises, and a lot to think about. All his past life on Earth takes on a completely new meaning...

Now he really wants to find God's Final Message to His Creation, and knows where to look.

Arthur Dent is going home.

Although a fascinating book outline, this is light-years away from the book that eventually came out.

Before starting the book, Douglas had received a lecture from Sonny Mehta, Pan's Editorial Director, and Ed Victor, his agent, on getting the book in on time.

"To begin with, I had been slightly unwilling to write another *Hitchhiker's* book. Then I went off to do long promotional tours, and got very involved in the writing of the computer game, which took a lot of time. And then I had to write another version of the screenplay.

"So I kept putting off the book over and over, taking on all these other things I would do, and then ended up having to write the book in a terribly short space of time, still not absolutely certain that I wanted to do it."

In order to make the deadline (remember, the presses had been booked to print the book, the quantities — even the reprint times — had been worked out in advance) the book had to be written in less than three weeks.

The last time a situation like this had occurred was with *The Restaurant at the End of the Universe*, when Douglas had wound up in monastic seclusion, hidden away from the world and doing nothing but writing for a month.

Once more the job of finding Douglas somewhere to write fell to Jacqueline Graham of Pan, who recalls, "I'd just got back from maternity leave and I was asked by Sonny Mehta to find a suite in a central London hotel — near to Hyde Park, so Douglas could go jogging — with air conditioning, and a Betamax video for Sonny. I rang around, and Sonny chose the Berkeley. They had a very posh suite, with a small bedroom and a big bedroom — Sonny gave Douglas the small bedroom, as, he said, Douglas wouldn't be needing it very much."

Sweating over his typewriter, Douglas sat and wrote. He was allowed out twice a day for exercise. Sonny Mehta sat next door, watching videos and acting as on-the-spot editor.

At this time, Douglas sent another synopsis of *So Long, and Thanks for All the Fish* to Pan and his American publishers. While this bore rather more relation to the book that eventually came out than the original synopsis, it concluded:

> Along the way they meet some new people and some old, including:
>
> Wonko the Sane and his remarkable Asylum.
>
> Noslenda Bivenda, the Galaxy's greatest Clam opener.
>
> An Ultra-Walrus with an embarrassing past.
>
> A lorry driver who has the most extraordinary reason for complaining about the weather.
>
> Marvin the Paranoid Android, for whom even the good times are bad.
>
> Zaphod Beeblebrox, ex-Galactic President with two heads, at least one of which is saner than an emu on acid.
>
> And introducing…
>
> A Leg.

It may be observed that not all of these characters made it into the book as it eventually came out.

Douglas explained: "The Leg was something I rather liked actually, and it came curiously enough, out of the film script. But as soon as I took it out of context it fell apart, and I couldn't get it to work elsewhere.

"Do you remember the robot who had the fight with Marvin? I never had any clear visual description of the battletank, but it was going to appear in the movie at one point, and I wanted to give it lots of mechanical legs. The idea was that it was like a dinosaur — a dinosaur has one subsidiary brain to control its tail, and I thought this machine would have lots of subsidiary brains to deal with different bits of it. After the thing smashed itself to bits, the one thing that would be left with some kind of independent existence would be one of its legs.

"It was actually one of my favourite new things that I came up with in the film script. Of course, we don't know what will happen with the film script, but that bit will almost certainly never make it into the completed version, not because it's not good, but because it's completely detachable from the rest and because the script's too long.

"The Galaxy's greatest Clam opener... I don't remember very much about that. It had something to do with a seafood restaurant in Paris. There was someone I had in mind for the character: he was the only person who could open this particular type of clam, which was one of the great gastronomic experiences. I'm not sure why it was one of the great gastronomic experiences, but I think it was because whenever you ate it you got a flicker of memory all the way back to the primeval ooze. It might have had some plot function, but I can't remember what, and anyway, it didn't make it beyond the very early version.

"The Ultra-Walrus with the embarrassing past... well, this is very self-indulgent, I'm afraid. I got the idea after watching *Let it Be* and feeling very sorry for this obviously very embarrassed policeman having to go and make the Beatles stop playing. I mean knowing this is actually an *extraordinary* moment: the Beatles are playing live on a rooftop in London. And this poor policeman's job was to go and tell them to stop it. I thought that somebody would be so mortified that they would do anything not to be in this embarrassing position.

"So I thought of someone who was placed in such an embarrassing position, one he hated so much, that he would just want not to be there. The thought goes through his mind, 'I would do *anything* rather than do what I now have to do,' whereupon someone appears and says to him, 'Look, you have the option to either go and do this thing you don't want to do... or I can offer you a life on a completely different planet.' So he opts to go and be this strange sort of walrus creature. And it's a rather dull life as a walrus, but on the other hand he's perpetually grateful for the fact that he wasn't in this incredibly embarrassing position, and had ended up a walrus.

"The reason I made it a walrus, was... well, first of all I didn't know what the alternative life would be, and then when Gary Day Ellison, who designed the cover, showed me that lenticular picture I thought, 'I might as well make him a walrus.' It's because Gary always designs a cover that can clearly not have any function in relation to the book, and if I still had a chance I'd always try and work it in somehow. Not that it ever actually happened that way."

In November the book was released in England and America. The English cover was all black, with a lenticular picture of a dinosaur that changed into a walrus (and vice versa) stuck on the front. (There are no dinosaurs or walruses in *So Long, and Thanks for All the Fish*.) The American cover, marginally more logically, showed some leaping dolphins. (There are no dolphins in *So Long, and Thanks for All the Fish*, but there are more dolphins than there are walruses or dinosaurs.)

It was in October that the world's most expensive *Hitchhiker's* book was sold. At a dinner-party at Douglas's, British inventorial entrepreneur Sir Clive Sinclair spotted a pre-publication copy of *So Long, and Thanks for All the Fish* and asked if he could have it. Douglas refused, pointing out it was the only copy he had, whereupon Sir Clive whipped out his cheque book, and offered Douglas £1,000 for the charity of his choice, providing he could have the book.

Douglas had him make the cheque out to Greenpeace.

However, Douglas's hesitation to give the book away may have had less to do with the fact it was his only copy, and more to do with the fact that it was not a book with which he was altogether happy.

So Long, and Thanks for All the Fish is very different from the other *Hitchhiker's* books, and the critical reaction to it was mixed. For many of the fans it was a disappointment: they wanted more Zaphod, more Marvin, more space; they wanted Arthur to make it with Trillian; they wanted to find out how the Agrajag problem resolved and why Arthur Dent was the most important being in the universe (and even funnier than the frogs); they wanted towel jokes and extracts from *The Hitchhiker's Guide to the Galaxy*.

What they got was a love story. *So Long, and Thanks for All the Fish* is no longer science fiction, and, for much of the book, it is no longer humour (although it is often funny, and has certain science fiction elements in it). It was not the book the fans were expecting, and many of them were disappointed.

Many of the mainstream critics, however, preferred it, finding the gentler pace and the relatively down-to-earth tone easier to cope with, and coming up with such quotes as "*Fish* is the best evidence yet that Adams is not simply a funny sci-fi writer but a bomb-heaving satirist" (*Time*); others commented that it read as if it had been written in a hotel room in two weeks, with such comments as "a work in which bits and pieces of different sketches orbit around a non-existent plot" (*The Times*). *So Long, and Thanks for All the Fish* went on to sell as well as any of the other books, and won the City Limits 'best book' award for 1985 (voted on by the readership of the London listings magazine).

Talking to Adams about the book, one would find a mix of emotions: relief and slight embarrassment that it sold as well as it did, added to the feeling that he had 'used up a life' with the book.

Why weren't the expected characters in the book? "Partly because they didn't fit, and partly because I didn't want to do them. It was like a chore — people were saying, 'Let's have a Zaphod bit,' and I didn't *feel* like doing a Zaphod bit!"

This attitude of "I am not going to buckle down to the wishes of the fans" comes across in the book, to its detriment, most obviously in Chapter 25, where, having asked, somewhat rhetorically, whether or not Arthur Dent ever indulges the pleasures of the senses other than flying and drinking tea, Douglas comments, "Those who wish to know should read on. Others may wish to skip on to the last chapter which is a good bit and has Marvin in it." It is patronising and unfair. And undoubtedly would have been cut from a later draft of the manuscript had there been one.

Douglas continued, "You see, I didn't even want to do Marvin, but then what happened was that I finally had an idea of something I wanted to do that would have to involve Marvin, which is the way it should be. I didn't have that with Zaphod, or I couldn't. But when I needed the extra element for that scene it looked like a job for Marvin.

"It's very strange, that walking across the desert scene, when they find the Message*. I felt very haunted by that when I wrote it — it's not particularly funny or anything, but curiously enough I was very proud of it. I actually felt very sorry for, and sympathetic with Marvin in that I felt close to the character in a way that sometimes I hadn't because I was just doing it out of duty.

"But yes, the book is lighter weight than the others. In a sense I came close to owning up to that on the last page."

It was hard not to see parallels between Arthur Dent's return from space — which involves him telling everybody he's just returned from California — and Douglas Adams's return from a not altogether happy year in Los Angeles to the safer environs of Islington. And while he maintains that Fenchurch is no relation to Jane (Adams's then fiancée and later wife), Fenchurch being based more on his memories of adolescent love, he admits there is an element of this in the book.

"It wouldn't be fanciful to say that there is an echo of my return from LA in there. But I do think that one problem with the book, and there are many, is that up to that point I had been writing pure fantasy, which I'd had to do as I'd destroyed the Earth in the first reel, so to speak. So my job was to make the fantastical and dreamlike appear to be as real and solid as possible, that was always the crux of *Hitchhiker's*.

"Whereas in *So Long, and Thanks for All the Fish* a curious kind of thing happened. I got back to the everyday and somehow for the first time it seemed to be unreal and dreamlike. It was rather in reverse. I think it's largely because I thought I'd get rid of this problem of not having the Earth there to relate to by just bringing it back, and I suppose a part of me knew, a part of me said that you can't really do that. So therefore it wasn't the real Earth, and therefore it was bound to become unreal and dreamlike, and that was

* This passage was read out at Douglas's memorial service.

really a problem with the book.

"Also, you see, the character of Arthur Dent has undergone a fundamental change by then, because up to that point he has been our representative in a fantastical world, he has been Everyman, the person we can relate to, and through whose eyes we have seen the strange things that have happened. Now suddenly it's been turned around, and we have a real everyday Earth, and this character who, far from being our representative, has just spent the last eight years of his life alternately living in a cave on prehistoric Earth or being flung around the galaxy.

"So he is no longer someone through whose eyes we can see things. The whole thing has turned upside down, and I don't think I had got to grips with that until I was too far committed.

"That's why I am starting afresh now, because I feel all the lines have gotten rather too tangled."

Whatever happened to the 'jumping off a cliff' plot? "It was a structural idea I came up with which I still think is neat as a structure, but doesn't work as a book. The book would start with him leaping off a cliff, with the idea that just before you die your life flashes before you. There was something he wanted to remember, and he'd deal with what happened when he got to the bottom when he got there. So the entire book would be a flashback which would come from what he thought and he remembered as he fell down the cliff. I decided after hacking away at that for a while that it's a short story structure, but not a novel structure. Some people might argue (and with, I think, a certain amount of justice) that I didn't achieve a novel structure in the end, so what was I making a fuss about?

"But I suppose one reason why a lot of that stuff went, why it never materialised, was I had the feeling during that period of the whole world looking over my shoulder while I was writing. Every time someone would write to me and say, 'What are you going to do with this character?' or, 'Why don't you do this to resolve this situation?' then you instantly shy away from it and think it's no longer yours to control.

"It seemed to me like there was too much to tie up and mop up in *Hitchhiker's*, so that trying to write it like that would just be a continual task of knotting up the loose ends, when in fact it might be better just to think of something completely different to do..."

So Long, and Thanks for All the Fish was to be the last word on *Hitchhiker's*. At least in novel form; there were still to be the computer games, the film, the towel, possibly more television and more radio — even this book. But in novel form the story had gone as far as it was going to go.

At least for then.

Douglas said so.

20

DO YOU KNOW WHERE YOUR TOWEL IS?

A towel, as explained at length in *The Hitchhiker's Guide to the Galaxy*, is a jolly useful thing.

A towel is also a fairly obvious piece of merchandising.

While the merchandising properties of a number of artefacts mentioned in the *Hitchhiker's Guide to the Galaxy* have obvious commercial potential — Joo Janta sunglasses, for example, which turn black when danger threatens, or Disaster Area records, or even the *Guide* itself — technology has not yet reached the point where these things could be manufactured in bulk nor, indeed, at all.

Not so with towels.

At one point Marks and Spencer* considered marketing the towel of the book; however, nothing came of this.

In 1984 Douglas had lunch with Eugene Beer, of Birmingham publicists Beer-Davies. (Eugene was handling the publicity for the *Hitchhiker's* computer game.) During the course of this lunch, Douglas mentioned the abortive Marks and Spencer towel project. Eugene immediately saw the potential in real, authorised, money-making towels, with the relevant page of *Hitchhiker's* emblazoned on it. He began marketing them, taking out an advert in *Private Eye*, and sending complimentary towels all over the place.

* A British chain store whose underwear can be found on two out of three British people.

The complimentary towels were intended to cause the writers who received them to recommend them in print, something which happened almost without exception.

The towels were originally available in a sort of purple and a sort of blue. They were large, strong, good value, and did all the things that hitchhikery towels are well known for doing, in addition to which they gave you something to read on long journeys, something that even Douglas Adams, in his initial treatise on towels, failed to think of. The second edition of towels were available in 'Squornshellous Silver' and 'Beeblebrox Brown', and were sixty inches by forty inches.*

---

* A wide variety of merchandise, such as T-shirts, pens, badges, stickers, etc, is available from ZZ9 Plural Z Alpha (4 The Sycamores, Hadfield, Glossop, Derbyshire SK13 2BS, UK). Though the 'official' Hitchhiker's towel is no longer available, ZZ9 Plural Z Alpha still sell a very nice 'Don't Panic' towel. They would like to sell even more of them so that they can have their spare bedroom back.

21

GAMES WITH COMPUTERS

Douglas Adams was always fascinated by gadgets of every kind. His home, and indeed his life, was awash with all those little devices designed to reduce the complications of the workaday world. Televisions and amplifiers, computers and cameras, tape players of all descriptions, electronic objects of every colour and size. "The tendency for me to take the piss out of technology is me taking the piss out of myself. Digital watches and a kitchen full of juice extractors — I'm a sucker for it!"

While the initial success of *Hitchhiker's* allowed him to indulge his passion for tape players, Walkmans and the like, he remained for a long time on a battered manual typewriter, neither liking nor trusting computers.

DEEP THOUGHT DESIGN:
THE COMPUTER IS BASICALLY A TALL WHITE TOWER WHICH TAPERS AS IT GOES UP. AS IT GOES DOWN IT WIDENS OUT SO THAT IT ACTUALLY BECOMES THE FLOOR. YOU QUITE LITERALLY WALK UP TO IT. TO EITHER SIDE OF IT AND SET SLIGHTLY FORWARD OF IT ARE TWO SIMILAR BUT SMALLER TOWERS. SET INTO THE FRONT OF EACH TOWER IS A TV SCREEN.

THE SCREEN ON THE MAIN TOWER HAS A PICTURE OF A MOUTH. WHEN DEEP THOUGHT TALKS, THE MOUTH MOVES IN SYNCH. ONE OF THE OTHER SCREENS SHOWS A SINGLE EYE, AND THE THIRD SCREEN SHOWS A SIDE VIEW OF A SINGLE EAR. EACH EYE AND EAR AND MOUTH SHOULD BE AS ANONYMOUS AS POSSIBLE, BUT IT SHOULD BE APPARENT THAT THEY ARE NOT FROM THE SAME PERSON.

— Deep Thought design (first version) from TV series script,

Episode Four.

In a 1982 interview he revealed that he considered computers to be, if not intrinsically malevolent, then useless — either HACTARs or EDDIEs. He had just moved into the Islington flat, and had found it impossible to convince the various utilities companies' computers that he had in fact moved. "Dealing with the American Express computer", he told the reporter, "has been beyond Kafka's worst nightmares".

In retaliation he had created a scenario for *Life, the Universe and Everything* in which a world much like our own is poised on the brink of nuclear Armageddon, and tipped over the brink not by a flock of geese or a madman's finger on a red button, but by a change-of-address card fouling up a computer. The scene never made it into the final draft.

He had tried to like computers, indeed had gone to a computer show earlier that year, but had been overcome by jargon and was forced to leave. His enthusiasm (bordering on messianic fervour) for computers did not really begin until 1983, when he spent seven months in Los Angeles, supposedly writing the *Hitchhiker's Guide to the Galaxy* film screenplay.

While it is true that he did write one and a half drafts of a screenplay over this time, it would be equally fair to say that he spent much of the time playing with his word processor and getting involved with interminable computer games.

Douglas had received many requests to turn *The Hitchhiker's Guide to the Galaxy* into a computer game, and had so far refused all of them. However, the time spent playing computer games had given him definite ideas: he knew he wanted the *Hitchhiker's* game to be far more a problem-solving, interactive novel than an arcade or space invaders game.

In late 1983 he contacted Infocom, a Massachusetts based company whose previous games had impressed him, and suggested a collaboration. They agreed enthusiastically, and by January 1984 Douglas was in a position to announce, "I'm going to get the computer game done this year which will give me an excuse for playing around with my computer. I'll be doing the work on a computer in Boston and accessing it from here on international packet-switching. I love all that!"

NEW DEEP THOUGHT DESIGN:

DEEP THOUGHT IS A HUGE EDIFICE, AS HUGE AS SET AND BUDGET LIMITATIONS WILL ALLOW. IT IS BRILLIANT GOLD. IT IS CLEARLY A COMPUTER, BUT IT BEARS AN UNCANNY RESEMBLANCE TO A HUGE FAT BUDDHA. THE FACT THAT IT DOES SO MUST LOOK AWESOME AND IMPRESSIVE.

— Deep Thought design (second version) from TV series script, Episode Four.

Douglas Adams's collaborator on the computer game was an American, Steve Meretzky. They began by corresponding via electronic bulletin board, and then met in February 1984 for initial discussions. Adams wrote chunks of material, sent them via computer to Meretzky, who programmed them and sent them back. Douglas Adams actually designed and wrote more than half the game; the rest was a joint effort, using Douglas's ideas and material, and Meretzky's computer experience. The game itself was released in late '84, and proved an immediate success. The packaging was imaginative, containing an illustrated booklet with pictures of the *Guide* and sundry alien phenomena, together with a 'Don't Panic' badge, Joo Janta sunglasses, fluff, a microscopic space fleet, demolition orders (real eager-beavers should take a very careful look at the signatures on them), and no tea.

The computer game, which Adams described as "bearing as much relationship to the books as *Rosencrantz and Guildenstern are Dead* does to *Hamlet*", opens much as the other versions of *Hitchhiker's*. You are Arthur Dent, waking with a hangover on the morning that your house is demolished, but you rapidly find yourself in a fiendish and phantasmagoric nightmare, in which the object seems to be as much to find out what the purpose of the game is as it is to play it.

As Adams explained, "It gets the player going and lulled into a false sense of security. And then all hell breaks loose and it goes through the most extraordinary number of directions. The game just glances at events which were a major part of the books, while things I used as one line throwaways are those that I used for the game's set pieces. The reason was to keep me interested in doing it, and I wanted to make it fair for the people who haven't read the books. So readers and non-readers were, as much as possible, on an equal footing... the game is equally difficult for both."

The response to the game was extraordinary. Described by the London *Times* as "without doubt the best adventure ever seen on computer", it became the bestselling adventure game in America on its release, selling over a quarter of a million copies. A major part of the game's success must have been due to the fact that a real-life author was, for the first time, actively involving himself in, indeed writing, a computer game based on his work; and also to Adams's own love of messing around with computers, and devising problems, doing crosswords and the like — not to mention his need to keep himself interested and amused by that game, which communicates itself to participants.

The game contains much that is new (and doubtless apocryphal); obscure, brain-baffling problems; and much new Adams text, including another opportunity to examine and rewrite the events of the first half of the first book. Doors, Babel fish, peanuts and tea (or lack therefore) take on a whole new lease of life.

Some sample passages include:

Of a pub cheese sandwich...

> The barman gives you a cheese sandwich. The bread is like the stuff that stereos come packed in, the cheese would be great for rubbing out spelling mistakes, and margarine and pickle have combined to produce something that shouldn't be, but is, turquoise. Since it is clearly unfit for human consumption you are grateful to be charged only a pound for it.

Of one of the many deaths of Arthur Dent...

> Your serious allergic reaction to protein loss from matter transference beams becomes a cause célèbre among various holistic pressure groups in the Galaxy and leads to a total ban on dematerialisation. Within fifty years, space travel is replaced by a keen interest in old furniture restoration and market gardening. In this new, quieter Galaxy, the art of telepathy flourishes as never before, creating a new universal harmony which brings all life together, converts all matter into thought and brings about the rebirth of the entire Universe on a higher and better plane of existence. However, none of this affects you, because you are dead.

Later in the game, when one obtains a copy of the *Guide*, it can be consulted on a number of subjects. Fluff, for example...

> Fluff is interesting stuff: a deadly poison on Bodega Minor, the diet staple of Frazelon V, the unit of currency on the moons of the Blurfoid System, and the major crop of the laundry supplies planet, Blastus 111. One ancient legend claims that four pieces of fluff lie scattered around the Galaxy: each forming one quarter of

the seedling of a tree with amazing properties, the sole survivor of the tropical planet Fuzzbol (Footnote 8). The ultimate source of fluff is still a mystery, with the scientific community divided between the Big Lint Bang theory and the White Lint Hole theory.

(Footnote 8, should you care to check, informs you that "it's not much of a legend really".)

The game is bizarre and improbable. It has the text of a short novel in its memory, and meant that a good part of Douglas Adams's mail subsequently consisted of heartfelt cries from people trapped on the bridge of the *Heart of Gold* or unable to obtain a Babel fish.

A second game was planned at the same time as the first, this to take place on the planet of Magrathea.

Whether or not the game is a valid part of the *Hitchhiker's* canon (for which the only requisite for joining would seem to be that it is completely different from any other versions) could be debated. But comparison is not really needed. As Douglas Adams explained, when interviewed about Interactive Literature, "You can't compare IL with literature. If you do, you can very easily make a fool of yourself. When Leo Fender first invented an electric guitar one could have said: 'But to what extent is this real music?' To which the answer is: 'All right, we're not going to play Beethoven on it, but at least let's see what we can do.' What matters is whether it's interesting and exciting.

"The thing I like about this is that I can sit down and know that I am the first person to be working in this specific field. When you are writing a novel, you are aware that you are manipulating your readers. Here you know you are going to have to make them think how you want them to reason. I don't regard it as being an abdication of creative art. Yes, at first I was horrified: in fact, there is a sense in which now the author is even more in control, because the 'reader' has more problems to solve. All the devices of the novel are still at your disposal, because a novel is simply a string of words, and words can mean whatever you want them to. It just offers the opportunity to have a lot of fun".

Adams enjoyed putting together and writing the computer game more than any other aspect of *Hitchhiker's*. Following the computer game, Adams's interest in computers, computer games and programming remained high, although at one point he found that he was spending so much time playing with his Apple Macintosh that he switched back to a manual typewriter, in order to get some work done and as a form of penance. Subsequent computer-related projects included *Bureaucracy**, *Starship Titanic* and h2g2.com. Projects that were slated to happen but never did include *Reagan*, *God*, *Hitchhiker's II* and *The Muppet Institute of Technology*.

The Muppet Institute of Technology was to have been a one-hour special for television, using the Muppets to promote the idea of computer literacy. The late Jim Henson, the Muppets' creator, flew Adams and twenty other people to New York for discussions, and while Douglas was enthused about the project, and found Henson Associates "extraordinarily nice people to work with", the project did not happen.

The idea for the *Reagan* program occurred to Douglas after watching one of the Reagan-Mondale debates in 1984: "It occurred to me that people who have to brief Reagan for a debate such as that have to provide him with the minimum number of facts and the maximum number of ways of getting to those facts, and the most all-embracing fallback positions — lines to come up with when he doesn't really know the answer to the question and maybe doesn't even understand the question, but has recognised some key phrase, and can come up with a phrase or line that will cover it.

"And I thought, 'This is exactly the way you program a computer to appear to be taking part in a conversation.' So, with a friend in New York, I was going to do a program to emulate Reagan, so you could sit down and talk to a computer and it would respond as Reagan would. And then we could do a Thatcher one, and after a while you could do all the world leaders, and get all the various modules to talk to each other.

"After that we were going to do a program called *God*, and program all God's attributes into it, and you'd have all the different

* The object of *Bureaucracy* being to persuade your bank to acknowledge a change-of-address card.

denominations of God on it... you know, a Methodist God, a Jewish God, and so on... I wanted to be the first person to have computer software burned in the Bible Belt, which I felt was a rite of passage that any young medium had to pass through.

"However, with the recession in the American computer industry, all that came to nothing, largely because the people who wanted to do it with me discovered they didn't have cars or money or jobs."

THE GAME ITSELF

It is difficult to say too much about the computer game without giving information away that could spoil it for somebody playing it. Essentially, it is based on the events in the first two-thirds of the book *The Hitchhiker's Guide to the Galaxy*. One starts out as Arthur Dent, in bed one morning in Tiverton in Devon, with an awful hangover. Initial problems include how to pick something up without it slipping through your fingers and how not to be killed when a large yellow bulldozer knocks down your house.

Things remain fairly faithful to the book until you reach the *Heart of Gold*, at which point Ford, Zaphod and Trillian go off to have a sauna and you are left to your own devices in a ship full of uncooperative GPP machines. After that things get very bizarre indeed: events are experienced from a multitude of viewpoints; problems to be solved occur in places as disparate as Damogran, a party in Islington, and the interior of a whale.

To get you through the game are your copy of *The Hitchhiker's Guide*, your Sub-Etha Sens-O-Matic and Electronic Thumb, and your towel — not to mention your native wit, luck, and a sense of humour. And a thing your aunt gave you that you don't know what it is.

The game is addictive: fiendishly hard, yet impossible to leave alone until every last problem is solved, which can only be done by paying attention to every piece of information that comes your way, and often by thinking extremely laterally. The game can be played by novices, who might in some ways have less difficulty than experienced computer gamers, who would not necessarily find it easy to tune in to the game's peculiar mind-set.

The weakest part of the game is the opening section of the packaging and manual: an eight-page advertisement for the *Guide* ("Yes! The Universe Can Be Yours For Less Than 30 Altairian Dollars Per Day!") which comes across as sophomoric — more like *Mad* magazine than Douglas Adams.

The game, however, is a major achievement, one that even the least computer literate *Hitchhiker's* fan should enjoy.

It is easy to see why Douglas Adams found this the most enjoyable part of *Hitchhiker's*; almost all aspects of it, from the adventure, to the *Guide* entries, to the footnotes, even to the Invisiclues Hints book, display a relaxed attitude missing from the books and radio series. Adams had a tendency to have ideas that didn't always fit into the framework of what he was doing at the time. The enjoyable thing about the computer game is that the most bizarre ideas could be incorporated into it with ease. Also Adams's love of problem-solving (crosswords and such) was given full rein.

Postscript: The *Hitchhiker's* computer game was subsequently re-released on a CD-ROM called *The Lost Treasures of Infocom* and was eventually made available over the web as part of the Comic Relief site.

22

LETTERS TO DOUGLAS ADAMS

"I'm terribly grateful for the fans — apart from anything else, they provide my bread and butter. I'm obviously delighted there are so many people who enjoy this stuff. But I try to keep a little bit of distance because I believe the most dangerous thing a person can do is believe their own publicity. I know, from people I look up to and admire — for instance, John Cleese: it took me a long time to be able to perceive him as an ordinary human being, and I know how very very easy it is to look at somebody who is actually a perfectly normal human being, who happens to have a particular talent, an ability or facility that puts them into the limelight, to see them as being some sort of very elevated and extraordinary person, which they're not. I think you do yourself a favour if you try not to expose yourself too much to people who are going to tell you you are God's gift to the human race, which you're not. The media present you as being some kind of superhuman, and you aren't, so you just have to keep all that at arm's length.

"It's rather curious when I discover that a phrase of mine has entered the language. I mean, one never seriously thinks that what one gets up to at home has much effect on anything else, and though you see the bestseller lists, and get letters and royalty statements it doesn't impinge on me that it has that kind of effect on other people. I don't want to believe that it does.

"People like me don't make the gossip pages because they don't know our faces. I get the advantages of being famous with none of the disadvantages. It's startling when somebody does recognise me — I feel slightly vulnerable when it occurs. I can understand why writers take a pseudonym. It's strange having an existence in other people's minds which has little to do with you. It's not the same me they wrote about on my school reports."

— Douglas Adams, on fame, 1985.

Browsing through Douglas Adams's letters file is a truly mind-expanding experience. All human life, and a fair amount of putative alien life, is there. Certain themes, however, tend to recur. Most people wanted to know where he got his ideas. (One American would-be author wanted to know if she could have any leftover ideas he didn't need.) Others asked questions, wanted advice, proposed marriage or sex, and occasionally offered solutions to matters raised in the books.

Three students from Huddersfield University, for example, claim to have discovered the Ultimate Question of Life, the Universe, and Everything...

The Answer to "The Ultimate Question of Life, the Universe, and Everything" is not in fact 42, but is stored in the reproductive cells of all life forms and this answer is found via 42. To explain better: all, or most, cells reproduce by splitting in two to form two cells.

Thus, one cell becomes two, two becomes four... and so on. It follows that the Answer must, therefore be some power of two. Deep Thought came up with the number 42, and this is indeed the power to which 2 must be raised to find this answer...

Thus, by obtaining 2^{42} — 4398046511104 — reducing it to morse code, turning the morse code into letters, rearranging the letters into passable words, and interpreting the Answer thus obtained they were able to work out what the question was. I would not dare to give the game away by revealing it, but will simply say that any Cabbalistic scholar would have been proud of their work. You may reproduce it if you wish.

These are some of the most common questions he was asked...

Q: What was the Dire Straits song from So Long, *and Thanks for All the Fish?*
A: The Dire Straits song is 'Tunnel of Love' and it's on the *Making Movies* album.

Q: Did you steal the biscuits story from Jeffrey Archer?
A: The origin of the story about the biscuits was that it actually happened to me at Cambridge Station, England, in 1976; since when I've told the story so often on radio and TV that people have begun to pinch it. This is why I wanted to put it down in black and white myself. I didn't know Jeffrey Archer had used a similar story in *A Quiver Full of Arrows* (1982) having never read the book. I would point out that the date, 1982, comes somewhat after the date 1976.

Q: What was the Question of "Life, the Universe, and Everything"?
A: The actual question for which Arthur Dent has been seeking has now been revealed to me. It is this:
As soon as I've managed to decipher it — and I'm waiting for someone to send me a primer for the language in which it is written, and it may be some time — I will let you know.

To a thirteen year-old young novelist, who was having great difficulty thinking up names for characters:
A: If you are having trouble in thinking up character names you are probably using the wrong kind of coffee. Have you tried an Italian blend?

Q: How do you mix a Pan Galactic Gargle Blaster?
A: I'm afraid it is impossible to mix a Pan Galactic Gargle Blaster in Earth's atmospheric conditions, but as an alternative I suggest you buy up the contents of your local liquor store, pour them into a large bucket and re-distil them three times. I'm sure your friends would appreciate this.

Q: What is the point of Doctor Who?
A: The whole point of *Doctor Who* is that, if you take the second letter of each of the fifty-ninth words of all the episodes over the last twenty years of broadcast and run them together backwards, the original location of the lost city of Atlantis is revealed. I hope this answers your question.

To a student who wished to do a thesis on scientific and philosophical themes in *Hitchhiker's*:
A: Most of the ideas in *Hitchhiker's* come from the logic of jokes, and any relation they bear to anything in the real world is usually completely coincidental.

To someone enquiring where Arthur got the copy of *The Hitchhiker's Guide to the Galaxy* in *So Long, and Thanks for All the Fish*, and in which pub in Taunton Fenchurch and Arthur met:
A: Although copies of the actual *Guide* have never been published on Earth, copies of it are freely (or rather, expensively) available throughout the Galaxy. Arthur acquired another one for himself on his journey back to Earth — in other words, between the end of *Life, the Universe and Everything* and *So Long, and Thanks for All the Fish*. Although I set the pub scene in Taunton, the pub I had in mind was in fact one in Gillingham in Dorset, the name of which (wisely) I forget.

Q: Will you ever novelise the Doctor Who *episodes you wrote?*
A: As far as *The Pirate Planet* or *City of Death* are concerned, although I wouldn't mind adapting them into books at some time in the future, there are far too many other things that I want to do in the meantime. Certainly I don't want anyone else doing them though!

As for *Shada* — no, I don't particularly want to see that done. I think that it's not such a great story, and has only gained the notoriety it has got because no one's seen it. If it had been finished and broadcast, it would have never have aroused so much interest.

Often he received numbered questions, which often got numbered answers:

Q:
1) *Why did you decide to start writing?*
2) *What aspects of science fiction are you 'ripping off'?*
3) *What experiences do you feel affected your attitudes and values?*
4) *Can your feelings be linked with those of any of the characters in your books?*
5) *What is your background?*
6) *Why do you write science fiction rather than normal fiction?*
7) *Do you enjoy writing?*
8) *What do you think is your 'style' of writing?*
A:
1) Because I couldn't think of anything else to do.
2) Are you sure you mean the same by 'ripping off' as I do?
3) All of them.
4) Some of them.
5) Varied.
6) I'm not sure.
7) No.
8) Both.

Q:
1) *How long did it take you to write* Life, the Universe and Everything?
2) *Are any of the characters designed from your own personality?*
3) *Have you ever considered doing a comic book?*
4) *Who is your favourite character in the trilogy?*
5) *Where did you get the inspiration to do your books?*
A:
1) Several months.

2) No.

3) No.

4) Don't have one.

5) From a mail order company in Iowa.

Q:

1) Why did you start to write?

2) Why do you write science fiction?

3) Where do you get your ideas from?

A:

1) Because I was broke.

2) I didn't mean to. I just exaggerate a lot.

3) A small mail order firm in Cleveland.

Q:

1) How do you come up with those names?

2) What gave you the idea to write the books?

3) Why this subject?

4) When did you decide to become an author and why?

5) Did you like the results of the books?

6) Why did you put Ford and Arthur on Ancient Earth?

7) How long did it take to write the books?

A:

1) Yes.

2) 37.5.

3) No.

4) Somerset.

5) Last Thursday morning.

6) French.

7) No.

And finally, a letter that Douglas scrawled answers on, but which was never posted, since the correspondent had omitted his name and address...

1) Do you parallel yourself on any of the main characters? How?

No.

2) How did working with the Monty Python Troupe affect your work?

I didn't. I knew them but did not work with them.

3) How often have you been railroaded or forced into doing something you just didn't want to do (as Arthur Dent in Life, the Universe and Everything*)?*

37 times.

4) Do you believe in fate, and do you try to put this idea across in your work?

No.

5) Could you include a short autobiography, including anything that you consider contributing to your work?

Born 1952. Haven't died yet.

6) What is your favourite planet?

Earth. It's the only one I know.

7) Did you do much research before doing the writing?

None.

8) Have you studied history in depth?

Semi-depth.

9) What is your main message in Life, the Universe and Everything*?*

No message. If I'd wanted to write a message I'd have written a message. I wrote a book.

10) Have you ever had experiences similar to that your characters have?

No.

11) Have you ever been hounded by the Galactic police for the where-abouts of one Zaphod Beeblebrox?

No. They are fictional characters.

SEX AND THE SINGLE HITCHHIKER

...Since I have such an in-depth knowledge of your work I feel I am worthy of meeting you and chatting to you about our dear friends Trill, Zaphod, and not forgetting miserable Marvin. Please write and let me know when and where you would like to arrange a meeting...

    (M.D. London)

I'm mostly to be found 33,000 feet above Iceland, but if you feel like popping up for a drink I'd be glad to say hello.

Dear Mr Adams,

Rest easy — I'm not a Beverly Hills real estate agent. If you're still unmarried and have no children and you're interested in girls, pick up the phone next time you're in New York City, dial (xxxxx) and ask for Marion. I would love to meet the man behind that silly grin. References furnished on request.

Dear Mr Adams,

Let me start by telling you I'm not a Surrey Estate Agent. (God, the number of letters you must have had starting with that.) I will get straight to the point. I'm formally offering you the opportunity of an affair with me, you have been selected out of many WORLD-FAMOUS writers of humerus [sic] prose to be the recipient of a romantic involvement with me, the duration of which will depend on:

a) Whether [sic] or not we speak the same language, and

b) How good you are at screwing.

The young lady in question said she was five feet eight, nine stone six, a brunette with multicoloured eyes, and described herself as *discreet, adventurous, agile, willing to do anything provided it doesn't do me permanent physical damage and I've a good phone manner.* Douglas did not reply.

Then there was the fan letter from an American writer, hopefully working on a film script, who explained: *It's a lot of work, but I break the monotony getting laid in the back bars by pretending to be you.*

Thanks.

FRUITCAKES

Dear Mr Adams,

Thank you for no longer writing about Zaphod Beeblebrox, because I grew to feel a keen sense of identification with him from acquiring two heads, a fleet, and experiencing the Flying City in the Pyramids, your HHGG Corporation Building. At least I deduce it was because the motto was 'Don't Panic' (see Daniel 4:34 because at that very hour the planets were in conjunction).

This is followed by a lengthy ramble through the Bible, and the works of Adams, Castenada and Moorcock, which proves that 42 is really 666, the number of the beast, and concludes...

Well, thanks for all the fish. A word from you might help matters with my girlfriend who doesn't seem to understand I actually lived through your books: If you don't understand this then I'll just give up ("The Gods don't dwell amongst men" Daniel 2:11)...

Dear Mr Adams,

I had a dream this morning that Jack Lemmon came up to me and asked directions to the Royal Albert Hall...

Dear Douglas Adams,

The Answer is not 42; it is 'NAM-MYOTO-RENGE-KYO'. This is the law of life as propounded by Nichiren Derishonin in about 1255 AD...

Dear Douglas,

What age will I be when mankind is born out of mother earth? I am now 34. Do you know Kit Williams's phone number?

Happy Christmas and many of them. I reckon about eight by my digital watch.

Love Muz.

"A number of people have said that *Hitchhiker's* belongs to the same genre as *Pilgrim's Progress*.

"That's not to compare the two, just to point out that there is a genre with a long history, which is that of the innocent abroad in a fantastical world.

"A graduate student sent me a long paper on one book that we know for sure that John Bunyan (author of *Pilgrim's Progress*) actually read. It's called *The Plain Man's Path to Heaven*, written by an English Puritan writer called Arthur Dent. He assumed that I was aware of this and was having some extraordinary academic joke.

"Once you've decided to find parallels you can find them all the time: you can add up numbers, you can compare images… you can pick up any two books and if you wished to prove they were parallel, you could do it. You could pick up the Bible and the telephone directory, and you could prove that each has a direct relationship to the other."

— Douglas Adams.

THE LAST WORD…

Dear Mr Adams,

You're weird. Or at least your writing is weird. That's okay by me. I'm a little weird myself. If you are really one of those terribly dull people who just write weird please keep it a secret, I hate being disillusioned…

23

DIRK GENTLY AND TIME FOR TEA

"I'm half inclined to look at other genres. I never set out to parody SF, but to use the trappings of SF to look at other things. I think I'd like to do a detective novel. Not as a parody, but to use those conventions to do something else. Then again, people could say, 'Why don't you do something else directly?' and I don't know the answer to that, except that I'd feel very nervous about it. I always have to dogleg around something to get somewhere.

"I'd like to do a mystery story or a detective story — not influenced by any one author — as soon as you do that you become a parodist, and I'm not a parodist — parody is one of the easier forms of writing, and it's one that is too easy to slip into when you aren't trying hard enough. I'm not saying I've not slipped into it, but when I did, it was usually one of my less successful moments."

— Douglas Adams, January 1984.

"I feel written out in *Hitchhiker's* and I don't feel I have anything more to say in that particular medium. There are other things I want to do. I've been thinking of writing in the horror/mystery/occult area. Really the whole thing is to find a whole new set of characters and a new environment — it isn't just that it's new, but that it's an environment and a set of characters that I, now at age 33, thought up, rather than what I came up with when I was 25. There's an awful lot of things I want to do, and the major thing, the core, is going to have to be writing books."

— Douglas Adams, October 1985.

"It's called *Dirk Gently's Holistic Detective Agency*."
— Douglas Adams, December 1985.

One morning in November 1985, Douglas Adams and his agent, Ed Victor, sat in a hotel room in which a number of phone lines had been set up, and waited for the phones to ring. By the end of the working day one lucky publisher had come away with the rights to *Dirk Gently's Holistic Detective Agency*, and its sequel, and Douglas was over two million dollars richer than he had been that morning. The first book was to be delivered in a year's time, and would be published in April 1987.

And after that?

"Well, the moment you always feel like writing a book is when you've just finished one, so now I've actually got a two-book deal, what I'd like to do is write this book, then immediately write the second book, and see if I can get them both done in a year. At the moment, the second book will be a Dirk Gently book as well — assuming the first one works."

From the original outline of *Dirk Gently's Holistic Detective Agency*, it was obviously a detective novel, an occult-ghost story, a dissertation on quantum physics, and a great deal of fun. As has already been commented on, certain characters and situations from *Shada* and *City of Death* recur.

"One of my objectives with this book is, although it is going to be a comedy, it is not, as *Hitchhiker's* was, going to be primarily a comedy, because with *Hitchhiker's* everything would have to bow and bend to the jokes, and often you would have to abandon bits of plot or turn them on their heads, or do real violence to a plot in order to get the joke to be funny.

"What I want to do with this, and am in the process of getting, is a tightly organised plot with a lot of ideas packed in it, and then write by that plot and allow it to be funny when it wants to be, but not force it to be funny, which was the problem with *Hitchhiker's*. Once that's straight, then all sorts of things become naturally funny, but there's never any sense of... well, it's like when you used to have to write essays at school you would always want to put in jokes, but the moment you've got to write a sketch you can't think of anything funny to save your life. So I'm setting this up in a different way this time.

"It will be apparent when you read it that being funny is an important part of it, but it's just not the prime mover any more."

In the UK, the bidding saw the book go to Heinemann, with Pan as the paperback house, something that Douglas saw as solving a problem he had faced hitherto.

"The problem was that I've always gone into paperback first, and even with *So Long, and Thanks...* which went into hardback first, it was still from a paperback house.

"But there's a different way that paperback houses are geared to doing things than hardbacks, because at a paperback house the schedule is so much tighter, because they are going to sell so many more copies of the book. And because everything a paperback house does is almost always after the hardback publication of the book, there's no need to build flexibility into the system.

"Hardback publishers on the other hand are completely geared to the fact that writers are always late and always difficult. In the past, every time I hit a problem (which was pretty frequently) there was no time to stop and get it right. It began to seem absurd to me that here I was, an author of incredibly popular books, so what I wrote was important not only to me but to a very large public, and I didn't have a chance to get it right, and this seemed absolutely crazy. The more successful you become the less chance there is of getting the stuff you are writing to work properly.

"Now I want to make it clear that I'm not being rude about Pan, who did a wonderful job in promoting and marketing and selling an enormous number of copies, but it is just not in the nature of a paperback house to deal with the problems of actual authorship. That's not what they are geared up to do. So now that I have a hard-back publisher I think this is going to make a huge difference to the way things go from now on."

"My lifestyle? It's very boring. I do spend a lot of money on things that I don't need, like fast cars, which is pretty silly, considering I only use them to pooter about town. I've been through this thing with cars before, as I'd always promised myself that when I had some money I *wouldn't* do something silly like buying a flashy car. So, as soon as *Hitchhiker's* went to number one in the bestseller lists, I went out and bought a Porsche 911. I hated it. Driving it around in London was like taking a Ming vase to a football match. Going for a drive was like setting out to invade Poland. I got rid of it after going into a skid coming out of Hyde Park and crashing into a wall by the Hard Rock Café... there was a huge queue of people outside, all of whom cheered loudly, so I got rid of it and got a Golf GTI. When I was in LA, I had a Saab Turbo, and when I came back to the UK with an LA state of mind I bought a BMW, which was nice, but I didn't need a car that cost £24,000. *Spendthrift* is part of my lifestyle.

"I spend a lot of my money in restaurants. Like Jane and I going off last year to France. We decided to have fun (which was about the only thing we failed to do). Everywhere we went the hotels were shut, so we decided to go down to Burgundy, where at least the meals would be good.

"We arrived there late at night, and I had one of the best omelettes I've ever tasted. Unfortunately, it had some strange mushrooms in it, and I was in bed for two days with food poisoning. We were booked into all these wonderful restaurants and I never got to any of them.

Then we drove back. As soon as my stomach was strong enough to hold anything down, we couldn't find anything decent to eat. Then it rained all the time and we missed the ferry and had to drive to Calais, and I was seasick all the way back home. That's the jetset lifestyle for you. Somehow it cost me a lot of money."

— Douglas Adams.

Adams spent most of 1986 editing *The Utterly Utterly Merry Comic Relief Christmas Book,* spending less time than he had hoped assisting in the writing of the *Bureaucracy* computer game ("it involves you in a bewildering series of adventures from your own home to the depths of the African jungle, but the object of the game is simply to get your bank to acknowledge a change-of-address card..."), and planning *Dirk Gently.*

"*Dirk Gently* has nothing at all to do with *Hitchhiker's.* It's a kind of ghost-horror-detective-time-travel-romantic-comedy-epic, mainly concerned with mud, music and quantum mechanics.

"The strange thing is that while I was working on *Hitchhiker's* I would always find myself telling people I wasn't a science fiction writer, simply a humour writer who happened to be using some science fiction ideas to tell jokes with. But *Dirk Gently* is changing my mind. I think maybe I *am* a science fiction writer. It's very strange..."

ON SCIENCE FICTION

Extract from an interview with Douglas Adams conducted by the author in November 1983:

I've read the first thirty pages of a tremendous amount of science fiction. One thing I've found is that, no matter how good the ideas are, a lot of it is terribly badly written. Years ago, I read Asimov's *Foundation* trilogy. The ideas are captivating, but the writing! I wouldn't employ him to write junk mail! I loved the film of *2001,* saw it six times and read the book twice. And then I read a book called *The Lost Worlds of 2001* in which Clarke chronicles the disagreements between himself and Kubrick — he goes through all the ideas left by the wayside, "Look at this idea he left out, and this idea!" and at the end of the book one has an intense admiration for Kubrick. I read *2010* when it came out, and it was like all the stuff that Kubrick had been sensible enough to leave out of *2001*.

What's good? Vonnegut, he's great, but he's not an SF writer. People criticise him for saying it, but it's true. He started with one or two ideas he wanted to convey and happened to find some conventions of SF that suited his purpose.

I thought The Sirens of Titan *was close in many ways to* Hitchhiker's. *The Chrono-synclastic infundibulum, for example, if I've got that right.*

That's right, yes. It's funny, people make this comparison, and I'm always incredibly flattered, because I don't think it's a fair comparison. It's unfair to Vonnegut, apart from anything else, because when you are talking about his best books (I'm not talking about his later books, where I can't understand how he gets the enthusiasm to get in front of the type-writer and actually write that stuff. It's like going through the motions of his own stylistic tricks), those first three were deeply serious books. My books aren't serious at that level — they are on some level — but there's a very clear disparity between them. Read a Vonnegut book next to one of mine and it's clear they're utterly different. People are tempted to compare them for three reasons. Firstly, they are both funny in some way, and secondly, they've got spaceships and robots in them. [No third was mentioned.] It's the labelling. A much, much stronger influence in my writing is P.G. Wodehouse; he didn't write about robots and spaceships, though, so people don't spot it. They are looking for labels.

There are Wodehousian turns of phrase in your writing. Like the line about "Aunt calling to Aunt like Dinosaurs across a marsh".

Yes, I actually pinched that line somewhere in the third book. I'm not sure where.

The mattresses?

Yes, it's at the end of the mattresses scene, in the swamp. But I have to point that out to people since no one noticed.

As regards good SF books, well *A Canticle for Leibowitz* [Walter Miller Jr] is a wonderful book. There's also someone I came across because of *Hitchhiker's* — people kept saying, "If you write this stuff you must know the work of Robert Sheckley?"

I assumed you must have read Sheckley's Dimension of Miracles.

People kept saying that, so I finally sat down and read it, and it was quite creepy. The guy who constructed Earth... it was completely fortuitous. Those are coincidences, and after all there are only a small number of ideas. I felt what I did was more akin to Sheckley than Vonnegut.

As with everything else Douglas did, *Dirk Gently* was late. By the time it was finished, there was no time to get it properly typeset and to get proof copies out — something that spurred Douglas to become a desktop publisher. The book was typeset on his Macintosh computer (indeed, the proof copies were printed on his laser printer) and came out on time in Spring 1987 — to mixed reviews. Some people found it more satisfying than a *Hitchhiker's* book. Others missed the non-stop cavalcade of jokes.

24

SAVING THE WORLD
AT NO EXTRA CHARGE

Dirk Gently is a detective and a rather improbable one at that. He's smug, he's fat, he's bespectacled, he's a smartass, he sends out ludicrous bills with positively ridiculous expenses claims and, worst of all, he's probably right. He's the kind of person you only ever want to know under the direst of circumstances.

Svald Cjelli. Popularly known as Dirk, though, again, "popular" was hardly right. Notorious, certainly; sought after, endlessly speculated about, those too were true. But popular? Only in the sense that a serious accident on the motorway might be popular — everyone slows down to have a good look, but no one will get too close to the flames. Infamous was more like it. Svald Cjelli, infamously known as Dirk.

— *Dirk Gently's Holistic Detective Agency.*

Douglas Adams knew nothing about detectives, or at least not very much.

Indeed, so woeful was his level of knowledge that *Dirk Gently's Holistic Detective Agency* was criticised for the sloppy way in which the author disentangled the problems he posed for the sleuth. ("Adams also violates cardinal rules of mystery writing by supplying readers with information insufficient to solve the crime and by introducing *deux ex machina* to bail out the plot logjams", according to the *Chicago Tribune*.) If Dirk Gently was *genuinely* a detective the criticism might have been valid. But then Gently is really a con-man who has a disproportionate interest in the "interconnectedness of all things" and the workings of quantum mechanics. That's what really fascinates Gently, and working as a private eye simply enables him to engage that passion and charge his clients for the privilege.

"Of course I will explain to you again why the trip to the Bahamas was so vitally necessary," said Dirk Gently soothingly. "Nothing could give me greater pleasure. I believe, as you know, Mrs Sauskind, in the fundamental interconnectedness of all things. Furthermore I have plotted and triangulated the vectors of the interconnectedness of all things and traced them to a beach in *the Bahamas* which it is therefore necessary for me to visit from time to time in the course of my investigations. I wish it were not the case, since, sadly, I am allergic to both the sun and rum punches, but then we all have our cross to bear, don't we, Mrs Sauskind?"

— *Dirk Gently's Holistic Detective Agency.*

As a whodunit, *Dirk Gently* doesn't really hang together, since there is only one murder and, if you were paying attention, it's fairly obvious who did it. Even if you weren't paying attention, you get told before too long. So, if *Dirk Gently* doesn't work as either a detective story or an archetypal whodunit, how does it engage any interest?

Well, like all Douglas Adams books, it is funny. It's an amusing and engaging romp through the spurious borders of the detective yarn. Within these parameters, Douglas constructs a hugely improbable tale which requires the introduction of a detective to unravel.

There's also Adams's fascination with science fiction, computers, ecology, quantum mechanics and even a touch of fractal mathematics. The story in which Dirk Gently finds himself is almost incidental. What's important is all the peripheral stuff which may, or may not, advance the plot.

Both reviewers and detective novel fans were annoyed by the introduction of a bit of science fiction to get out of some of the tricky plot twists. This is understandable, or at least it would be understandable if *Dirk Gently's Holistic Detective Agency* was, in fact, a detective novel. But it isn't. It's a Douglas Adams novel, where the rules aren't quite the same.

Even so, Adams does take liberties, and using the time-travel trick is perhaps an easy way out.

But there is plenty to enjoy. For a start, there's Dirk himself, a thoroughly wretched character with few redeeming features.

And then there's the Electric Monk, perhaps Adams's finest creation since Marvin the Paranoid Android. The Electric Monk was created to believe things, which would save their creators the trouble of believing them themselves. This is such a mind-meldingly brilliant ploy it's a wonder no one ever thought of it before. But then no one ever thought of writing a fully realised "ghost-horror-detective-whodunit-time-travel-romantic-comedy-epic" before either.

The Electric Monk's only flaw is that it has developed a fault and insists on believing the most ludicrous things, even if only for twenty-four hours. But when an Electric Monk believes something it will believe it up to the hilt, and nothing will shake its fundamental certainty until such time as it finds something more interesting to believe in.

This Monk had first gone wrong when it was simply given too much to believe in one day. It was, by mistake, cross-connected to a video recorder that was watching eleven TV channels simultaneously, and this caused it to blow a bank of illogic circuits. The video recorder only had to watch them, of course. It didn't have to believe them all as well. This is why instruction manuals are so important.

So after a hectic week of believing that war was peace, that good was bad, that the moon was made of blue cheese, and that God needed a lot of money sent to a certain box number, the Monk started to believe that thirty-five per cent of all tables were hermaphrodites, and then broke down.

— Dirk Gently's Holistic Detective Agency.

Dust had not even begun to think about settling on *Dirk Gently's Holistic Detective Agency* when Douglas produced a follow-up, *The Long Dark Tea-Time of the Soul.*

Here Dirk continues to explore the interconnectedness of all things. This time, the things that are interconnected include a new fridge, a Coca-Cola drinks dispensing machine (an echo, perhaps, of some previous episode), a self-immolating airline check-in desk, and the Gods of Asgard, one of whom, Thor, is currently an unhappy patient of the NHS. Now, normally that might be enough to spoil anyone's day, but what *really* upsets Dirk is that his client is dead — so who's going to pay the bill? Dirk is never one to let anything so trivial as saving the world interfere with the important stuff, like getting paid promptly and by someone living.

The plot frailties of the first book were largely remedied in the sequel and Dirk Gently at one point looked set to become at least as long-running as *Hitchhiker's**. As many novelists have discovered, the public loves a good detective. What's more, they're damn diffi-cult to kill off. Just ask Sir Arthur Conan Doyle.

The Long Dark Tea-Time of the Soul was dedicated to Jane Belson, a barrister and Douglas's long-term companion. The book was published in October 1988, but it still took them another three years to get married. This took place on 25th November 1991 at Islington Town Hall in North London. The only reason it probably hadn't happened earlier was that Douglas was, well, not exactly noticeable by his presence.

---

* In fact Dirk Gently's only subsequent appearance was in one draft of *The Salmon of Doubt*, and by the time that book was (posthumously) published he was nowhere to be seen. Attempts to transfer the character onto TV or film came to nothing, although there was a successful stage play, which Douglas greatly enjoyed, and *Long Dark Tea-Time* was adapted into a Finnish radio series.

Throughout the entire Dirk Gently episode Douglas was in constant contact with a zoologist called Mark Carwardine. They were organising, or attempting to organise, a series of expeditions to track down some of the world's rarest animals. But, what with one thing and another, books coming out and needing to undertake world tours to promote them, that sort of thing, this would be another episode that would be three years in the making.

25

DOUGLAS AND OTHER ANIMALS

In 1985 Mark Carwardine, the zoologist, and Douglas Adams, the extremely ignorant non-zoologist, went to Madagascar in search of the Aye-Aye, a creature no one had actually seen for years, at the behest of *The Observer* colour supplement and the World Wildlife Fund. Setting off for an island in pursuit of the near-extinct lemur, they caught a twenty second glimpse of the creature on the island of Neco Mangabo on the first night, photographed it and returned feeling remarkably pleased with themselves.

In fact, they were so remarkably pleased, they decided to do it all again, only this time with some different species of endangered animal and in places other than Madagascar.

But, as Mark Carwardine was to discover, getting himself, Douglas Adams and a bunch of threatened animals together in the same place at the same time was to prove a logistical nightmare. And since logistics were not Douglas's strong point, this was all left to Mark.

> "It was several years before we both had the time, as we were both involved in other projects, to set off and undertake *Last Chance to See*. But when we actually sat down to do it, it was amazing. We actually worked out that if we had three weeks to search for each endangered species and went for all the main ones in the world, it

would take us 300 years. And that's just the animals. If we had decided to include threatened plants as well, it would have taken another thousand years.

"So we decided we'd be selective. We just sat down and I said: 'Well, how about going to the Congo?' And Douglas would say: 'Well, I'd rather go to the Seychelles.' And so we'd hit on a happy medium and go to Mauritius. It was a bit like that. We picked a whole variety so we'd get different kinds of animal. We had the Komodo dragon, which is a reptile; we had the Rodrigues fruitbat, which is a mammal; we went to look for the Yangtze River dolphin in China; the Kakapo, which is a bird, a kind of parrot, in New Zealand; the Juan Fernandez fur seal in Chile; the manatee in the Amazon, in Brazil; and the northern white rhino in Zaire."

— Mark Carwardine.

Once they had decided where they were going to go, and in search of which animals, all they had to do was arrange a time. This was not to prove an easy task. But, by May 1988, after a year of anxious juggling and rearranging, the pair were ready to probe the darker recesses of man's inhumanity to everything else he shares the planet with.

With a self-imposed time limit of just three weeks for each trip, they set off in search of dolphins and dragons. And, on and off, they weren't to re-emerge until mid-1989.

Meanwhile, as is the way in all these things, other forces were at work. Heinemann had been persuaded to stump up a staggeringly huge advance to enable the intrepid explorers to go off exploring intrepidly. They also thought it would make a fairly nifty TV series.

This idea was quickly dismissed after a conversation with the Chinese authorities. As Mark Carwardine explains: "The first expedition we tried to set up was the Yangtze River dolphin. We started making investigations, enquiring with the right people in China about permits for filming and all that kind of thing, and we got a reply back saying: 'Sure, we can arrange for you to come and film, it'll take at least nine months to organise the permit and it'll cost you £200,000.' So we put a stop to that straight away and then started thinking about radio."

And so, armed with only a BBC radio sound engineer, the pair set off for the far corners of the planet. Sometimes they were successful, sometimes not. Either way, the BBC managed to get themselves six wildlife programmes for next to nothing as the zoologist began to realise the benefits of recording for radio and the non-zoologist began to get wet.

"We were trying to land on an island off the coast of Mauritius called Round Island which, they reckon, has more endangered species per square metre than anywhere else in the world. It's a tiny little island, very hard to land on because of the swell and there's no good landing points. We all had our gear wrapped up, but the soundman just had a microphone sticking out and was recording when Douglas fell out of the boat and was being smashed against the rock. There was blood everywhere and it was all quite dramatic. We got the whole thing on tape, but if we'd had a TV crew there we'd have had to dry Douglas off, mop up all the blood and then get him to do it again, and it just wouldn't have been the same.

"Initially we were thinking about radio as a second choice but in retrospect it worked much better than television. And they always say about radio you get better pictures. There was an occasion when we were just checking into the lodge on the island of Komodo in Indonesia. We had three chickens with us for food and a Komodo dragon came and grabbed the chickens and ran off. And the sounds of all this, the squawking of the chicken and the three of us chasing after the dragon and the shouting of the guards and scrabbling in the dust, comes across so well on radio. Maybe we'd have got some of it on telly if we'd have had the cameras ready by chance. But I think it's more impressive when you sit back, eyes closed, and just listen to it and build up your own picture. So I think in retrospect radio worked better than television could have."

— Mark Carwardine.

With Douglas dried off and mopped down, they returned to civilization and the south of France, where Douglas had been exiled for a year by his accountant for tax reasons. There the explorers were to write of their adventures.

Instead, as the zoologist confesses, they became strenuously involved in, "Lots of sitting in French cafés discussing it. We just spent hours and hours and hours talking it through, listening to the tapes — they were really useful for sorting information. We kept notes about facts and figures and what happened and quotes from people and that kind of thing. But just listening to some of the sounds on the tapes brought back memories of our impressions and a feeling for places rather than the pure facts and figures. We spent hours listening to those, discussing it all, talking it through. Then we sat down and Douglas did most of the writing, with me feeding ideas and information and checking facts while he was sitting at the word processor with me looking over his shoulder.

"That was basically how it was done. We did it in different ways, it was done in bits, basically, and then put together with a mad period of twenty-four-hour days at the end."

In fact, the south of France proved a less than productive environment for the pair — too many distractions, too many cafés to sit in. After four months they had produced a total of one page.

But, one way or another, the book eventually got written.

Heinemann published *Last Chance to See*, a bizarre combination of travelogue and conservation, in October 1990 to good reviews. *The Times* considered it "descriptive writing of a high order... this is an extremely intelligent book". The Pan paperback followed thirteen months later.

Last Chance to See was also made available on CD-ROM by The Voyager Company, providing hundreds of colour stills, interviews and audio essays by Mark Carwardine, and extracts from the radio series to accompany the text. Lazier readers could simply listen to Douglas reading the book. Voyager have also published *The Complete Hitchhiker's Guide to the Galaxy* (at least it was complete until *Mostly Harmless* put in an appearance) as an Expanded Book for use on a Macintosh computer.

The BBC broadcast the *Last Chance to See* programmes weekly on Radio 4 between 4th October and 8th November 1989, with repeats later the same week.

Curiously enough, four of the programmes were re-broadcast the following year, though what happened to the Kakapo and the fruitbat tapes can only be guessed*. Also lost, it seems, was a ten-minute programme called *Natural Selection: In Search of the Aye-Aye*, broadcast on 1st November 1985, recalling that first expedition.

But the question remains, after all this, did they do any good? Mark Carwardine thinks so: "When we went to New Zealand to look for the Kakapo — which is this ground-living parrot which can't fly, but it's forgotten that it can't fly; it jumps out of trees and just lands on the ground with a thud. It's down to roughly the last forty to forty-five birds, that's all that's surviving and people had sort of half given up in New Zealand. There were a few dedicated scientists, but the powers-that-be weren't really putting enough resources into it and the scientists were having a hard time getting what they needed to save the bird from extinction. When we went there, for some reason, our visit got a lot of interest and there was a lot of publicity. And one thing led to another over the weeks we were there and the bird was suddenly put as top priority and more resources were made available to help it. So that was good.

"In other parts of the world where the book's been published it's really hard to say. My general view is that if you can aim a book like *Last Chance to See* at people who wouldn't normally buy a wildlife book and get a radio series out to people who wouldn't normally listen to one, then you're reaching a completely different audience, and if you can capture just one per cent of them then it's doing

* Even more curiously, five further programmes, also called *Last Chance to See*, were broadcast on Radio 4 in May 1997, which proved to be simply Douglas reading extracts from the book.

some good. The more people you can make aware of the problems the wildlife's facing and what's being done about it and what needs to be done, the better. From that point of view I think it probably has done some good."

The captured chickens on Komodo might have had other ideas.

26

ANYTHING THAT HAPPENS, HAPPENS

It goes something like this: after *The Hitchhiker's Guide to the Galaxy* trilogy is completed it, well, isn't, not really. There are too many loose ends left dangling out there in hyper-space that need tying together. So Douglas Adams is locked into a room and told not to come out until he has completed the fourth and absolutely final book in the trilogy. All those dangling plot threads have to be clipped and tied off, there has to be no going back, ever, at all, not even slightly.

So, after *So Long, and Thanks for All the Fish*, wherein God's Final Message to His Creation is revealed and Marvin at last relieves the pain in all the diodes down his left side by finally dying, things were supposed to have been wrapped up neatly and conclusively.

But then...

Anything that happens, happens.

Anything that, in happening, causes something else to happen, causes something else to happen.

Anything that, in happening, causes itself to happen again, happens again.

It doesn't necessarily do it in chronological order, though.

— Preamble to *Mostly Harmless*.

Then there was *Mostly Harmless*.

After Douglas's travels undertaken for *Last Chance to See*, his outlook on the world and its mercurial workings were altered irrevocably. This is hardly surprising given the staggering vista those expeditions had opened to the author. Adams took this new perspective, and naturally began writing it into his books.

And there were also those tantalisingly unanswered questions lingering from *So Long, and Thanks for All the Fish*, such as:

What was to become of Arthur Dent and his new-found love, Fenchurch?

What had become of Ford Prefect, Zaphod Beeblebrox and Trillian, the other occupants of the *Heart of Gold*?

What was to become of that most successful book ever to come out of the great publishing corporations of Ursa Minor, *The Hitchhiker's Guide to the Galaxy*?

And, perhaps most importantly, could Marvin *really* be dead?

There is a positive answer to at least one of these questions. But, in order that some sense of mystery remain to those who have not read *Mostly Harmless*, it won't be revealed which question this answer relates to until the end of this chapter.

1992 was bookended by *Hitchhiker's* activity. At the beginning of the year the BBC finally issued the TV series on video, having previously been prevented by the uncertain contractual situation between Douglas and the movie moguls in Hollywood, to whom he had sold the film rights. To recoup these rights cost Douglas something in the region of £200,000, with a bunch of other catch-22 clauses thrown in for good — or bad — measure.

The original series was released on video in a two-volume set, eleven years after its initial transmission. The second volume even contained 'previously unseen material', a few minutes that were cut to make the programmes fit their time-slot. The BBC also managed to re-master the mono soundtrack into stereo. And on radio the BBC re-broadcast the second *Hitchhiker's* series.

At the end of the year came *Mostly Harmless*, fifth in the "increasingly inaccurately named *Hitchhiker's Guide to the Galaxy* trilogy". While many fans may have been disturbed by *So Long, and Thanks for All the Fish's* lack of science fiction — it was, after all, a love story, kind of — *Mostly Harmless* has a whole truck-load of SF. And there's the occasional passage you just know could not have been written by Douglas prior to his ecological jaunt around the world.

It was a sight that Arthur never quite got used to, or tired of. He and Ford had tracked their way swiftly along the side of the small river that flowed down along the bed of the valley, and when at last they reached the margin of the plains they pulled themselves up into the branches of a large tree to get a better view of one of the stranger and more wonderful visions that the Galaxy has to offer.

The great thunderous herd of thousand upon thousand of Perfectly Normal Beasts was sweeping in magnificent array across the Anhondo Plain. In the early pale light of the morning, as the great animals charged through the fine steam of the sweat of their bodies mingled with the muddy mist churned up by their pounding hooves, their appearance seemed a little unreal and ghostly anyway, but what was heart-stopping about them was where they came from and where they went to, which appeared to be, simply, nowhere.

— *Mostly Harmless.*

There's also some bizarre physics and temporal paradoxes that may, or may not, have come about since the Earth, or what we popularly believe to be the Earth, was destroyed by the Vogons way back when.

The Hitchhiker's Guide to the Galaxy has, in what we laughingly call the past, had a great deal to say on the subject of parallel universes. Very little of this is, however, at all comprehensible to anyone below the level of Advanced God, and since it is now well-established that all known gods came into existence a good three millionths of a second after the Universe began rather than, as they usually claimed, the previous week, they already have a great deal of explaining to do as it is, and are therefore not available for comment on matters of deep physics at this time.

— Mostly Harmless.

Mostly Harmless delves into that decidedly murky pool of parallel universes, so you're never entirely sure whether the Arthur Dent featured here is in fact the same Arthur Dent as popped up elsewhere. After all, there's an astro-physicist called Trillian in the stars and also a thrusting young TV reporter called Tricia McMillan, and they may be related, in some way or other. And the TV reporter, who once met an extra-terrestrial called Zaphod at a party in Islington but didn't go with him, is apparently a TV reporter on Earth. At least *an* Earth, although which one is anybody's guess. This Earth hasn't been destroyed, or if it has it is showing a remarkable reluctance to disappear altogether.

Meanwhile, aside from tackling such weighty SF/cosmological/ scientific questions as parallel universes, there's a little astrology, plus some aliens called Grebulons. The Grebulons are currently stationed on the recently discovered tenth planet in the Solar System named, after nothing much in particular, Rupert*. The Grebulons, who set out to wreak havoc or something, met with a slight accident courtesy of a meteor storm on the way and have since entirely forgotten what it was that they were supposed to do when they got wherever it was they were meant to be going. So they watch TV instead.

In the meantime, Arthur, having singularly failed to find the Earth, or at least an Earth that remotely resembles the one we still presume the Vogons to have blown up, settles on a pleasant little planet after his ship crashlands and he is the only survivor. There he becomes the Sandwich Maker and is reasonably happy. Reasonably happy, that is, for a man who has managed to lose not only his planet but also, since then, the love of his life, Fenchurch, in an accident involving Improbability Drive, however improbable that may seem. But Arthur manages to remain stoical throughout since he

* In Germany the book was entitled *Einmal Rupert und Zuruck* — 'Round Trip to Rupert'.

knows he can't die until he meets the hapless Agrajag on the anarchically named Stavromula Beta, as he discovered during the unfolding plot of *Life, the Universe and Everything*. And yes, if nothing else, this is a story that does manage to resolve itself.

Elsewhere, Ford is having huge problems with the new owners of *The Hitchhiker's Guide to the Galaxy*, InfiniDim Enterprises. They are not only no fun to be with at parties, but are also, horror upon horror, in the process of replacing the *Guide* with the *Guide Mark II*, which comes in a box on which is printed, in large, unfriendly letters, the word PANIC. Ford, unable to go to a party, is understandably not at all happy. And the more he learns of InfiniDim Enterprises, the less happy he is. He engages the services of a mechanical friend called Colin and attempts to get to the bottom of the mystery — that is, why there are no parties or even drink at the *Hitchhiker's* offices anymore — by leaping out of the building a lot and eventually going off in search of Arthur.

While all that is happening, Arthur discovers, to his shock, that he has become a father. His daughter has the unlikely name of Random, and is generally surly and bad-tempered and has a mother called Trillian. And, if you're wondering, no they didn't, it was all down to DNA sampling and stuff like that. Anyway, Random is definitely not the sort of person you want to lend a watch to and Arthur is a little taken aback when his peaceful existence as Sandwich Maker is interrupted by the arrival of Trillian, who dumps their daughter on him and disappears into the stratosphere once again. Arthur loses happiness and gains responsibility. He isn't happy.

All this goes on between the covers of *Mostly Harmless*, which contains only mentions of Zaphod Beeblebrox and not a single appearance.

Oh yes, and if you are still wondering, and haven't bought *Mostly Harmless* yet — and shame on you if you haven't — yes, Marvin really is dead and doesn't appear in the book at all. Of such exclusions are great tragedies made.

27

GUIDES TO THE GUIDE

In today's world of electronic press kits, DVDs and CD-ROMs, every film and TV series produced seems to be accompanied by a 'Making of' documentary, whether anybody would actually be interested in how the thing was made or not. (Ironically, sometimes the 'Making of' is actually better than its subject.)

When the TV series of *Hitchhiker's* was in production in 1980, such an extravagance was unheard of, but fortunately Kevin Davies had the foresight to record much of the behind-the-scenes action on tape, just in case the BBC should consider producing a 'Making of' documentary at some point in the future.

Thirteen years later, the BBC decided that the time was exactly right to produce a documentary entitled *The Making of The Hitchhiker's Guide to the Galaxy*.

Strictly speaking, Kevin Davies's job on the TV series was as an animator, working under Rod Lord at Pearce Studios. But being a huge fan of science fiction in general and *Hitchhiker's* in particular, he took every opportunity to visit the set, where he was allowed to wander around, laden down with a domestic video unit. This being 1980, long before the invention of the term 'palmcorder', Kevin's equipment consisted of a bulky camera attached by a cable to a heavy recording unit, slung over his shoulder like Ford Prefect's satchel. His ubiquity on set actually earned him a couple of spoof credits in the end titles — as 'Mouse Trainer' and 'Bath Supervisor'.

When the BBC planned the video release of the *Hitchhiker's* TV series in 1992, Kevin suggested to them that some of his archive footage could be included as a little ten-minute 'Making of' piece. The corporation decided that a full-length documentary would be a better proposal, but only if the fans wanted it, so initial copies of the *Hitchhiker's* videos carried a caption asking purchasers to write in if they would be interested in purchasing a *Making of Hitchhiker's* video. Apparently enough did.

Kevin was appointed director on the recommendation of John Lloyd* and, under the producer's hand of Alan J. W. Bell, wrote and directed a documentary which not only celebrated *Hitchhiker's* but also became — to some extent — part of the canon.

The Making of The Hitchhiker's Guide to the Galaxy begins with Arthur Dent being dropped off back on Earth after hitching a lift on a passing spaceship (to the delight of SF fans, this was shown to be the Liberator from *Blake's 7*, which was being chased by a familiar-looking police box!). He returns home, where he finds a pile of junk mail (as in *So Long, and Thanks for All the Fish*) and a copy of that indispensable electronic companion, *The Hitchhiker's Guide to the Galaxy*. It is on the screen of the *Guide* that Arthur — and the viewers — see the documentary about how the TV series was made.

As well as Kevin's own archive footage and clips from *Hitchhiker's* segments on shows like *Pebble Mill at One* and *Tomorrow's World*, there were new interviews with Douglas Adams, Sandra Dickinson, David Dixon, Martin Benson, Mark Wing-Davey, David Learner, Alan J. W. Bell, Rod Lord, composer Paddy Kingsland, designer Andrew Howe-Davies, effects supervisor Jim Francis and — to Arthur's surprise — Simon Jones.

The section about the creation of the animated graphics is truly inspired. Arthur pulls a cartoon Babel fish from his ear** who shows

* Kevin Davies had worked on some commercials with special effects producer Sean Broughton, whose girlfriend was John Lloyd's former PA. Unusually, no secretaries were involved.

** Like most British animators, Kevin had worked on *Who Framed Roger Rabbit*, animating part of the scene where Roger hides in a sink.

him a scratchy 'educational' film about how the graphics were brought to life. The Babel fish's voice and the 1940s-style narration on the 'film' were both provided by Michael Cule, who also reprised his role as the Vogon Guard. Dressed in the original costume (borrowed from the fan who bought it at a BBC auction) but with new head, hands and boots, Cule stamped into the room and grabbed Arthur/Simon, before morphing into David Dixon as Ford (in slightly the wrong jacket).

As Ford leads Arthur out of the house and past Marvin the Paranoid Android, he explains that the whole thing is a virtual environment, calling up control panels which switch off Marvin, the road and indeed everything.

The very first batch of videos of *The Making of The Hitchhiker's Guide to the Galaxy* had a major fault with the soundtrack, with the result that Peter Jones's narration is missing in several places. Swiftly recalled, a few were sold and, depending on your point of view, are either (a) important collector's items or (b) defective.

The initial edit of *The Making of* ran to ninety minutes, but the US distributor requested a last-minute cut to sixty minutes. However, in 2001 Kevin Davies was able to compile another thirty minutes of material as a sort of *Making of (Part II)* which was included, along with the original documentary and complete versions of the *Tomorrow's World* and *Pebble Mill* segments, on the 2002 DVD release of the series.

The Making of The Hitchhiker's Guide to the Galaxy was first released in March 1993, to tie in with the fifteenth anniversary of the original radio series. Five years later, Radio 4 broadcast a one-hour documentary about the radio series. Mooted at one point to have the oft-suggested but never used title *The Hitchhiker's Guide to The Hitchhiker's Guide to the Galaxy*, it was broadcast as *The Guide to Twenty Years' Hitchhiking* and subsequently released on cassette as *Douglas Adams' Guide to The Hitchhiker's Guide to the Galaxy*.

Narrated, like the *Making of* video, by Peter Jones, the programme was written by Debbie Barham whose script paraphrased many memorable passages from *Hitchhiker's* — a technique that had also been used by Kevin Davies and Andrew Pixley in a quite startlingly detailed article about the TV series which they wrote for *Time Screen* magazine. Douglas Adams, Simon Brett, Geoffrey Perkins, Simon Jones, Geoffrey McGivern, Stephen Moore, Paddy Kingsland and others were interviewed, and the cassette release included a second tape with the entire fifty-minute Adams interview on it.

Although Douglas Adams was interviewed many, many times, one of the most notable occasions was when he was the subject of *The South Bank Show* in January 1992. Like the *Making of* video two years later, this interwove real and fictional worlds, with Simon Jones and David Dixon reprising their roles from the TV series. The script, by Douglas himself, also featured narration by Peter Jones, Marvin (voiced by Stephen Moore)*, and three characters from *Dirk Gently's Holistic Detective Agency*: the eponymous detective (played by humorist Michael Bywater, on whom the character was based), Richard MacDuff and the Electric Monk. And an eagle.

The various fictional characters sat upstairs in Douglas's Islington flat, cynically discussing what they thought he would be saying to Melvyn Bragg in the room below. The programme also featured Douglas's friend Professor Richard Dawkins and his editor Sue Freestone.

Possibly the most memorable event of the whole programme occurred off-camera when Douglas found himself in his own kitchen, desperately trying to remember what he had come in for. Actors, crew and assorted hangers-on who had gathered in the kitchen to keep out of the way wracked their brains over Douglas's statement that he was looking for something which was, "like a pub, only smaller". It eventually turned out to be a fridge.

Postscript: Readers seeking further detailed information on *The Hitchhiker's Guide to the Galaxy* are directed to the excellent BBC site at www.bbc.co.uk/cult/hitchhikers and to MJ Simpson's book *The Pocket Essential Hitchhiker's Guide* (wherein the co-author of this work, being definitively inaccurate, describes *Don't Panic* as "out of print").

* Dressed in a long, brown overcoat, Marvin complained that even his own body had eventually left him. This was supposedly because everything except his head had been junked by the BBC. Quite how he was able to appear whole in the *Making of* video two years later remains a mystery.

28

THE MOVIES THAT DON'T MOVE

As well as the TV series and the various theatrical incarnations of *The Hitchhiker's Guide to the Galaxy*, there have been two other attempts to present the story visually. One was done with very little involvement by Douglas Adams, received hardly any publicity, met a decidedly mixed response from the fans, and was reasonably successful. The other was carefully overseen by Douglas (who even made a cameo appearance), was heavily promoted, received laudatory reviews by both fans and critics, and was a huge financial bomb.

First there were the comics. The idea of presenting *Hitchhiker's* in comic-strip form had long been a staple of fans' discussion, given the enormity of the ideas in the story, the vast scope of many scenes, and the fact that neither the BBC nor Hollywood showed any sign of doing the story justice any time soon.

In 1992, out of the blue, it was announced that a three-issue adaptation of the first novel would be published the following year by DC Comics, home of Superman, Batman, Wonder Woman *et al*. A page of artwork by Hawaiian-based artist Steve Leialoha appeared in the trade press, showing the central characters, and it was announced that the adaptation would be written by John Carnell, best known up to that point for a comic called *The Sleaze Brothers*.

The comics appeared in late 1993, lavishly presented in full-colour, glossy, perfect-bound format. This made them look very nice but gave them a hefty price tag of £4.50 when imported into Britain, which was rather a shock for *Hitchhiker's* fans more used to buying *The Beano* or *2000 AD*. And having shelled out £13.50 for the set, they were disappointed to find that all they had was an edited version of the novel. With pictures.

Essentially, there were two problems with the comics. One was that, although the project was supposedly 'overseen' by Douglas Adams, he had neither the time nor the inclination to be actively involved (nor, it must be said, any discernible interest in comic books as a medium). Writer John Carnell, an experienced comics scripter and admirer of Douglas's work, was looking forward to helping his hero to create yet another version of *Hitchhiker's*. He was therefore rather disappointed to find that his job was simply to adapt the book.

The other problem, which stemmed from the first, was that no attempt was made to remould the story to fit the medium. On radio, on record, on TV, in print and on stage, *Hitchhiker's* has always shown no respect for itself, changing — and often contradicting its previous versions — to make full use of the possibilities of whatever medium it found itself in. But without Douglas's involvement, this simply wasn't possible in the comics.

Leialoha's artwork met with general disdain. Clean, crisp and colourful though it was, to a generation of science fiction fans raised on the gritty imagery of *2000 AD* the pages of the *Hitchhiker's* comic were simply too... well, clean, crisp and colourful. Zaphod was a bleached blond beach bum; the Vogons looked like large, humanoid toads; Ford was overly oddball rather than just slightly disconcerting; the Babel fish didn't look like anything you would want near your head, let alone in your ear; Arthur was clearly far, far too young; and Marvin seemed to be an extraordinarily expressionless robo-waiter. The only aspects where the comic design scored over that of the TV series were Trillian — a brunette in flowing, Arabic-style dresses — and Zaphod's second head, which at least looked alive.

But in fact the comics could have been a lot worse. Published as they were by an American company, there was a serious attempt (not by Carnell) to Americanise and update the dialogue. However, Douglas's minimal involvement did mean that everything had to be okayed by him and though a few Americanisms slipped through, important points — like references to Rickmansworth or digital watches — were restored on Adams's say-so.

Despite general indifference, the comics were apparently successful. A three-part adaptation of *The Restaurant at the End of the Universe* was published the next year, followed by *Life, the Universe and Everything* twelve months later. The first three comics were collected into a graphic novel, and a set of a hundred trading cards was also made available.

While the comics went largely unnoticed by many people, few can have failed to spot the frankly enormous, silver-jacketed book that appeared in September 1994, entitled *The Illustrated Hitchhiker's Guide to the Galaxy*.

The idea was first raised in 1993 — a new edition of the first *Hitchhiker's* novel, illustrated through the wonders of computer technology. Not drawings or paintings, but photographs of people and models, manipulated by computer in such a way as to create images previously unimagined. It would be lavish, it would be groundbreaking, it would be (in the words of the publisher) "The Movie That Doesn't Move".

The first thing required was a creative consultant, and Douglas turned to Kevin Davies*, who had done such a sterling job on *The Making of The Hitchhiker's Guide to the Galaxy*. Kevin gathered around him a skilful and enthusiastic team of designers, model-makers and artists, and started thinking which bits of the story could be most imaginatively depicted.

But first the book had to be sold. Such an expensive project required overseas investment — just like movies that *do* move — so a test photograph was created and shown at the Frankfurt Book Fair. This depicted Arthur and Ford cowering before a bulldozer as a Vogon Constructor Ship flew overhead. It was similar to the picture used on pages 18 and 19 of the finished book, but with David Dixon

* Kevin Davies's final credit was 'Concept Art Director'.

as Ford and Alastair Lock as Arthur (Simon Jones being unavailable). The publishers in Frankfurt *ooh*-ed and *ah*-ed over the image, and deals were signed.

Uniquely among novels, *The Illustrated Hitchhiker's Guide to the Galaxy* has a cast of actors. Tom Finnis and Jonathan Lermit were cast as Ford and Arthur, it having been decided to remove any connection with the TV series. Janos Kuruz (who was starring at the time in the West End production of *The Phantom of the Opera*) played Slartibartfast, with Francis Johnson as the first black Zaphod (an idea long mooted by Douglas) and Tali — the only model among a cast of actors — as Trillian. Michael Cule, a veteran of the TV series, the *Making of* video and the Rainbow stage production, played Mr Prosser. Shooty and Bang Bang, the Galactic Cops, were played by Douglas Adams and his agent Ed Victor, while Kevin Davies made an unbilled cameo as the bulldozer driver.

He was roughly humanoid in appearance except for the extra head and third arm. His fair tousled hair stood out in random directions, his blue eyes glinted with something completely unidentifiable, and his chins were almost always unshaven.

— Description of Zaphod Beeblebrox from
The Hitchhiker's Guide to the Galaxy.

Subjective impressions may vary according to local reality miscalibrations and the perceptual systems of the observer. For instance, any entity suffering from HSSE, or Mad Human Disease, will probably perceive the President's hair as being short and dark, and should consult a qualified Peripsychosemiolothanatician immediately.

— Footnote added to *The Illustrated
Hitchhiker's Guide to the Galaxy.*

Principal models were designed by Martin Bower (of *Space: 1999* fame) and Jonathan Saville, and the actual photographs were taken by the legendary Michael Joseph, before being mucked about with on the computer by Colin Hards. Two external locations were used — Southend Pier and Stringfellows nightclub.

There is much to enjoy in the book, among both the images and the layout of the text itself, and a great number of details which can be easily missed and only found on subsequent visits. Really tonto fans of science fiction television may enjoy spotting a number of props borrowed from other shows.

The downside of the book, of course, was that it cost £25*. It could, in fact, have cost even more if the rumours that it would include a talking computer chip had proved founded. This was about twice as much as an average hardback novel and had the additional disadvantage that everyone who bought it already owned at least one copy of the novel. Added to which, the book was frankly *huge* — too big to read comfortably or indeed to fit on the average bookshelf.

Sadly — and despite universal acclaim — the book was heavily remaindered, quashing any hopes of a paperback edition or *The Illustrated Restaurant at the End of the Universe*. Furthermore, the wow-factor of the images rapidly faded as such computer manipulation became commonplace. What Colin Hards slaved over in 1994 can now be done at home in an afternoon by most of the people reading this book. On the other hand, the overall design of the spaceships, props, costumes, aliens and settings remains a thing of beauty, certainly far more imaginative and memorable than the comics. Marvin in particular — built as a half-size model — is certainly the best design ever created for the Paranoid Android.

Of passing interest is the fact that a suggestion for a photograph involving dolphins was dropped when it was discovered that there were no dolphins in captivity in the UK. Which is a Good Thing.

* The American edition, which was otherwise identical, cost $42.

29

THE DOT.COM THAT CANNOT POSSIBLY GO WRONG

I think online publishing is the most exciting new area to be working in. It's rather like being in the film industry in about 1905, when the whole industry is actually being invented around you, and every idea you have is a new one.

— Douglas Adams, MSN webchat, July 1995.

Douglas Adams's love of computers — his passion for information technology of all sorts — is well documented. It therefore seemed natural that, at some point, he should set up his own multimedia company.

Except that The Digital Village (TDV) was not Douglas's company, and as he was at pains to point out, it was actually a "multiple media" company (he never explained precisely what the difference was).

Douglas was 'Chief Fantasist' of TDV, which meant that he was the public face, a newsworthy name, and charged with thinking up great ideas. His partners, while they may not have had the public presence of Douglas, had plenty of business experience and knew that if anyone could make a company work in the world of dot.coms, it was Douglas Adams. The CEO was Robbie Stamp, whom Douglas had met when searching for a producer for a proposed TV series.

TDV was founded in 1994 as an idea and officially launched in 1996, amid much ballyhoo. It lasted nearly five years.

The first product from TDV was *Starship Titanic*, a book-and-game franchise which took its name and basic idea from a throwaway reference in *Life, the Universe and Everything* about a fabulous starship which, immediately after launch, underwent Spontaneous Massive Existence Failure. Enamoured with the visual delights of the game *Myst*, Douglas sought to combine the marvel of late 1990s graphics with the mental stimulation of the early 1980s Infocom games.

The result was a massive starliner — many stories high and serviced from fore to aft by, of all things, a canal (replete with robotic gondoliers). The Oscar-winning team of Isabel Molina and Oscar Chichoni created the look of the game, while Douglas was one of several writers who created the storyline and nearly six hours of pre-recorded speech. When the player 'conversed' with the game's characters, a program called TrueTalk was able to select the most appropriate speech and combine it in such a way as to give the appearance of genuine conversation.

> "The problem with text-to-speech at the moment is not that it doesn't work. It actually does work, but it becomes very, very tiresome on the ear after a while, simply because it's not natural speech rhythms and all the characters tend to end up sounding like either Stephen Hawking or a semi-concussed Scandinavian."
> — Douglas Adams, June 1997.

To support the game, there was the novel. This was going to be not just a novel based on a game, but fifty per cent of a novel-game combination, so that each supported the other*.

"When I was thinking about the novel, I first decided 'We'll get somebody else to do it,'" explained Douglas. "Then about halfway

---

* The obvious precedent is *2001: A Space Odyssey*. Arthur C. Clarke and Stanley Kubrick created the novel and film simultaneously, and neither makes much sense unless one has read/watched the other. Of course, for many people they still don't make much sense after that.

through the process I panicked and thought, 'No, no — this is what I know, this is what I do, so I should write the novel.' But then because it had to be out at the same time as the game, the question was: 'Am I going to now dive out of work on the game, leave that to everybody else and do the novel?' But that would have been changing horses in mid-stream and probably not to the benefit of either. So I was then coming up against the problem of the number of hours in a day and the number of days in a week, and the unfortunate necessity of getting regular amounts of sleep."

After all this shilly-shallying, and despite the game having been delayed from its original launch date, a novel was suddenly needed very quickly.

Step forward Terry Jones, who was already involved in the enterprise, providing the voice of a parrot. Though he had written screenplays, children's books and even serious academic books such as his famous analysis of the *Canterbury Tales*, *Chaucer's Knight*, Jones had never written a full-length novel. But he busied himself on a tale of the great Blerontinian starship, empty except for a variety of eccentric robots, a talking bomb and a manic parrot. In the novel, three humans board the ship — for no very good reason — and have to upgrade themselves in an attempt to find and defuse the bomb*.

The book was published as '*Douglas Adams's Starship Titanic* — a novel by Terry Jones'** and was frankly bedeviled with problems. The formatting of Douglas's introduction was all over the shop — something which the harried editors at Pan either didn't notice or spotted but assumed was deliberate. Despite a wide-ranging US promotional tour, the UK edition was delayed and given very little publicity. In fact the delay was *because* of the wide-ranging US tour, with Pan executives chasing after Terry and Douglas to get back the corrected proof.

Neither the novel nor the game received particularly laudatory reviews — although the game did win at least one award — and

---

* In the game, the player boards the ship — for no very good reason — and has to upgrade him/herself in an attempt to find and defuse the bomb.

** In Germany (where it was very successful) and France the book was published as '*Starship Titanic* — a novel by Douglas Adams and Terry Jones'.

since neither was really by Douglas, we shall skip over them here and move on to TDV's second creation, h2g2.com.

> I really didn't foresee the Internet. But then, neither did the computer industry. Not that that tells us very much of course — the computer industry didn't even foresee that the century was going to end.
>
> — Douglas Adams, introduction to h2g2.com.

For years, Douglas had talked about marketing some sort of search engine called 'The Hitchhiker's Guide to the Internet', and in April 1999 — live on a special edition of *Tomorrow's World* — he finally achieved this goal, although by then the name had been sensibly shortened to h2g2. In respect of this, TDV changed its name to h2g2 Ltd.

But this wasn't just a search engine for the web. Instead, it was an attempt to create a global repository of knowledge — serious, irreverent, essential or arcane — which could be read by anyone and — more importantly — written by anyone. It was a sort of microcosm of the Internet, on the Internet — a situation strangely redolent of Zarniwoop's creation of an artificial universe in his office in the second radio series of *Hitchhiker's*.

Anyone (anyone with net access, at least) could sign up to become a field researcher for the *Guide* and submit entries on any subject. An army of voluntary editors ensured that material was properly spelt and not libelous, obscene, offensive, advertising or really, really lame jokes. A small team was employed to head the whole operation — and for the first time ever a select few people were able to genuinely cite their profession as 'writer for *The Hitchhiker's Guide to the Galaxy'*.

h2g2.com's launch generated great interest, with more than three thousand researchers registering themselves within twenty-four hours of the *Tomorrow's World* programme. Douglas worked tirelessly to promote the site and its "global Internet community" and there was even a deal signed to allow access via WAP mobile phones. By December 1999, with exactly two weeks left to go in the twentieth century (Douglas poured great scorn on millennial pedants), a constantly updated databank of information and opinion from thousands of roving researchers was available anywhere in the world via a small, handheld device. Okay, so nobody was selling mobile phones with the words 'Don't Panic' in large, friendly letters on the front, but other than that it was a remarkable thing to happen — especially to a writer who had always been at pains to point out that his science fiction stories were in no way meant to be predictive.

The only fly in the ointment was that, like most dot.com companies, it was not entirely clear where h2g2 Ltd was actually making *money*. It was notable that the only advertising banners on the h2g2.com site were for *Starship Titanic*, which was not exactly a cash-cow, so where was the revenue coming from? In December 2000, the first crack appeared when the merchandise page of the site announced: "Having survived the Christmas rush, the h2g2 Shop will now be temporarily closed while we restructure the e-commerce side of the business. We apologise for any inconvenience this may cause."

h2g2.com closed on 29th January 2001, another victim of the dot.com boom.

Or was it? On 21st February it was announced that h2g2 would be re-opening — as part of the BBC. And indeed, on 12th March, the whole affair went back online at www.bbc.co.uk, where it has remained happily ever since, gradually increasing in size. Many observers noted the irony of *The Hitchhiker's Guide to the Galaxy* coming home, twenty-three years later, to the BBC where it had all started at 10.30 pm on that Wednesday night.

> The launch of www.bbc.co.uk/h2g2 represents a significant step towards 'engaging with' rather than 'broadcasting to' our consumers. As a key part of our public service offering in building communities on the web we want to ensure that we will offer something of interest to the diverse tastes of the UK's online community.
>
> — Ashley Highfield, Director of New Media, BBC.

The BBC is where *Hitchhiker's* first started, and I am delighted — in the words of the hot new pop combo we've been hearing so much about recently — to get back to where I once belonged.

— Douglas Adams, in the same press release.

30

A SORT OF APRÈS-VIE

"Jesus said, 'Blessed are those who mourn, for they shall
be comforted.' Ford Prefect said, 'What I need now is a
strong drink and a peer group.'"

— Blessing by the Reverend Anthony Hurst
at Douglas Adams's memorial service.

Douglas Adams died.

It was that sudden, that surprising, that much of a "Where did
that come from?" slap in the face. One minute he was in California,
working on the *Hitchhiker's* screenplay, the next he was gone.

The specific circumstances were that Douglas Adams suffered a
fatal heart attack while exercising in his gym* in Santa Barbara on
11th May 2001. But that wasn't really the point. The point was that
one of the most popular, most influential, most important British
humorists of the twentieth century, who actually produced books
only infrequently, wasn't going to produce any more. Obituaries and
tributes from around the world demonstrated the love that people
felt for Douglas and the shock of his sudden passing. Thousands of
e-mailed tributes appeared on the douglasadams.com website.

Douglas's funeral was held in California, with music from Bach

---

* It was observed by one fan that, with an irony Douglas would have loved, right
at the very end he at least knew precisely where his towel was.

and the Beatles, and readings from Simon Jones, Terry Jones, Michael Nesmith and others. A memorial service was held in London a few months later, attended by many well-known faces from the worlds of publishing, broadcasting, comedy, science and rock music. Speakers included Professor Richard Dawkins, Simon Jones and Ed Victor. The choir sang Bach, and David Gilmour's solo acoustic rendition of 'Wish You Were Here' brought a tear to every eye. But even death couldn't stop Douglas from breaking new ground in communications technology: this was the first church service broadcast live over the web by the BBC.

> It is unfinished not just in the sense that it suddenly, heartbreakingly for those of us who love this man and his work, stops in mid-flow, but in the more important sense that the text up to that point is also unfinished.
> — Douglas Adams, from his introduction to *Sunset at Blandings* by P. G. Wodehouse (Penguin, 2000).

When Douglas had first mentioned *The Salmon of Doubt* many years previously, he had described it as a third adventure for Dirk Gently. In later interviews he said that the book was not working as a Dirk Gently novel, and that the Holistic Detective had been removed, leaving a book unconnected with any of his previous works. Still later, he said that he had realised that his ideas for the book actually fitted the *Hitchhiker's* universe better, and it had now become a sequel to *Mostly Harmless*. At the memorial service it was announced that this final, unfinished novel would be published posthumously.

When Douglas's various hard drives were examined, several different versions of *Salmon* were discovered. The version eventually published — the Dirk Gently version — was pieced together from three separate files by Peter Guzzardi, Douglas's New York editor. Chapters 2 to 8, 10 and 11 are from one file, with Chapter 1 being an earlier draft and Chapter 9 being Douglas's last known piece of writing.

So what is *The Salmon of Doubt* actually about? Briefly, Dirk is approached by a client who wants him to find the back half of her cat (the front half is doing very well, oblivious to its ignominy or indeed the basic laws of biology and physics). At the same time, Dirk discovers that somebody is paying $5,000 into his bank account every week. Feeling that he should do something to earn this money, he follows somebody at random and finds himself in California, where he meets a rhinoceros named Desmond. The first chapter, entirely unconnected with any of the above, is an enigmatic, unexplained piece about someone called Dave, hang-gliding in California (or Daveland, as it is now called) 1.2 million years after the extinction of the human race.

Misleadingly described by the press as an unfinished novel, *The Salmon of Doubt* is a fragment, a few chapters of working notes. It has some good bits, such as a taxi driver who has never been asked to "Follow that cab!" and has come to the conclusion that his is the cab all the other cabbies are following, and it has some bad bits, notably an unconnected description of a Los Angeles car-jacking, for which Douglas incongruously and unnecessarily lurches into first person narrative, and which would almost certainly never have made it into a finished novel. Probably the most interesting part of the story is in Chapter 9, in which the rhinoceros's rampage through a party is described from Desmond's point of view. Douglas had often commented that a rhino's view of the world is primarily olfactory rather than visual or aural, and this is a bold attempt to describe an event through smell.

The Salmon of Doubt (the fragment) is of peripheral interest to completists but it is only one of many items in *The Salmon of Doubt* (the book), which also contains two short stories ('Young Zaphod Plays It Safe' and 'The Private Life of Genghis Khan'), thirty-three non-fiction pieces and two and a half interviews. The non-fiction includes a description of a charity walk up Kilimanjaro dressed as a rhinoceros, written for *Esquire*; some speculations on the millennium from *The Independent on Sunday*; the inlay notes to a J. S. Bach CD; and an h2g2.com piece on how to make a cup of tea. Plus some snippets, the sources or precise topics of which, frankly, nobody involved with the book could identify, but which are enjoyable anyway.

The best piece in the book is 'Riding the Rays', a lengthy description of a 1992 trip to Australia to investigate whether the Sub Bug, a one-man underwater motive device, is as good as being dragged through the water by a manta ray. This is non-fiction writing of the highest calibre, on a par with *Last Chance to See*, combining Douglas's love of travel, gizmos, scuba diving and nature with a supremely accurate observational eye.

Douglas's passing also precipitated a deluge of *Hitchhiker's*-related items, starting with tribute programmes on BBC 2 (*Omnibus: Douglas Adams — The Man Who Blew Up the Earth*) and Radio 4 (*So Long and Thanks for All the Fish: A Tribute to Douglas Adams*, presented by Geoffrey Perkins). The TV series was released as a lavish two-disc DVD, including *The Making of The Hitchhiker's Guide to the Galaxy* and numerous other clips and oddments. A graphical computer game of *The Hitchhiker's Guide* was announced for May 2002, developed by the team behind *Starship Titanic* (Douglas had been involved in the early stages of the project), but although images from this 'towel-'em-up' adventure appeared on the web, it was put on hold in February 2002 and its eventual fate remains unknown.

In early 2002 a biography of Douglas Adams was announced, to be written by *Hitchhiker's Guide* expert MJ Simpson and published in March 2003 on the 25th anniversary of the radio series's first broadcast. An authorised feature-length documentary, provisionally entitled *Douglas Adams: Heart of Gold*, was also produced, including interviews with many of Douglas's friends, relatives and colleagues, and clips from some of the many speeches which he had made to business conferences (he was one of the most popular speakers on the international business circuit and frequently talked on the subjects of ecology and information technology).

Plus, a third edition of the official *Hitchhiker's Guide* companion, *Don't Panic*, was published. Obviously.

With the movie version of *Hitchhiker's* back in development — a new draft of the screenplay was commissioned from a leading Hollywood scriptwriter in February 2002 — and the books, videos and CDs continuing to sell, it is clear that interest in the works of Douglas Adams remains as high as ever. The tragedy is that Douglas

Noel Adams himself isn't here to enjoy that interest. The world is a poorer place for his passing.

> The lights went out in his eyes for absolutely the very last time ever. — from *So Long, and Thanks for All the Fish*
> — Posted on the Digital Village website, 11th May 2001.

APPENDIX I

HITCHHIKER'S — THE ORIGINAL SYNOPSIS

THE HITCH-HIKER'S GUIDE TO THE GALAXY.

Douglas Adams.

The show is a science fiction comedy adventure in time and space, which weaves in and out of fantasy, jokes, satire, parallel universes and time warps, in the wake of two men who are researching the New Revised Edition of the Hitch Hiker's Guide to the Galaxy, an electronic 'book' designed to help the footloose wanderer find his way round the marvels of the Universe for less than thirty Altairian dollars a day.

One of the men is an extraterrestrial who has spent some years living incognito on the Earth. When he first arrived the minimal research he had done suggested to him that the name Ford Prefect would be nicely inconspicuous. The other is an Earthman, Arthur D. J. who was a friend of Ford's for years without realising that he wasn't a perfectly ordinary human being.

The first episode tells of how Ford reveals the truth about himself to an incredulous Arthur, and how they both escape from a doomed Earth to begin their wanderings.

The story starts as ~~Alexis~~ Arthur is lying on the ground in the path of a
bulldozer which is about to demolish his house to make away for a new
by-pass. Having fought the plans at every level, this is his last
ditch effort. He is arguing with a man from the council who is
pointing out to him in a Godfatherly way that the bulldozer driver is
is a rather careless gentleman who isn't too fussy about what he drives
over. In the middle of this confrontation Ford arrives in a rather anxious
state and asks ~~Alexis~~ Arthur is he's busy at all, and if there's somewhere they
can go and have a chat. ~~Alexis~~ Arthur, astonished, refuses to move. Ford is
very insistent and eventually ~~Alexis~~ Arthur calls the man from the council
and asks him if they could decide a truce for half an hour. The
councilman very charmingly agrees and says that if he likes to slip
away for half an hour he'll make sure they don't try and knock his house
till he gets back, word of honour. Ford and ~~Alexis~~ Arthur repair to a nearby
pub, where Ford asks ~~Alexis~~ Arthur how he would react if he told him that he
wasn't from Guildford at all but from a small planet in the vicinity
of Betelgeuse.

As soon as they're out of the way the councilman orders the demolition
ceremony to start. A local lady dignitary makes a very moving speech
about how wonderful life will suddenly become as soon as the bypass is
built, and swings a bottle of champagne against the bulldozer, which
moves in for the kill.

The sound of the crashing building reaches ~~Alexis~~ Arthur who is in the middle
of not believing a word that Ford is telling him, and he charges back
to his ex-house shouting about what a naughty world we live in.

At that moment the sky is suddenly torn apart by the scream of jets,
and a fleet of flying saucers streak towards the Earth. As everyone
flees in panic an unearthly voice rings through the air announcing that
due to redevelopment of this sector of the galaxy they are building a
new hyperspace bypass and the Earth will unfortunately have to be demolished

demolished. In answer to appalled cries of protest the voice says that
the plans have been on public display in the planning office in Alpha
Centauri for ten years, so it's far too late to start making a fuss now.
He orders the demolition to start. A low rumble slowly builds into an
earshattering explosion, followed by silence.

&

Arthur wakes, not knowing where he is. Ford tells him they've managed
to get a lift aboard one of the ships of the Vogon Constructor Fleet.
Not to worry about the Earth, he says, there are an infinite multi-
plicity of parallel universes in which the Earth is still alive and
well. He explains how they got on the ship by producing a copy of an
electronic book called the Hitch Hiker's Guide to the Galaxy. Under the
entry marked 'Vogon Constructors' it gives detailed instructions as to
the best way of hitching a ride from one of their ships - you have to
play on Vogon psychology, which it describes. Ford explains that it's
his job to research a new edition of the book, which is now a little
out of date. Would Arthur like to accompany him in the task? Arthur
only wants to get back to Earth, or at least, it's nearest equivalent.
However, he is fascinated to browse through this strange book. He is
suddenly appalled when he discovers Earth's entry. Though the book is
over a million pages long, the inhabitants of the Earth only warrant a
one word entry - 'Harmless'. Ford, rather embarrassed, explains that
the reason he had been on Earth was to gather a bit more material.
He'd had a bit of an argument with the editor over it, but finally he'd
been allowed to expand the entry to 'Mostly harmless'. They are very
short of space.

Arthur is stung to the quick. He agrees to go with Ford.

END OF EPISODE ONE.

HITCH HIKER'S GUIDE TO THE GALAXY

Some suggestions for future development.

Each episode should be more or less self contained, but lead on quite naturally to the next one, perhaps with a 'cliff hanger'.

A narrative structure can be achieved by having short extracts read from the Guide itself, since much of its information would naturally be presented in the form of anecdote.

Ford and Aleric frequently have to subsidise their travels by taking odd jobs along the way; as well as strange new worlds they can visit parallel alternatives of Earth which are more or less the same, but not quite...; they find that many of the eccentric alien races they encounter epitomise some particular human folly such as greed, pretentiousness etc., rather in the manner of Gulliver's Travels.

In one episode they are hired by a fabulously wealthy but rather nervous man to act as 'internal body guards'. For this they are reduced to microscopic size in order to escort meals through his digestive system.

In another they encounter a race of dentists, exiled from their home planet for having pronounced that everything you can possibly eat or breathe, up to and including toothpaste, is bad for your teeth. They have been told not to return till they have successfully evolved an entirely new way of life that is both hygienic and fun.

In another episode they find themselves on an 'alternative' Earth which is receiving its first visitation from alien beings who announce that they have come to pay court at the home of the most intelligent life form in the Galaxy. After a lot of self satisfied parading by the humans it turns out that it was the dolphins the aliens actually had in mind.

The 'Guide' structure should allow for the almost unlimited development of freewheeling ideas whilst at the same time retaining a fairly simple and coherent shape and purpose.

APPENDIX II

THE VARIANT TEXTS
OF HITCHHIKER'S:
WHAT HAPPENS WHERE AND WHY

The First Radio Series

1) Arthur Dent wakes up to find his house is about to be knocked down. Ford Prefect takes him to the pub. Just before the Earth is destroyed, they hitchhike their way onto one of the spaceships of the Vogon Destructor Fleet. The Vogon Captain throws them out of the airlock, having read them some poetry.

2) They are rescued by the starship *Heart of Gold*, piloted by Zaphod Beeblebrox and Trillian, inhabited by Marvin the Paranoid Android, Eddie the ship's computer and a number of Doors.

3) Arriving in orbit around the legendary planet of Magrathea, they are fired on by an automatic defence system, resulting in the bruising of someone's upper arm and the creation and demise of a bowl of petunias and a sperm while. Exploring Magrathea reveals Slartibartfast, a planetary designer who is very keen on fjords, and is about to design the Earth Mark II.

4) Arthur discovers that white mice really ran the Earth as an experiment in behavioural psychology set up by the computer Deep Thought, to find the Question to the Great Answer of Life, the Universe, and Everything (the Answer being 42). Shooty and Bang Bang, two enlightened and liberal cops, interrupt a meeting with the Mice, who want Trillian and Arthur to find the Question for them. The cops blow up a computer bank behind which our heroes are hiding.

5) The fearless four find themselves in the Restaurant at the End of the Universe... actually a far-future Magrathea. Marvin has been parking cars there. Abandoning Arthur's Pears Gallumbit they steal a small black spaceship, which turns out to belong to an Admiral of the Fleet and drops them in the vanguard of a major inter-galactic war.

6) In which it is revealed that Arthur Dent's only brother was nibbled to death by an Okapi. The chair in the ship they are in is actually one of the Haggunenons of Vicissitus Three, a shape-shifting race who evolve several times over lunch. Arthur and Ford escape in a hyperspace capsule, while the others are eaten by the Ravenous Bugblatter Beast of Traal (aka the Haggunenon Admiral). Arthur and Ford, having materialised inside the hold of the Golgafrincham 'B' Ark, crash land on Earth two million years before the Vogons destroy it. An experiment with Scrabble shows that the Question is, or might be, "What do you get if you multiply six by nine?"

Christmas Special Episode

7) Zaphod Beeblebrox is picked up by a freighter taking copies of *Playbeing* to Ursa Minor Beta (the Haggunenon having evolved into an escape capsule). Arthur Dent and Ford Prefect get drunk on Old Earth and start seeing a spaceship. Zaphod tries to see Zarniwoop, editor of the *Guide*. He meets Roosta as the building is attacked by Frogstar fighters: while Marvin saves the day, the building is kidnapped and taken to the Frogstar...

The Second Radio Series

8) Zaphod discovers that he is going to be fed to the Total Perspective Vortex. Zaphod, despite two hangovers, rescues Ford and Arthur, having discovered their fossilised towel. Zaphod (still on board the Frogstar-snatched building) goes to a robot disco, lands on the Frogstar, is fed to the Total Perspective Vortex, and eats some fairy cake.

9) On board the *Heart of Gold*, Zaphod, Ford and Arthur find themselves under attack from the Vogon Fleet, under orders from

Gag Halfrunt, Zaphod's psychiatrist. Arthur flings away a cup of Nutrimatic drink, and the computer's circuits occupy themselves with the problem of why Arthur likes tea. A seance summons Zaphod's great-grandfather, who tells him to find the person really running the universe, and rescues them.

10) Finding themselves in a cave on the planet Brontitall, they soon find themselves falling through the air thirteen miles above the ground. Arthur is rescued by a bird, and discovers that he has fallen from the cup in the Statue of Arthur Dent Flinging the Nutrimatic Cup. Taken to the bird colony which lives in his car, he is told by a Wise Old Bird the significance of the statue. 'Belgium' is discovered to be a very rude word indeed. Ford and Zaphod land on a passing bird. Arthur discovers the planet to be the property of the Dolmansaxlil Corporation, and is attacked by limping footwarriors, then rescued by a Lintilla, a bright and sexy girl archaeologist.

11) Ford and Zaphod reach the ground relatively safely. Arthur discovers that the Lintilla he met is one of three identical Lintillas, or rather one of 578,000,000,000 Lintillas, due to problems with a cloning machine. Hig Hurtenflurst of the Dolmansaxlil Corporation threatens Arthur and the Lintillas with revocation, then shows them what happened to Brontitall; a Shoe Shop Intensifier Ray caused the planet's inhabitants to build shoe shops and sell shoes. Marvin, who was not rescued by a bird, falls to the ground creating a hole, but gets out and rescues Arthur and a Lintilla. Meanwhile, Zaphod and Ford find a derelict space port and a curious ship...

12) Poodoo shows up with a priest and three Allitnils, while Arthur and the Lintillas are under attack. The Allitnils and two Lintillas fall in love, are married, kiss and explode. Zaphod and Ford discover a spaceship full of people going nowhere, and also Zarniwoop. Arthur kills the third Allitnil (an anticlone) and sets off with Marvin and a Lintilla. Zarniwoop explains some of the plot to Zaphod (Ford is getting drunk and isn't listening). They all go and visit the Man in the Shack, who runs the universe. He reveals that Zaphod was in collusion with the consortium of psychiatrists who ordered the Earth destroyed in order to prevent the Question from

coming out. In a huff, Arthur takes the *Heart of Gold*, and leaves with a Lintilla and Marvin, abandoning Zaphod, Ford and Zarniwoop on the Man in the Shack's planet...

The TV Series/Records

Essentially the plot of the first six episodes; only instead of all the Haggunenon stuff, they have escaped in a stuntship belonging to the rock group Disaster Area (whose lead Ajuitarist Hotblack Desiato is no longer talking to his old friend Ford Prefect, because he is dead), which is going to be fired into the sun. They escape through a wonky transporter unit, operated by Marvin, sending Zaphod and Trillian heaven knows where and Ford and Arthur to the 'B' Ark. It was also established that the Mice were quite keen on slice-and-dicing Arthur's brain to extract the Answer from it.

The Books

i) *The Hitchhiker's Guide to the Galaxy*

In terms of plot, this resembles the first four radio episodes. At the end, however, Marvin depresses Shooty and Bang Bang's ship to death, blowing up each of the cop's life support units, and they leave Magrathea.

ii) *The Restaurant at the End of the Universe*

This starts off with Arthur trying to get a cup of tea from the *Heart of Gold*, tying up all its circuits as the Vogons attack (a bit like Episode Nine of the radio series). Zaphod's great-grandfather transports Zaphod and Marvin to Ursa Minor Beta where events similar to Episode Seven of the radio series occur. Once more Zaphod is taken to Frogstar B, and fed into the Total Perspective Vortex. Once more he eats the cake. Then he discovers Zarniwoop and the spaceship (as in Episode Twelve). Then they visit the Restaurant at the End of the Universe, steal Hotblack Desiato's ship (as in records/TV) and wind up in a predicament.

From there, Ford and Arthur go to prehistoric Earth, while Trillian and Zaphod go to the Man in the Shack, this time abandoning Zarniwoop there. (Shoes and the Shoe Event Horizon, which merited rather more than an episode of the second radio series, get a paragraph in this book.)

iii) *Life, the Universe and Everything*

Ford and Arthur are rescued from two million years ago by a sofa which dumps them at Lord's Cricket Ground a few days before the Earth was/is/will be destroyed. Trillian and Zaphod, on the *Heart of Gold*, sort of split up. Marvin has spent a long time in a swamp. There's a plot about the robots of Krikkit, but I'm not giving anything away. There's also a statue of Arthur Dent, but for a different reason from the radio series.

Variations between the British and American editions include a certain amount of translation ('lolly' becomes 'popsicle'), the respelling of a sound effect ('wop!' becomes 'whop!' throughout) and an extra 400 words are added to Chapter 21, adapted from radio Episode Ten, concerning 'Belgium' as term of profanity. (The British edition just goes right ahead and uses the word 'fuck', thus avoiding the problem entirely.)

iv) *So Long, and Thanks for All the Fish*

The Dolphins restore the Earth. Arthur Dent falls in love and discovers God's final message to His creation.

v) *Mostly Harmless*

Arthur Dent loses both his planet and the woman he loves, and unexpectedly gains a daughter. And a new version of the *Guide*, which behaves in an altogether more mysterious and sinister manner, puts in an appearance.

vi) *The Hitchhiker's Trilogy*

American collection of the first three books (American editions). Contains 'Introduction — a Guide to the *Guide*' Douglas's essay on *Hitchhiker's* origins, and the first few paragraphs of 'How to Leave the Planet'.

vii) *The Compleat Hitchhiker*

This was what Pan called *The Hitchhiker's Guide to the Galaxy: A Trilogy in Four Parts* when they were publishing it. Seeing as they never published it, or even came close, because the book went instead to Heinemann, Douglas's new hardback publishers, this is positively the rarest *Hitchhiker's* book available. If you have a copy, hold onto it, and auction it before returning to whichever parallel universe you bought it in.

viii) *The Hitchhiker's Guide to the Galaxy: A Trilogy in Four Parts*

The same as the *Hitchhiker's Trilogy*, only in English editions, and with an extra three lines of introduction and *So Long, and Thanks for All the Fish* added.

The Expanded Books
The Complete Hitchhiker's Guide to the Galaxy

A collection of the first four books, for use on a Macintosh computer.

APPENDIX III

WHO'S WHO IN THE GALAXY: SOME COMMENTS BY DOUGLAS ADAMS

ARTHUR DENT

"Arthur wasn't based on Simon Jones. Simon is convinced I've said this at some point, whereas what I've said was very similar, which was that I wrote the part with him in mind. Which is a very different thing to say about an actor. I wrote the part for him, and I wrote the part with his voice in mind and with an idea of what he was strong on playing and so on. But there's only the slightest echo of Simon himself in it. He isn't based on Simon, but he is based on what I thought Simon's strengths as an actor were, which is a very different thing. Nor, by the same token, is it autobiographical; having said that, Arthur Dent is not so remote from myself that it's impossible to use things which have happened to me in writing about him."

DEEP THOUGHT

"The name is a very obvious joke."

FENCHURCH

"She isn't based on any particular person, but on a number of different thoughts or observations of people or incidents. It was a bit of a parody of the Oscar Wilde thing in *The Importance of Being Earnest* — being found in a bag at the left luggage office at Victoria. When in fact it's Paddington Station, where the ticket queues are always insane and you can't understand why it happens like that every single day, why it isn't sorted out. Paddington was the station I had in mind, but I couldn't call her that, because there's already a bear named Paddington after the station, so I just went through the various names of the London termini, and Fenchurch seemed a nice name. I just selected the one that seemed the most fun as a name. I don't think it's even a station I've ever been to. That was where that came from, it was just an idea I'd had floating around for a character, whereas I was also looking for a character who was going to be the girl who'd been in the café in Rickmansworth. I put the two things together. Then the whole thing of Arthur falling in love with her was sort of going very much into adolescent memories really."

FORD PREFECT

"I remember the idea I had when I created Ford, which was that he is a reaction against Doctor Who, because Doctor Who is always rushing about saving people and planets and generally doing good works, so to speak; and I thought the keynote of the character of Ford Prefect was that given the choice between getting involved and saving the world from some disaster on the one hand, and on the other hand going to a party, he'd go to the party every time, assuming that the world, if it were worth anything, would take care of itself. So that was the departure point for Ford. He wasn't based on any particular character but come to think of it, aspects of Ford's later behaviour became more and more based on memories of Geoffrey McGivern's more extreme behaviour in pubs."

HOTBLACK DESIATO

"I had this appalling overblown rockstar character, and I couldn't come up with a name for him. Then I saw an estate agent's board up outside a house. Well, I nearly crashed my car with delight! I couldn't get the name out of my mind. Eventually I phoned them up and said, 'Can I use your name? I can't come up with anything nearly as good!' They said fine. It hasn't done them any harm, except it's terribly unfair, as people keep phoning them up and saying, 'Come on, it's a bit cheeky, nicking a name from *Hitchhiker's* to call your estate agents by, isn't it?' And they were a bit upset, when I moved back to England, that I didn't buy my house from them."

THE MAN IN THE SHACK

"I suppose he came from a discussion I had with someone about this not entirely original observation that everyone's experience of the world, on which we build this enormous edifice of what we consider the world is, of what we think the universe is, and our place in it, and how matter behaves, and everything, is actually a construct which we put on little electrical signals that we get. When you think of what we know about the universe, and the data we have to go on, it's a pretty huge gap. Even the information we have is not only just what we happen to have been told but the interpretation that we have put on the little electrical signals which tell us that somebody's told us this.

"We really have nothing to go on at all. So that character was someone who took that observation to the ultimate extreme, which is that he would take absolutely nothing on trust at all. He wouldn't accept anything as being proved or assumed, and therefore responds absolutely intuitively, if you like, thoughtlessly, to whatever happens. He makes everything up as he goes along. Because he makes no assumptions about anything he really is the best qualified person to rule, to exercise power, because he's completely disinterested. On the other hand, that level of disinterest makes him completely unable to produce any rational or useful decisions whatsoever. As I say in the passage that introduces him, who can possibly rule if no one who wants to do it can be allowed to?"

MARVIN

"Marvin came from Andrew Marshall. He's another comedy writer, and he is exactly like that. When I set out to write the character, I wanted to write a robot who was Andrew Marshall, and in the first draft I actually called the robot Marshall. It only got changed on the way to the studio because Geoffrey Perkins thought that the word Marshall suggested other things. Andrew was the sort of guy you are afraid to introduce to people in pubs because you know he's going to be rude to them. His wife recognised him first time. He's cheered up a lot recently.

"But I said that on the radio once — that Marvin was Marshall, and my mother heard it. Next time I spoke to her she said, 'Marvin isn't Andrew Marshall — he's Eeyore!' I said 'What?' She said, 'Marvin is just like Eeyore, go and look.' So I did, and blow me! But literature is full of depressives. Marvin is simply the latest and most metal.

"The other place that a lot of Marvin comes from is from me. I get awfully gloomy, and a lot of that comes out in Marvin. But I haven't been that depressed in a year or so: I haven't had one of these terrible depressions.

"Curiously enough, I never had a very clear idea of what Marvin looked like, and I still don't have one. I don't think the TV one quite got it. I described him differently for the film script — he's not silver any more, he's the colour of a black Saab Turbo. He isn't so square, either, he needs a kind of stooping quality: on the one hand, he's been designed to be dynamic and streamlined and beautiful. But he holds himself the wrong way, so the design has gone completely to naught because he looks pathetic. Utterly pathetic. The patheticness comes from his attitude to himself rather than any inherent design. As far as his design is concerned he looks very sleek. A hi-tech robot.

"People ask me what my favourite character is, to which the answer has usually been, after a long 'Umm' and a pause, 'probably Marvin'. It's not something I strongly feel."

Marvin was interviewed in the Sunday Times *colour supplement in July 1981:*

Q: Would you like to be a human being?

A: If I was a human being I'd be very depressed, but then I'm very depressed already, so it hardly matters. Sometimes I think it might be quite pleasant to be a chair.

Q: How does it feel to have a brain the size of a planet?

A: Ghastly, but only someone with a brain the size of a planet could hope to understand exactly how appalling it really is.

Q: Why are you so miserable?

A: I've been in precisely the same mood ever since I was switched on. It's just the way my circuits are connected. Very badly.

Q: *Can you repair yourself?*

A: Why should I want to do that? I'd just as soon rust.

Q: *Do you like reading?*

A: I read everything there was to read on the day I was switched on. It was all so dull I don't see any point in reading it again.

Q: *Music?*

A: Hate it.

Q: *Hobbies?*

A: Hating music.

Q: *What do you like the least?*

A: The entire multi-dimensional infinity of all creation. I don't like that at all.

OOLON COLLUPHID

"See Yooden Vranx."

ROOSTA

"The guy who played Roosta wasn't very certain what kind of person Roosta was meant to be, because I wasn't either. It happens from time to time when you're writing serially, when you introduce a character at the end of a show and you're going to bring him back at the start of the next show and get him working properly, that you can leave a character dangling like that. You realise that you don't need the character or it's not the right character or whatever, but in the meantime you've already got the actor there, so have to have him do something."

SLARTIBARTFAST

"Slartibartfast was actually a favourite character of mine in the first book, though I think I slightly misused that character in the third book. One thing I don't think I explained in the script book was that I was also teasing the typist, Geoffrey's secretary, because the character had actually been on stage for quite a long time before you know what his name is. I was teasing the typist because she'd be typing out this long and extraordinary name which would be quite an effort to type and right at the beginning he says, 'My name is not important, and I'm not going to tell you what it is.' I was just being mean to Geoffrey's secretary."

TRILLIAN

"Her name was a sort of feeble little twist actually. When she is introduced to the audience you think, 'Trillian — she must be an alien.' Then later you realise it was just a nickname for her real name. Tricia Macmillan, and that she was actually from Earth. It's a feeble surprise, isn't it?

"I thought it would be useful to have somebody else from Earth so that Arthur could have somebody that he could have some kind of normal conversation with, otherwise he is going to be totally lost, and the reader/viewer/listener/whoever will be utterly lost as well. There has to be someone who will understand when Arthur mentions something which is Earth-specific, therefore there must be someone else who survived Earth. But in fact that wasn't really necessary, because obviously Ford fulfils that function, so I'm afraid the main problem with Trillian is that the part wasn't really required. It was superfluous.

"She makes less noise than the others do, but she comes very much to the fore at the end of the third book. She is far more acute, perceptive, aware and able than most of the rest of them put together. That was something I finally spotted about her, and I was pleased about that. Everyone always asked me, why is Trillian such a cipher of a character. It's because I never really knew anything about her. And I always find women very mysterious anyway — I never know what they want. And I always get very nervous about writing one as I think I'll do something terribly wrong. You read other male accounts of women and you think, 'He's got them wrong!' and I feel very nervous about going into that area."

VOGONS

"The name was just a sort of code name — they sound like the typical baddies from *Doctor Who* or *Star Trek* or wherever, don't they?"

WONKO THE SANE

"The whole notion of this character actually came from this thing about toothpicks. I came across this packet of toothpicks which had instructions for use inside. I just imagined somebody who might feel that this was the final thing which just tipped them over the edge in terms of what they thought of the world, and how they thought you could live in a world which had such a thing in it. So from that came the idea of the universe turned inside out, if you like — he built this house to enclose the universe, which he called the Asylum, and he really thought that was what the universe should be put into, an asylum, and that he would live outside the Asylum and look after it. That was where it came from, really, toothpicks."

THE WORST POET IN THE UNIVERSE

"He was a bloke I was at school with. He used to write appalling stuff about dead swans in stagnant pools. Dreadful garbage." [The name of this character was changed to Paula Nancy Millstone Jennings after complaints by Paul Neil Milne Johnson, an ex-schoolfriend of Douglas Adams.]

CAPTAIN: Thy micturations are to me
As plurdled gabbleblotchits in a lurgid bee
Now the jurpling slayjid agrocrustles
Are slurping hagrilly up the axlegrurte
And livid glupules frart and slipulate
Like jowling meated liverslime
— Unused variant of poem from early draft of TV series script.

YOODEN VRANX

"Yooden Vranx was a character who was introduced in order to pave the way to some bit of plot which then didn't get properly pursued because something funny happened and I thought, 'Well, I'll go with that instead.'

"In a way, it's more interesting to keep a character on the sidelines and never bring him out on stage. Like Oolon Colluphid who only appears as an author, and you just keep adding books... I think some of these characters become so popular because there's this hint of who the person might be the whole time. The audience have to use their imaginations. If I were to sit down and explore them in the same depth it would probably be disappointing. You select the characters you are interested in and deal with them fully, but it's the little characters on the fringes, that the audience can make of what they will, that really involve the audience."

ZAPHOD BEEBLEBROX

"Zaphod was originally based on somebody I knew at Cambridge called Johnny Simpson, who I think is now a bloodstock agent. He had that nervous sort of hyperenergetic way of trying to appear relaxed. That in a way is where it came from, he was always trying to be so cool and relaxed, but he could never sit still. Having said that, none of my characters are really based on actual people. They start with an idea, then they take on a life of their own, or they fizzle out.

"The two heads, three arms was a one-off radio gag. If I'd known the problems it was going to cause... I've had lots of rationales for where the extra head and arms came from, and they all contradict each other. In one version I suggested that he had always had two heads, in the other I suggest he had it fitted. And I suggested somewhere he had the extra arm fitted to help with his skiboxing. Then there was the question of how he managed to pass himself off on Earth. Arthur says in early versions, rather inexplicably, that he only had one head and two arms and called himself Phil, but I never really explained that. In the computer game I actually dealt with that, and Zaphod is there at the party, but it's actually a fancy dress party and he claims to have a parrot on his shoulder. He has a cage for it, with a drape over it, and his second head is sitting under the drape saying 'Pretty Polly!'

"There's a scene in which Trillian can't understand why Zaphod seems on the one hand quite bright and on the other appallingly dumb. That was a bit of self-portraiture. I sometimes strike myself as being quite a clever guy, and sometimes cannot imagine how I can be so slow-witted and stupid, so dull and brainless. I can't understand why I should be able to write something which everybody thinks is terribly clever, and at the same time be personally so dumb. I think I'm schizophrenic."

APPENDIX IV

THE DEFINITIVE
'HOW TO LEAVE THE PLANET'

You have been carefully selected as a totally random member of the Human Race. This chapter is for you. Before you read it:

1) Find a stout chair.

2) Sit on it.

This chapter has been spontaneously generated by the PASSING ACQUAINTANCES OF THE EARTH computer. It will appear in this book when the computer judges that the Earth has passed the P.O.S.T.O.S.E.H.*

If you have this chapter you may assume that the crucial point has now been passed, and that you are one of those chosen to be the future of the Human Race.

The following instructions are for you:

Leave the planet as quickly as possible.

Do not procrastinate.

Do not panic.

Do not take the Whole Earth Catalog.

HOW TO LEAVE THE PLANET

1) Phone NASA (tel. 0101 713 483 0123). Explain that it's very important that you get away as quickly as possible.

---

* P.O.S.T.O.S.E.H. — Possibility Of Sorting Things Out Sensibly Event Horizon.

2) If they do not cooperate, then try to get someone at the White House (tel. 0101 202 456 1414) to bring some pressure to bear on them.

3) If you don't get any joy out of them, phone the Kremlin (tel. 0107 095 295 9051) and ask them to bring a little pressure to bear on the White House on your behalf.

4) If that too fails, phone the Pope (tel. 010 396 6982) for guidance.

5) If all these attempts fail, flag down a passing flying saucer and explain that it's vitally important that you get away before your phone bill arrives.

WHERE YOU SHOULD BE HEADING

Where everyone else in the Galaxy is heading. Stay in the swim, hang out in bars, keep your ear to the sub-etha. Send all information home on postcards for the benefit of the next wave of Earth emigrants. Current information says that everyone else in the Galaxy is heading for a small planet in Galactic Sector JPG71248. It is clearly the most wonderfully trendy zillion tons of hunky rock in the known sky.

WHAT YOUR TRAVELS WILL BE LIKE

Difficult and unbelievably dangerous.

Space is notorious for having all sorts of terribly frightening things happening in it, most of which are best dealt with by running away very fast.

You should therefore take with you:

1) A pair of strong running shoes. The most useful type are of outrageous design and mind-mangling colours; experience has shown that if, while strolling through the ancient swampworld of Slurmgurst you come unexpectedly across an appalling alien monster with Lasero-Zap eyes, Swivel-Shear teeth, several dozen tungsten-carbide Vast-Pain claws forged in the sun furnaces of Zangrijad, and a terrible temper, it is in your immediate best interests that the monster should be for a moment

a) startled, and

b) looking downwards.

2) A towel. Whilst the monster is temporarily confused by your footwear you should wrap the towel round its head and strike it with a blunt instrument.

3) A blunt instrument (see above).

4) A green Eezi-Mind Anti-Guilt jacket or sweat shirt, for wearing after incidents such as the above. Guilt is now known to be an electromagnetic wave-form which is reflected and diffused by the material from which these shirts are made. Wearing them protects you from worrying about all sorts of things, including your unpaid phone bill.

5) A pair of Joo Janta 200 Super Chromatic Peril-Sensitive Sunglasses. These will help you to develop a relaxed attitude to danger. At the first hint of trouble they turn totally black, thus preventing you from seeing anything which might alarm you.

6) All the lyrics to any songs you like to sing whilst travelling. It is very easy to make enemies by continually singing a song you don't know all the words to, particularly on long space journeys.

7) A bottle of something. There are very few people in the Galaxy who won't be more pleased to see you if you are carrying a bottle of something.

MEDICAL KIT

In case of physical injury, press the buttons relating to

   A) part affected and   B) nature of injury simultaneously

❑ leg   ❑ broken

❑ arm   ❑ bruised

❑ head   ❑ wrenched off

❑ chest   ❑ mauled by Algolian suntiger

❑ other   ❑ insulted

This page will instantly exude appropriate waves of sympathy and understanding.

REASSURANCE PANEL

In case of doubt, confusion or alarm, please touch this panel.

> # HI THERE!

At times of stress it is often reassuring to make physical contact with friendly objects. This panel is your friend.

NB: On the assumption that nothing terrible is going to happen to the world and everything's suddenly going to be alright really, all the advise in this chapter may be safely ignored.

Douglas Adams originally wrote 'How to Leave the Planet' under the title of *The Abandon Earth Kit*, which appeared as a fourteen-sided figure — a quatuordecahedron — of a silvery-blue colour, which was "issued partly in the interests of assuring some reasonably relaxed and pleasant future for the human race, partly to introduce the world to Athleisure," the footwear company who distributed the Kit as a marketing ploy, "and partly because it's a rather nice shape."*

He then rewrote bits of it, changing the concept of the planet Athleisure to Ursa Minor Beta, for *The Restaurant at the End of the Universe*. He then rewrote the whole of it, leaving out some bits, for the liner notes of the American editions of the *Hitchhiker's* albums. He then took the first section and rewrote that not very much for the American (three book) *Hitchhiker's Trilogy* introduction, and not at all for the English (four book) *Hitchhiker's Trilogy* introduction.

The version above is a pretty definitive compilation of all the others.

---

* One of these, possibly the last one still held in shape by its original internal rubber bands, was auctioned for a considerable sum of money at the twentieth anniversary *Hitchhiker's Guide* convention in 1998.

APPENDIX V

DOCTOR WHO AND THE KRIKKITMEN: AN EXCERPT FROM THE FILM TREATMENT BY DOUGLAS ADAMS

Cricket at Lord's — the last day of the final Test. England need just a few more runs to beat Australia.

The Tardis lands — in the Members' Enclosure; very bad form. The members are only slightly mollified when the Doctor emerges (with Sarah Jane Smith) wearing a hastily donned tie and waving a very old membership card.

Three runs still needed. The batsman hits a six and the crowd goes wild.

In the middle of the pitch, the Ashes are presented to the England captain. The Doctor causes a sensation by strolling over and asking if he could possibly take them as they are rather important for the future of the Galaxy. Confusion reigns, along with bewilderment, indignation, and all the other things the English are so good at.

Then, whilst the Doctor is discussing the matter quite pleasantly with one or two red-faced blustering gentlemen, something far more extraordinary happens:

A small Cricket Pavilion materialises on the centre of the pitch. Its doors open and eleven automata, all apparently wearing cricket whites, caps, pads and carrying cricket bats file out onto the pitch.

Bewilderment turns to horror as these automata, moving as a tightly drilled and emotionless team, club those in their immediate vicinity with their bats, seize the urn containing the Ashes and file back towards their Pavilion.

Before they depart two of them use their bats as beam projectors to fire a few warning shots of stunray into the crowd. Another tosses what appears to be a red ball into the air, and with a devastating hook smacks it straight into a Tea Tent which promptly explodes.

The doors of the Pavilion close behind them and it vanishes again.

After a few seconds of stunned shock the Doctor struggles back to his feet.

"My God," he breathes, "so they've come back..."

"But it's preposterous... absurd!" people exclaim.

"It is neither," pronounces the Doctor. "It is the single most frightening thing I have seen in my entire existence. Oh, I've heard of the Krikkitmen, I used to be frightened with stories of them when I was a child. But till now I've never seen them. They were supposed to have been destroyed over two million years ago."

"But why," people demand, "were they dressed as a cricket team? It's ridiculous!"

The Doctor brusquely explains that the English game of cricket derives from one of those curious freaks of racial memory which can keep images alive in the mind eons after their true significance has been lost in the mists of time. Of all the races in the Galaxy only the English could possibly revive the memory of the most horrific star wars that ever sundered the Universe and transform it into what is generally regarded as an incomprehensibly dull and pointless game. It is for that reason that the Earth has always been regarded slightly askance by the rest of the Galaxy — it has inadvertently been guilty of the most grotesquely bad taste.

The Doctor smiles again for a moment and says that he did enjoy the match, and could he possibly take the ball as a souvenir?

The Doctor and Sarah leave in the Tardis. During the next couple of scenes we learn some of the background history of the Krikkitmen from the Doctor's explanation to Sarah and his arguments with the Time Lords. If it can be done partly using flashback and archive recordings from Gallifrey then so much the better.

BRIEF HISTORY OF KRIKKIT

The Planet of Krikkit lies in an isolated position on the very outskirts of the Galaxy.

Its isolation is increased by the fact that it is obscured from the rest of the Galaxy by a large opaque Dust Cloud.

For millions of years it developed a sophisticated scientific culture in all fields except that of astronomy of which it, understandably, had virtually no knowledge.

In all their history it never once occurred to the people of Krikkit that they were not totally alone. Therefore the day that the wreckage of a spacecraft floated through the Dust Cloud and into their vicinity was one of such extreme shock as to totally traumatise the whole race.

It was as if a biological trigger had been tripped. From out of nowhere, the most primitive form of racial consciousness had hit them like a hammer blow. Overnight they were transformed from intelligent, sophisticated, charming, normal people into intelligent, sophisticated, charming manic xenophobes.

Quietly, implacably, the people of Krikkit aligned themselves to their new purpose — the simple and absolute annihilation of all alien life forms.

For a thousand years they worked with almost miraculous speed. They researched, perfected and built the technology to wage vast interstellar war.

They mastered the technique of instantaneous travel in space.

And they built the Krikkitmen.

The Krikkitmen were anthropomorphic automata. They wore white uniforms, peaked skull helmets which housed scything laser beams, carried bat-shaped weapons which combined the functions of devastating ray guns and hand-to-hand clubs. The lower half of their legs were in ribbed rocket engines which enabled them to fly.

By an ingenious piece of systems economy they were enabled to launch grenades with phenomenal accuracy and power simply by striking them with their bats.

These grenades, which were small, red and spherical, and varied between minor incendiaries and nuclear devices were detonated by impact — once their fuses had been primed by being struck by a bat. Finally, all preparations were complete, and with no warning at all the forces of Krikkit launched a massive blitz attack on all the major centres of the Galaxy simultaneously.

The Galaxy reeled.

At this time, the Galaxy was enjoying a period of great harmony and prosperity. This was often represented by the symbol of the Wicket Gate — three long vertical rods supporting two short horizontal ones. The left upright of STEEL, represented strength and power; the right upright, of PERSPEX, represented science and reason; the centre upright, WOOD, represented nature and spirituality. Between them they supported the GOLD bail of prosperity and the SILVER bail of peace.

The star wars between Krikkit and the combined forces of the rest of the Galaxy lasted for a thousand years and wreaked havoc throughout the known Universe.

After a thousand years of warfare, the Galactic forces, after some heavy initial defeats, eventually defeat the people of Krikkit. Then they have to face...

THE GREAT DILEMMA
The unswerving militant xenophobia of the Krikkitas rules out any possibility of reaching any modus vivendi, any peaceful co-existence. They continue to believe their sacred purpose is the obliteration of all other life forms.

However, they are quite clearly not inherently evil but simply the victims of a freakish accident of history. It is therefore impossible to consider simply destroying them all. What can be done?

THE SOLUTION
The planet of Krikkit is to be encased for perpetuity in an envelope of Slow Time, inside which life will continue almost infinitely slowly. All light is deflected round the envelope so that it remains entirely invisible and impenetrable to the rest of the Universe. Escape from the envelope is impossible until it is unlocked from the outside.

The action of Entropy dictates that eventually the whole Universe will run itself down, and at some point in the unimaginably distant future first life and then matter will simply cease to exist. At that time the planet of Krikkit and its sun will emerge from the Slow Time envelope and continue a solitary existence in the twilight of the Universe.

The Lock which holds the envelope in place is on an asteroid which slowly orbits the envelope.

The key was the symbol of the unity of the Galaxy — a Wicket of Steel, Wood, Perspex, Gold, and Silver.

Shortly after the envelope had been locked, a group of escaped Krikkitmen had attempted to steal the Key in the process of which it was blasted apart and fell into the Space Time Vortex. The passage of each separate component was monitored by the Time Lords.

The ship containing the escaped Krikkitmen had been blasted out of the sky.

All the other millions of Krikkitmen were destroyed.

The Doctor and Sarah go to Gallifrey to try and find some answers.

The Doctor is furious with the bureaucratic incompetence of the Time Lords. The last component of the Wicket to emerge from the Space Time Vortex was the wooden centre stump which materialised in Melbourne, Australia in 1882 and was burnt the following year and presented as a trophy to the English cricket team.

Only now, a hundred years later, have the Time Lords woken up to the fact that every part of the Wicket is now back in circulation and should be collected up and kept safely.

The Time Lords at first refuse to believe the Doctor's story that the Krikkitmen have stolen the Ashes of the wooden stump. They say that every single Krikkitman was accounted for, and they are all safe.

"Safe!" exclaims the Doctor, "I thought they were all destroyed two million years ago!"

"Ah well, not exactly destroyed, as such…" begins one of the Time Lords, and a rather curious story emerges.

The Krikkitmen, it seems, were in fact sentient androids rather than mere robots. The difference is crucial, particularly in war time.

A robot, however complex, is basically a programmable fighting machine, even if an almost infinitely large number of response patterns give it the appearance of intelligent thought.

On the other hand, a sentient android is taught rather than programmed, it has a capacity for actual initiative and creative thought, and a corresponding slight reduction in efficiency and obedience — they are in fact artificial men and as such protected under the Galactic equivalent of the Geneva Convention. It was therefore not possible to exterminate the Krikkitmen, and they were instead placed in a specially constructed Suspended Animation Vault buried in Deep Time, an area of the Space Time Vortex under the absolutely exclusive control of the Time Lords. And no Krikkitman has ever left it.

Suddenly, news arrives that the Perspex stump has disappeared from its hiding place. The Time Lords are forced to admit that the Doctor's story may be true and tell him the locations of the other components of the Wicket.

The Doctor and Sarah hurriedly visit the planets where the other components are stored.

First, the Steel Stump. They are too late. It is gone.

Second, the Gold Bail. It is gone.

Third, the Silver Bail... it is still there! If they can retrieve it the Key is useless and the Universe is safe.

It is worshipped as a sacred relic on the planet of Bethselamin. The Bethselamini are predictably a little upset when the Doctor and Sarah materialise in the chamber of worship and remove the Sacred Silver Bail. The Doctor cannot stay to argue the point but gives them all a little bow just as he is about to leave the chamber, thus fortuitously ducking his head at the precise moment that a Krikkit bat swings at him from the open door.

They have arrived.

A pitched battle ensues in which the Bethselamini are rather forced to conjoin on the Doctor's side.

During the Battle, the Doctor finds his way into the Krikkitmen's Pavilion, where he has to fight for his life. Just as a death blow is apparently about to be struck, the Doctor, half dazed, falls against a lever, and the Krikkitman slumps forward, paralysed.

The Doctor has inadvertently switched them all off.

The battle is over. The Doctor is incredulous. If it is possible simply to turn them off then they can't possibly be sentient androids, they must be robots — so what were the Time Lords talking about? Why weren't the Krikkitmen destroyed?

The Bethselamini are recovering. Sarah seems to be slightly dazed, staring into the face of a paralysed Krikkitman. She soon recovers. We gather (though the Doctor doesn't notice) that she may have been hypnotised.

The Doctor dismantles one Krikkitman to examine its interior. He discovers that it is cunningly disguised as an android, but that in all crucial respects the circuitry is robotic, a fact that anyone making a thorough examination would quickly notice. Unless, of course, he didn't want to look very hard...

The Doctor and Sarah return to the Tardis. The next step is clear. If the Krikkitmen are merely robots after all, then they must all be destroyed at once. So — off to the Deep Time Vault.

Sarah points out that they shouldn't leave the Pavilion and paralysed Krikkitmen on Bethselamin, but take them back to Gallifrey for safe keeping and/or destruction.

The Doctor complains that he can't do both things at once. Sarah's bright idea: if the Doctor will preset all the controls in the Pavilion and guarantee that all the Krikkitmen are now absolutely harmless, then she will take them back to Gallifrey and wait for him there.

Nothing basically wrong with that, says the Doctor, and agrees. What he doesn't see is that while his back is turned for a few moments Sarah quickly and quietly switches a few of the Tardis's controls, whilst a foreign intelligence flickers briefly though her eyes.

As they leave the Tardis, Sarah surreptitiously hangs her hat over a panel of lights.

The Doctor sets the controls of the Pavilion, and rather reluctantly leaves her to it.

As soon as she is alone, Sarah completely resets the Pavilion controls, and it dematerialises.

The Doctor watches the Pavilion leave and then returns to the

Tardis. Whilst he is setting the controls, he notices that one or two of them are in the wrong position. With a momentary frown, he resets them and dematerialises the Tardis.

It is clear that the journey into Deep Time is immediately complicated, and actually requires the active assistance of the Time Lords on Gallifrey.

Eventually the Tardis materialises in a large chamber full of life support sarcophagi. The chamber is clearly just one of a very large number.

He leaves the Tardis. He passes Sarah's hat, but fails to notice that underneath it a bright warning light is flashing. After he has gone a hand picks up the hat. Under it a lighted panel reads, "SCREENS BREACHED: INTRUDERS IN TARDIS".

The hand is Sarah's. Keeping carefully out of sight, she follows the Doctor out of the Tardis.

The Doctor has passed through into the next chamber. Sarah goes to a large control panel set in the wall of the chamber, and carefully, quietly, moves a switch.

Krikkitmen are coming out of the Tardis.

The Doctor has opened a sarcophagus and is examining the internal workings of the Krikkitman within it.

Not far behind him another sarcophagus begins to open...

The Doctor is intent on his work. This Krikkitman is also quite definitely a robot.

A voice says, "Hello Doctor". He starts and looks up. There in front of him is Sarah Jane. Around them are several dozen functioning Krikkitmen. All the sarcophagi are opening.

A bat swings and connects with the back of the Doctor's head. He falls.

He comes to, lying in the Tardis, surrounded by Sarah and the Krikkitmen.

"You should be on Gallifrey," he says to her, "how did you get here? The Pavilion isn't a Tardis machine, it can't possibly travel into Deep Time."

Then he catches sight of the flashing panel which Sarah's hat had previously obscured and the penny drops. He struggles to his feet and presses a button. A wall drops away and there behind it stands the Pavilion. Inside the Tardis.

"So that's why the switches were off. You lowered the Tardis's defence field, and then reset the Pavilion's controls so that instead of going to Gallifrey you materialised a few seconds later inside the Tardis. In fact I gave you all a free ride into Deep Time," says the Doctor.

A Krikkitman announces that the entire Krikkit army has now been revived — all five million of them, the Vault has been shifted out of Deep Time into normal space, and they must now go to release their masters on Krikkit.

He orders the Doctor to transport the Tardis to the asteroid which holds the Lock.

"And if I refuse?" asks the Doctor.

"I will kill myself," says the hypnotised Sarah Jane, holding a knife to her own throat.

The Doctor complies.

As soon as the Tardis materialises on the asteroid, Sarah slumps over. She is of no further use to the Krikkitmen. When she comes to, she can remember nothing since the battle in Bethselamin.

The Krikkitmen have reconstituted the Ashes into the original stump shape, and reconstructed the Wicket Key.

They bear it before them out onto the surface of the asteroid.

The Doctor explains to Sarah that there, in front of them yet totally invisible, is the star and single planet of Krikkit. It has remained invisible and isolated for two million years, during which time it has only known the passage of five years. In another direction, they can see the great Dust Cloud that obscures the rest of the Galaxy.

A very large altar-like structure rises out of the surface of the asteroid. A Krikkitman climbs up to and pulls a lever. A perspex block rises up out of the altar. It has deep grooves carved in it, evidently designed to hold the upright Wicket. The Wicket is inserted. Lights glow. Power hums. In a scene that would make Kubrick weep like a baby, the star slowly re-appears before them, with its planet tiny, but visible, in the distance.

All the Krikkitmen turn to face the awe-inspiring sight and together chant, "Krikkit! Krikkit! Krikkit!"

In that moment of distraction, the Doctor grabs Sarah and makes a dash for the Tardis. They escape leaving that small group of Krikkitmen stranded on the asteroid. The Doctor explains that there's no point in trying to fight the robots now that they've all been released. Their only chance now is to go to the centre of it all... Krikkit. The Doctor is palpably scared stiff: Krikkit is about the most dangerous place that anyone other than a Krikkita could possibly go to. And they've got to go and make them change their minds...

They land on the planet...

Picking their way carefully through the back streets of a city, they suddenly inadvertently walk into a main square and come face to face with a large number of people.

There is stunned shock on all the faces...

After a few seconds on both sides, a howling cry starts up in the crowd — of pure animal fear and hatred. The Doctor and Sarah run for their lives with the crowd in hot pursuit.

They duck down a side street — and suddenly find themselves ambushed from in front. They are knocked senseless...

ACKNOWLEDGEMENTS

I owe a debt of thanks to all who helped with this book — not only those who gave interviews, who helped with the research, who made suggestions, but also to the people who made it easier for the book to be written by lending computers, making coffee, or just being nice at the right time.

Thanks especially are due to:

Alan Bell, Simon Brett, Kevin Davies, Jacqui Graham, Paddy Kingsland, John Lloyd, Geoffrey Perkins, and Cliff Pinnock for interviews above and beyond the call of duty.

Hitchhiker librarian and unpaid archivist Terry Platt, and ZZ9 Plural Z Alpha, the Official *Hitchhiker's Guide to the Galaxy* Appreciation Society (c/o 4 The Sycamores, Hadfield, Glossop, Derbyshire SK13 2BS, UK).

Wendy Graham, Ian Pemble, John Peel, Richard Holliss (who once started writing it), John Brosnan (who once started editing it), Roz Kaveney, Bernie Jaye and Nick Landau, Igor Goldkind, Peter Hogan and all at Titan, Ken Burr and Julian Marks at Rapid Computers, and Eugene Beer at Beer-Davies.

Two women with the same name: Mary Gaiman, my wife, who transcribed interviews fairly cheaply and put up with me for nothing; and my late grandmother, Mary Gaiman.

Finally, the man without whom this book would have been highly improbable: Douglas Adams, who never made any jokes about how late I was with the manuscript.

Neil. 1987. Late.

Coming Soon From
TITAN BOOKS

Tales From
Development Hell
David Hughes

Why did trying to make Neil Gaiman's acclaimed
graphic novel series, *Sandman*, into a movie become a
nightmare? Why have there been so many scripts
written over the years for the still in-development
Indiana Jones 4? What's Quentin Tarantino's
connection with the *James Bond* movie franchise?
Were the Beatles once really set to star in
The Lord of the Rings?

All these lost projects and more are uncovered in this
major new book, which features many exclusive new
interviews with the writers and directors involved.

'Hughes is a thorough, informed writer' SFX

www.titanbooks.com

Also Available From
TITAN BOOKS

Writing Science Fiction and Fantasy Television
Joe Nazzaro

What's it like putting words in Buffy's mouth? And how do you come up with a mission for the crew of the *Enterprise*, or invent your own X-File? Journalist Joe Nazzaro uncovers the answers to all these questions and more in this collection of revealing, in-depth interviews with writers and producers from television's hottest sci-fi and fantasy shows.

Some of the biggest names in the business talk candidly about how they started out, their inspirations and influences, and what it's really like to create the incredible and the impossible on a daily basis.

'If you've got any interest at all in TV sci-fi, and especially if you've got any ambitions to write the stuff, buy this book.' **DREAMWATCH**

www.titanbooks.com